BLACK COLLEGES
AND
UNIVERSITIES

CHALLENGES

FOR THE

FUTURE

EDITED BY

ANTOINE GARIBALDI

PRAEGER

PRAEGER SPECIAL STUDIES • PRAEGER SCIENTIFIC

New York • Philadelphia • Eastbourne, UK
Toronto • Hong Kong • Tokyo • Sydney

Library of Congress Cataloging in Publication Data
Main entry under title:

Black colleges and universities.
    Includes bibliographies and index.
    1. Afro-American universities and colleges — Addresses,
essays, lectures. I. Garibaldi, Antoine M.
LC2781.B43   1984   378.73   83-22943
ISBN 0-03-070302-6 (alk. paper)

Published in 1984 by Praeger Publishers
CBS Educational and Professional Publishing,
a Division of CBS Inc.
521 Fifth Avenue, New York, NY 10175 USA

456789 052 9876545321

Printed in the United States of America
on acid-free paper

Foreword

In June 1980, the National Institute of Education (NIE), then a part of the Department of Health, Education and Welfare, convened a group of educators from across the nation as participants in a seminar on black colleges. The seminar, "Current and Emerging Roles of Black Colleges and Universities," explored the historical and potential roles of black colleges, research at these institutions, external conditions and policies affecting their well-being, and methods of strengthening them as an increasingly important part of the nation's system of higher education. Fourteen of the participants were asked by Antoine Garibaldi of NIE to write papers on topics related to the theme of current and future roles for black colleges. These papers make up the major chapters of this book.

The historically black colleges that this book focuses on are those institutions established primarily for the education of blacks, although in most cases their charters were not exclusionary. These schools are located principally in the southern states, where the bulk of the black population originally resided, and today are living testimonies of a restrictive and oppressive system of higher education that left blacks little option but to develop their own institutions. It was never their policy to have a student body and faculty of one race only and, where the law allowed, integrated faculties were the rule rather than the exception (National Advisory Committee on Black Higher Education and Black Colleges and Universities [NACBHEBCU] 1979, p. 11).

The Civil Rights Movement of the 1960s succeeded in making the predominantly white institutions accessible to the majority of black students, and the Adams vs. Califano decision, which eliminated racially segregated higher education systems in ten states in violation of the 1964 Civil Rights Act, placed a new emphasis on institutional diversification by encouraging institutions to develop new programs and urging those schools in close proximity to avoid academic program duplication and attempt consortial arrangements instead. As a result, black higher education now encompasses all approaches: public, private, predominantly black, community, and historically black institutions, of which the latter is one of the most, if not the most significant. Indeed, the 105 black institutions accounted for almost 20 percent of all blacks enrolled in higher education throughout the nation at the beginning of the 1978-79 academic year (NACBHEBCU 1979, p. 12). An even more impressive picture emerges in the 17 states and the District of Columbia where these institutions are located. There, blacks were awarded 9.8 percent of the 363,000 baccalaureate degrees conferred on all students. The historically black colleges accounted for the major share, 61.5 percent of all baccalaureate degrees awarded to blacks (35,700). Moreover, in 13 of the 17 states and the District of Columbia, they accounted for over half of all baccalaureates awarded to blacks, 22.3 percent of the master's degrees, 4.1 percent of the doctorates, and 20.2 percent of the first professional degrees (NACBHEBCU 1980, p. 11).

While undergraduate degree production is important, the pivotal role of these institutions in black education is revealed in the share of advanced degrees they confer. Graduate programs were offered in historically black colleges and universities located in 13 states and the District of Columbia in 1975-76 (NACBHEBCU 1980, p. 15). In those states, blacks received 10.7 percent of all master's degrees, double the national average, and the historically black colleges accounted for 45.1 percent of all master's degrees awarded to blacks. In first-professional degree programs, they were responsible for 62 percent of the 876 degrees awarded to blacks in the seven states and the District of Columbia where they offered professional study. In the District of Columbia and Tennessee, the share was over two-thirds, largely due to the medical program of Meharry Medical College and to the medical and other professional programs at Howard University (NACBHEBCU 1980, pp. 16, 20).

The financial solvency of the nation's historically black colleges and universities is a major concern of these schools since a majority of their students depend, in varying degrees, on federal aid to attend college, especially Title IV programs. The fact that the median income of black families is only about 60 percent of the median income of white families makes equal access to higher education an even more urgent issue (Institute for the Study of Educational Policy (ISE) 1980, p. 27). This inequality between blacks and whites cannot be adequately assessed or compensated for by a simple calculation of cost and income ratios between the races. Financial aid can be very important in reducing the resulting disparities in distribution and persistence among college students, and in opening the door for equal access to equal educational opportunity.

What are the challenges for the historically black colleges in the near future? Since the establishment in 1854 of the first historically black college, these institutions have been the greatest producers of college-trained black Americans, the most consistent source of black leadership. "Blacks accounted for over 87 percent of the total of 29,497 degrees above the associate level conferred by the HBCs in 1976-77. Just over 8 percent went to whites, and less

than 5 percent to nonresident aliens and other minorities"
(NACBHEBCU 1979, p. 16; NACBHEBCU 1980, p. 125). Their
influence has been felt at home and abroad, in all corporate, phil-
anthropic, private or sectarian sectors of U.S. society, as well as
throughout the government. The position of blacks in U.S. society
is due, in no small way, directly to the influence of these institutions. Without question, their graduates have contributed to the
solutions of basic problems in U.S. society. If the past serves as
a valid indicator of these institutions' future, then their destiny
should be one of productivity.

One of the most pressing challenges is to produce more black
physicians, dentists, and lawyers. Black professionals are dra-
matically underrepresented in the total population. If the situation
remains static, there will be a deficit of approximately 42,000 black
physicians, 11,000 black dentists, and 19,000 black lawyers in the
year 2000. Ninety-two percent of black physicians (compared to 73
percent of white physicians) are located in metropolitan areas,
where there are large concentrations of the black population. Further, 90 percent of black physicians serve primarily nonwhite patients, whereas only 9.5 percent of the patients of nonblack physicians are nonwhite (NACBHEBCU 1978, pp. 13-14). Proximity of
health care is also important in assuring that blacks and other urban
poor receive adequate services.

Unless new solutions are offered and the numbers of first-
year black students in law, medical, and dental schools is increased,
the need for black professionals will not be filled. Considering the
estimated rates of completion and the difficulty blacks have had in
passing the bar and professional licensing examinations, there will
continue to be an inadequate number of blacks in these professions.
To produce the ideal number of physicians, dentists, and lawyers by
the year 2000, a tremendous increase will be necessary in the number of black first-year professional students beginning in the fall of
1984 and every year thereafter. Further, obtaining more master's
and doctoral degrees will require a large increase in the number of
students entering graduate school. Even though the total number
required to achieve parity seems great, if we spread that number
over all of the institutions, it will not be a great burden for them to
accommodate the additional students. However, without immediate
and drastic changes in education and counseling in the admissions
process and in completion rates, the problems will not be alleviated
by the year 2000, and we will continue to witness these stark inequities.

The shortage of health professionals among blacks is comple-
mented by a dreary picture for overall black employment. There
will be a marked slowdown in the expansion of the labor force between

1980 and 1990, and black representation in the professions and in high-technology fields will continue to be low (NACBHEBCU 1978, p. xii). Unless we target programs to increase opportunities for higher education for blacks in fields where future labor needs will be great, we will perpetuate the unemployment and underemployment of blacks and prevent the economic mobility of the black population.

If these conditions persist, it is imperative that black colleges and universities offer a traditional education under a broadened mandate. They must have the capabilities to respond to new areas of technology, biogenetics, analytical chemistry, new social thought, and new philosophies. This expanded mission should include greater emphasis on research. Unlike the major research institutions of higher education in the United States, the traditional focus of the historically black colleges and universities has been on teaching. This is understandable considering their history and the needs they have had to fulfill. Nevertheless, one of the great new frontiers for black colleges and universities will be the development of basic research.

One type of research that is clearly needed is socioethnic research, a field that is almost completely ignored by many other higher education institutions. The historically black colleges and universities, with their talented faculties and their sensitivity to social change, should be encouraged to address some of today's significant socioeconomic problems. Black college faculty can actively help to improve the quality of education in public and private schools in addition to preparing more students for careers in the sciences, engineering, medicine, and, most importantly today, elementary and secondary teaching. There is also a role to be played in the conduct of research on the public's attitudes toward social, political, and economic issues, particularly those that are having or may have a far-reaching impact on black communities and black Americans. Research and community service by black colleges must be intensified since these are two roles that are essential to their survival as well as importance in their respective communities.

The historically black colleges and universities continue to proclaim their readiness to be the linchpin of a very complex system of higher education in the United States. They say that they intend to be a part of the research community which seeks answers to grave problems that confront our nation. In the following chapters, some of the most brilliant minds in education explore these issues.

REFERENCES

Breneman, David W., Chester E. Finn, Jr., and Susan C. Nelson. Public policy and private higher education. Washington, D.C.: Brookings Institution, 1978.

Institute for the Study of Educational Policy (ISE). Equal educational opportunity: The status of black Americans in higher education. Washington, D.C.: Howard University Press, 1980.

National Advisory Committee on Black Higher Education and Black Colleges and Universities (NACBHEBCU). Target date 2000 A.D.: Goals for achieving higher education equity for black Americans. Washington, D.C.: NACBHEBCU, 1978.

_____. Black colleges and universities: An essential component of a diverse system of higher education. Washington, D.C.: NACBHEBCU, September 1979.

_____. Access of black Americans to higher education: How open is the door? Washington, D.C.: NACBHEBCU, June 1979a.

_____. Still a lifeline: The status of historically black colleges and universities. Washington, D.C.: NACBHEBCU, June 1980.

National Center for Education Statistics (NCES). Traditionally black institutions. A profile and an institutional directory. Washington, D.C.: NCES, 1979.

Preface

In November 1979, when the Seminar on Black Colleges and Universities convened for the first time in Nashville, Tennessee, it was privileged to have as one of its members Dr. John Warren Davis, former president of West Virginia State University. His participation in a study group designed to discuss future missions of black colleges was extremely important; while the other members could talk about the emergence of black colleges from what they had read in history books, John Davis could provide firsthand knowledge from his extensive experiences. This book is dedicated to Dr. Davis who, only three weeks after the study group's final meeting, passed away quietly at the age of 92 while he was preparing to go to his office.

Dr. Davis was born on February 11, 1888 in Milledgeville, Georgia, and attended elementary school there. Because there was no public high school for blacks in the entire State of Georgia at that time, John Davis went to Morehouse College in Atlanta in 1903, worked his way through high school and college, and graduated with honors in 1911.

He attended Morehouse while the well-known debate between Booker T. Washington and W. E. B. DuBois on the issue of industrial versus academic education for blacks was occurring. He roomed with Mordecai Johnson, who later served as president of Howard University from 1927 to 1960. From this association with Washington and DuBois, he began to formulate his lifetime philosophies and commitment to the educational development of the black community. Throughout his life he fought vigorously for improved relations among all Americans, for civil rights, and for more positive relationships between the United States and the black nations of the third world. He benefited greatly from the counsel he received from both Washington and DuBois and remained a lifelong friend of DuBois.

After receiving his bachelor's and master's degrees from Morehouse, he served on its faculty, and was registrar there from 1914 to 1917. He completed graduate studies in Physics and Chemistry at the University of Chicago. In 1919, at the age of 31, Dr. Davis became the president of West Virginia State College, a small school with only 21 students, which grew to 1,900 students by the time he left in 1953. During his 34-year tenure as president, John Davis not only increased enrollment but also guided the growth and development of West Virginia State and built its academic accreditation as one of the country's outstanding land-grant colleges. West Virginia State was also the first historically black college to enroll large numbers of white students.

At the age of 65, when he stepped down from the presidency of West Virginia State, Dr. Davis began a second career as a foreign-service officer. He was appointed by President Truman to serve under this country's first black Ambassador, Edward R. Dudley, as Director of American Technical Services Assistance to Liberia. Three years later, he began a third career as Director of Education of the NAACP Legal Defense and Education Fund. During his 24-year involvement with these programs, more than 1,300 scholarships and grants were awarded to black students pursuing under-graduate, graduate, and professional education.

An advisor to five U.S. presidents and recipient of 14 honorary doctorates, John Warren Davis was active in the struggle for civil rights and social justice. He was one of the founders of the first NAACP chapters in Atlanta; active in the National Urban League; assisted Carter G. Woodson in the establishment of the Association for the Study of Negro Life and History; and accompanied Mary McCleod Bethune on her initial visit to the White House when she presented the problems of black Americans to President Franklin Roosevelt.

Dr. Davis was appointed by President Truman to the first board of directors of the National Science Foundation and by President Hoover to the Organization of Unemployment Relief. He was a member of Prince Hall Masons (33rd Degree), Phi Beta Kappa, and Sigma Pi Phi Boule.

John W. Davis' insightful comments on these chapters as they were being prepared and his remarks during the work sessions were of inestimable value to the writers. Even at 92, he was still pro-gressive and provocative in his thinking and believed as strongly as any member of the group that black colleges would have to alter their missions to adapt to a changing clientele of students, changing demographics and political trends, and economic conditions that have adversely affected the financial health of most institutions of higher learning. Dr. Davis leaves a legacy for all educators to emulate. He will be missed by all those who had the good fortune to know him, but his contributions to education, to civil rights, and to the United States will live on.

Acknowledgments

The initial idea and plans for this book began in earnest in the fall of 1978, and thus there are many people that I would like to acknowledge for their assistance, cooperation, and support over the five years of this project.

First, I would like to especially thank my colleague and friend at the National Institute of Education, John Wirt, whose untiring efforts and commitment to the black college seminar series made this book a reality. Similar thanks go to my former supervisor at NIE, Berlin Kelly. I wish to give special thanks to Gertrude Martin for her editorial assistance on every chapter in this volume and her thoughtful comments on every issue discussed here. Her efforts added greatly to the organization, coherence, and clarity of each article. Special thanks too must go to each of the chapter authors and the auxiliary members of the seminar group for taking time from their busy schedules to attend the working meetings, review the early drafts of each paper, and, most importantly, for their patience with me when numerous requests were made to rewrite and revise their articles.

I am also indebted to my former NIE colleagues—Cliff Adelman, Cynthia Smith, and Joan Snyder—for reading and offering comments on the initial and final drafts of the articles. I also wish to thank my secretary at NIE, Janet Hawkins, and also my secretary at Xavier, Denise Watson, for typing some of the manuscripts and organizing the material. Thanks, too, to my work/study students, Ann Legaux and Rhonda Haydel, for their valuable assistance in helping me to meet the publication deadline during the summer of 1983.

I would also like to thank a very special person, Lynise Kennedy, who gave me encouragement and support during the editing of this volume. And lastly, thanks to my parents, Marie and Gary, and all of the staff at Praeger, especially Barbara Leffel, who believed in the importance of this book and saw to it that the ideas and suggestions in the following pages were shared with a larger audience.

AMG

Contents

PART I

INTRODUCTION

Black Colleges:
An Overview

Antoine Garibaldi

The slightly more than 100 black colleges and universities represented about 3 percent of the 3,325 postsecondary institutions in the United States during the 1982-83 academic year. Most of these historically black institutions were established after the Civil War for the exclusive purpose of educating black Americans. During the long period of segregation that followed, black colleges, by legal mandate, performed the useful function of providing higher education for blacks. Over the last 25 years, however, the removal of barriers of racial segregation, greater access to educational opportunities for racial minorities, and the rapid expansion of the higher-education system have led many to question the need for black colleges and universities.

The authors in this volume do not deal explicitly with the issue of whether the historically black colleges should exist in this society. All agree that the answer to that question is yes, but not clear-cut, since the universe of black colleges comprises a unique set of institutions possessing distinct characteristics and varied historical traditions.

The theme of this book—current and emerging roles of black colleges—developed from a proactive stance, rather than from the traditional reactive and defensive arguments for the existence of black colleges in America. We recognize that black colleges have made substantial contributions to this society, but we also realize that black colleges can no longer rest on their laurels to justify their existence today. The theme of roles and missions was chosen because the needs of black students have changed just as have social conditions in the United States. The fundamental thesis of the book is that black colleges, in order to remain vital, will need to expand, alter, or reinforce their traditional missions and goals so that they can carve niches for themselves in the American system of post-secondary education. In many ways, this premise is neither unusual nor impossible to achieve, since there is tremendous diversity among this group of institutions and many have succeeded historically in different roles and with varied objectives.

Most of the chapters in this volume focus on external factors that are likely to influence the direction in which an institution may choose to go. Two of the papers deal with issues that relate specifically to the implementation of roles, namely, governance, management, and leadership, and give examples of how an institution might develop a supporting structure of academic programs to meet its institutional goals. And, finally, three papers discuss the importance of research on black colleges, the importance of having research by black college faculty, and the pivotal role black colleges should play in identifying and conducting research on topics of concern to black people.

A PROFILE OF BLACK COLLEGES AND UNIVERSITIES

The group of colleges and universities that are discussed in this book are the historically black institutions of higher education in the United States. These institutions were founded for the education of black Americans and, by virtue of this special purpose, differ from the estimated 50 U.S. colleges and universities, commonly called predominantly black institutions, with enrollments of more than 50 percent of black students, e.g., the University of the District of Columbia, City College of New York, or Malcolm X College in Chicago. The purpose of this introduction is to provide an overview of the historically black colleges and universities as a way of accentuating their diversity and delineating some of their general characteristics.

Location, Level, and Control

There are 105 historically black institutions of higher education: eighty-three are located in the southeastern United States, ten in the Southwest, and the remainder in states outside of the South. The entire group of colleges is distributed across 19 states and the District of Columbia. Eighty-nine are four-year colleges, three of which—Florida A&M, Howard, and Atlanta—are universities, and 16 are two-year colleges. Sixty-two are privately controlled and the remaining 43 are publicly supported. Fourteen of the 62 private

institutions are independent and nonprofit; the other 48 are under
religious control (see Turner et al. 1979 for a listing of the 17 de-
nominations which support these institutions).

Enrollments

Most of the historically black colleges are small institutions:
eighty-four enroll less than 3,000 students and 41 of these enroll
less than 1,000. These average enrollments are not very different
from those of most private colleges in this country since 85 percent
of America's 1,408 private four-year colleges have enrollments of
less than 2,500 students (Eiden 1981). The remaining 21 black institutions enroll between 3,000 and 8,000 students; 11 have enrollments of more than 5,000 (Turner et al. 1979).

Student Characteristics

The majority of the students who attended historically black
institutions during the 1980 academic year were black (83 percent)
and fulltime (79 percent). All told, black colleges and universities
enrolled about one-fifth, or 212,000, of the more than one million
black students in institutions of higher education in this country in
the fall of 1980.

A recent study by Brazziel and Brazziel (1981) indicates that
black student enrollment in historically black four-year institutions
in 19 states declined by approximately 5,000 between 1976 and 1978.
Nine percent of the colleges' enrollment was white and 3 percent
were nonresident aliens. About 90 percent of the schools have student bodies that are at least 80 percent black and all but three of the
105 have enrollments that are more than 50 percent black. The
three which no longer serve a predominantly black population are:
Lincoln University in Missouri (37 percent black), West Virginia
State College (20 percent black), and Bluefield State College in West
Virginia (16 percent black).

Degrees Awarded

During the 1975-76 academic year, traditionally black institutions awarded 23 percent, or about 29,000, of all degrees blacks
received in the United States. That 23 percent included about
22,000 bachelor's degrees, 4,500 master's, 50 doctoral, 1,600
associate, and more than 500 first-professional degrees. These

figures, especially those for graduate degrees, may not seem significant, until one recognizes that only 28 of the black colleges offered master's degrees and only five offered doctorates. Yet, during 1975-76, black colleges awarded about a quarter of all master's degrees blacks received from institutions of higher education in this country. Finally, it should be noted that 75 percent of the master's and roughly 25 percent of the doctoral degrees awarded to blacks at black colleges were in the field of education (Turner et al. 1979).

Black colleges are not monolithic. Although they are similar to predominantly white institutions in many ways, their historical traditions and their levels and types of support make them distinct. Like many other institutions of higher learning, black colleges reflect the diversity that is so characteristic of the United States' postsecondary education system. This diversity should always be remembered when considering their past, their current conditions, and their future roles in American higher education.

HIGHER EDUCATION AND THE ROLE OF
BLACK COLLEGES TODAY

Ironically, many of the gains black Americans have achieved, especially between 1960 and 1980 through the impetus of the black colleges and their graduates, have prompted questions about whether these institutions are still needed. It is a serious dilemma for individuals who believe in the preservation of these institutions but reject segregation. Public and private postsecondary institutions no longer refuse black students and more colleges and universities actively recruit them. Despite their great contributions many black colleges and universities face serious threats—declining enrollments, potential mergers, and unhealthy fiscal situations—brought on largely by the expansion of, and changes within, the higher education system during the 1960s and 1970s.

Open admissions policies and an ever-expanding number of postsecondary institutions have provided youth with more opportunities to obtain a college education. Over the last 30 years, the total number of colleges and universities in this country has increased by more than 60 percent (from slightly less than 2,000 to more than 3,000 institutions) and enrollment has multiplied approximately five times (from slightly more than two million students in 1950 to more than twelve million students in 1981). A few of the obvious reasons for the expansion of the higher education system are the greater number of 18 to 24 year olds in the population during the 1960s and 1970s, an increased concern for more diversity in postsecondary education, and the drive toward equal educational opportunity for a larger segment of the population. The increase in numbers and the advances in educational equity are commendable, but black colleges and the rest of the higher education system must now face many new problems.

Forecasters of the future of higher education point to a number of negative factors that undoubtedly will affect the stability of most colleges and universities. These include:

— Scarcity of financial resources
— Substantial declines in enrollment of 18 to 24 year olds
— Intense competition for more able students
— More dropouts and stopouts among first-time enrolling students
— Consequences of court-ordered desegregation for many public institutions
— Increased cost of a college education
— Fewer and smaller educational grants and loans for students

The recognition of these factors has caused many postsecondary institutions to reexamine their roles and consider new missions and strategies for the future. Private black colleges are in no way immune to these problems and it is clear that the strains on these institutions will be much more acute, since they have been for some time underfinanced and heavily dependent on federal government funds, mostly in the form of student financial aid. They are predominantly small institutions with very little enrollment growth and are in a higher education market that has become increasingly competitive and affected by fiscal constraints. Many of the private black colleges especially have little or no endowments through which substantial income can be generated, and their students come from families with incomes significantly below the nation's mean average. Public institutions are in similar uncertain environments as state appropriations continue to fluctuate from year to year and as federal institutional and student support decline.

RESEARCH ON ROLES

Given these impending serious external pressures over which institutions have little control, black college administrators, boards of trustees, faculty, and students will have to make ultimate decisions about the future roles and missions of black colleges. There is no easy way to decide whether an institution should maintain or change its traditional mission. But research that attempts to clarify management and governance issues and speculates on new roles will help in making this decision. Even though this kind of theoretical research has certain limitations, the process can still be a useful tool in making sound judgments, provided that the correct trends are identified and analyzed before situations become hopeless. Pinpointing early decline in enrollments or noting shifts in the competition for students are examples of this type of research. It is also difficult for research to develop models that will fit all or most institutions. The papers which follow make few generalizations since each article implicitly recognizes the diversity within the community of traditionally black colleges: public and private, undergraduate and graduate, two-year and four-year, rural and urban, and small and large.

The current and prospective roles identified and the research issues presented in the book are illustrative rather than exhaustive. Other researchers, administrators, and faculty may conceive of a different set of roles for particular institutions as well as very different ways of approaching the research topics. The papers are intended to be speculative with the expectation that readers will study the theories and substantiate the premises. Researchers may then consider designing research and academic programs that will flow logically from them, and finally identify other roles that these institutions might choose to strengthen their position in higher-education circles. Throughout the book, the reader will find very few places where the past contributions of the black colleges are enumerated. That purposeful omission is not intended to deny those accomplishments; rather, the goal of this book is to discuss the future of black colleges in light of present-day conditions and situations. The fate of the majority of these institutions will not be determined by what they have done in the past, but instead by what important contributions they can make to society and higher education today during a period of contraction and retrenchment.

REFERENCES

Bowles, F. and F. A. DeCosta. Between two worlds. New York: McGraw-Hill, 1971.

Brazziel, W. F. and M. E. Brazziel. Recent college and university enrollment patterns of black students in states affected by Adams-Califano litigation. Atlanta, Georgia: Southern Education Foundation, 1981.

DuBois, W. E. B. The souls of black folk. In Three Negro Classics. New York: Avon Books, 1965.

Eiden, Leo J. Education in the United States: Statistical highlights through 1979-80. Washington, D.C.: National Center for Education Statistics, 1981.

McGrath, Earl J. The predominantly Negro colleges and universities in transition. New York: Columbia University, Teachers College Press, 1965.

Turner, William H. and John A. Michael. Traditionally black institutions: Their identification and selected characteristics. Washington, D.C.: National Center for Education Statistics, 1978.

Turner, W. H., N. L. Rosen, and B. Darrough Dixon. Traditionally black institutions: A profile and an institutional directory. Washington, D.C.: National Center for Education Statistics, 1979.

Winston, Michael R. "Through the back door: Academic racism and the Negro scholar in historical perspective." Daedalus, 100 (Summer 1971).

PART II

ADVANCING TRADITIONAL ROLES OF BLACK COLLEGES

This section of the book is devoted to discussions of two roles black colleges have played throughout their history and accomplishments for which they are customarily acknowledged: educating and training leaders and providing community service. But as the majority of black students choose to go to predominantly white and community colleges, how realistic is it to foster these traditional roles?

Sidney Barthelemy's chapter focuses on the inextricable relationship between education and leadership and argues that black colleges should preserve their mission of nurturing the leadership potential of their students. He recognizes that competition for students, especially minority students, is very intense today and that black colleges now enroll only about one-fifth of the black students who are in colleges and universities. Nevertheless, he emphasizes the maintenance and preservation of two important goals: first, that black colleges continue to train a critical mass of students for leadership roles; and, second, that these institutions utilize the expertise on their campuses to provide historical, political, and economic information and advice to elected and appointed local, state, and federal officials on issues that affect the total community and the black community specifically.

Charles U. Smith's chapter is devoted to the important contributions black colleges can make by providing extensive service to the communities in which they are located and also to the nation at large. Smith emphasizes that community service and development, like teaching and research, are fundamental responsibilities intricately tied to the mission of any university and acknowledges a few of the many contributions historically black colleges have made in this arena. However, he discusses and lists a panoply of contemporary service and development activities in order to accentuate the fact that historically black colleges may be able to carve out meaningful missions and roles for themselves that will have currency for society in the years ahead. But only through the development of long- and short-range plans will these objectives be achieved.

2

The Role of Black Colleges
in Nurturing Leadership

Sidney J. Barthelemy

Black colleges and universities were established after the
abolition of slavery for the express purpose of educating black
people. Over the years, these institutions have produced the vast
majority of black professionals and those whom the black community and society in general have acknowledged as "black leaders."
Many proponents and graduates of black colleges have claimed that
the chief role of these institutions was to produce leaders; but, in
fact, their primary mission was to train and educate students.
The fact that many of these institutions produced outstanding individuals in a variety of disciplines, who later assumed positions of
leadership, undoubtedly reflects on their history, the quality of
their faculty, their campus milieus that transmitted values of social
and personal significance, and also the contributions of alumni who
served as role models for younger students. Personal and family
characteristics also contributed to the intellectual growth of those
who became leaders, but black colleges motivated students, faced
with segregation and discrimination, to achieve regardless of the
barriers they confronted.

Recognizing that black colleges over the last three decades
are no longer the only institutions of higher education that prepare
young black men and women for professional careers and leadership
positions, black colleges should nonetheless preserve their manifest mission of educating students and of preparing those graduates
for leadership roles. Because I am limiting my discussion of leadership to political and public-service positions, I also recommend
that black colleges utilize the expertise on their campuses to provide historical, political, and economic information, and to advise
elected and appointed local, state, and federal officials on issues
that affect the total community and the black community specifically.

The word education is derived from the Latin verb <u>educare</u>, which means "to lead." History has shown us that there has always been an inextricable relationship between education and leadership. Thus, through education, leaders are trained and they, in turn, guide, direct, and influence the actions of others. There are, however, different kinds of leaders. Some are appointed, others are elected, and still others personify so completely the spirit and ideals of a movement that they become "leaders" by common consent. Often in the case of black leaders, they are characterized as such by some external forces such as the mass media and other organized groups. When speaking about "black leaders," it is important to note Charles Hamilton's observation that the term "black leader" tends to

> take on an additional meaning; one who is racially black in a leadership role and who speaks and acts on matters of specific (but not, necessarily, exclusive) concern to black people as a direct purpose of occupying that role. (Hamilton 1981)

Hamilton's point here is that the connotation of the term "black leader" refers not only to racial and role characteristics but also depicts issue orientation. This is a semantic distinction, but Hamilton has attempted to show that the mistake is often made of referring to prominent black people, who he calls "leading blacks," as "black leaders." Our concern in this chapter is with "black leaders."

BLACK COLLEGES AND THE DUBOIS-WASHINGTON DEBATE

In the early days of the black colleges, there were different, but not necessarily contradictory, viewpoints about the kind of education these institutions should provide and, in turn, the types of "leaders" they should be producing. The two educators who spurred this debate were Booker T. Washington, who founded Tuskegee Institute, and W.E.B. DuBois, one of the founders in 1910 of the National Association for the Advancement of Colored People (NAACP). Washington envisioned these schools' roles as institutions that would train black people to become self-sufficient, self-reliant, and able to cope with the conditions that existed during that period. His educational philosophy stressed agricultural, domestic, and mechanical work by students, focusing on the value in manual labor while exposing students to modern techniques and methods. DuBois, on the other hand, promoted the development of a cadre of black intellectuals, a "talented tenth," who would become the black leaders and professionals of the land. DuBois emphasized the close relationship between systems of higher education and the molding of leadership characteristics. Thus, he used many opportunities to argue forcefully for his belief that a university should transmit knowledge and culture from generation to generation. Nevertheless, despite this fundamental difference in opinion between Washington and DuBois, many students from both types of institutions rose to positions of leadership, prominence, and professional standing.

CHARACTERISTICS OF INSTITUTIONS THAT PRODUCE LEADERS

It is extremely difficult for any institution of higher education to make the bold statement that it produces "leaders," because it is not easy to identify measurable characteristics which support this assertion. Certainly graduation alone does not suffice, because there will be just as many nonleaders as leaders who graduate from a particular institution. But there are many positive and important aspects of institutions which permit them to take credit for the preparation and training of students who become leaders in society. One factor is the institution's past track record of outstanding alumni who students emulate in their professional careers. Another critical variable is the school's faculty—committed and dedicated men and women who not only teach and demand academic excellence, but also spend a considerable amount of time with their students. These individuals are usually the students' most significant role models and, from their example and inspiration, students recognize important academic and personal values. Another important feature is the campus milieu, the "inner life of the institution." The characteristics of the "inner life" are not easy to discern, but we can point to the esprit de corps that is evident among students, the interactions among faculty, and between faculty and students outside the classroom, and above all, the philosophy and value orientation of the institution.

Many alumni of black colleges would agree that these characteristics are typical of their alma maters. It was during their college years that they internalized values of social consciousness, of justice, of the struggle for equality that exuded from the speeches and teachings of administrators and faculty. As an example, we can single out the work of the law school at Howard University in the late 1940s and early 1950s, when students and faculty members

together prepared legal cases that eventually led to the Supreme
Court's decision that segregation and discrimination were unconstitutional in American society. The careful preparation of these
cases was vital and the results were tangible, but the spirit which
pervaded this group of individuals is difficult to measure. This is
the type of intrinsic motivation that brings about individual and group
success.

BLACK LEADERS TRAINED AT BLACK INSTITUTIONS

Today, blacks hold leadership positions in every aspect of
American life, both public and private, but if it were not for the
predominantly black universities, there would be very few black
leaders:

> It was not until 1954 that separate education of the
> races in the U.S. was formally declared to be uncon-
> stitutional, and educational opportunities thereafter in
> most colleges began slowly to become available, a
> process which accelerated after 1965. Today, the
> nation would have virtually no black leadership had
> these schools not existed. (Lincoln University 1972)

There is a great deal of literature on the history of black colleges and how they educated the freed slaves after the Civil War and
the great many blacks who have made significant accomplishments
in today's world. Vernon Jordan noted in 1975:

> It is the black colleges that have graduated 75 percent
> of all black Ph.D.s, 75 percent of all black army
> officers, 80 percent of all black federal judges, and
> 85 percent of all black doctors. (Vernon Jordan 1975)

A close examination of the educational backgrounds of blacks
who have served in leadership positions, or who currently occupy
those positions, shows that most have attended or taught at black
colleges. Justice Thurgood Marshall of the Supreme Court is a
graduate of Howard University; Andrew Young, now Mayor of Atlanta
and former United Nations Ambassador is a graduate of Dillard
University; Maynard Jackson, former Mayor of Atlanta is a graduate of Morehouse College; Ernest Morial, Mayor of New Orleans,
is an alumnus of Xavier University; and Richard Arrington, Mayor
of Birmingham, Alabama, is a former black college professor and
dean at Miles College. There are probably many more graduates of

black universities among the 180 black mayors who hold office in
the United States (Joint Center for Political Studies 1980). Several
members of Congress also are graduates of black colleges. As one
moves to the local government level, the numbers of black elected
and appointed officials who have graduated from black colleges increase. More than half the black legislators in the Louisiana State
House and Senate graduated from black colleges. Leonard Spearman,
a former federal official in the Department of Education and now
President of Texas Southern University, reported in 1975 that 64
percent of all blacks in state legislatures are graduates of black
colleges.

Historically, segregation kept most blacks out of the major
white institutions; the black colleges were the only places blacks
could go for education and career preparation. Segregation and
racism, however, reinforced the production of black leadership,
because these hurdles provided the motivation to overcome barriers:

> The goal of the black college is not education for its
> own sake, but for a continual challenge of the status
> quo in oppressive race relations and social behavior.
> The historical preeminence of this mission is attested
> to both in number and quality of black political, educa-
> tional and religious leaders who have graduated from
> predominantly black colleges. (Hedgepeth, Edmonds,
> and Craig 1979, p. 18)

These black institutions were established not only to educate
black students, but also to cull from their number potential leaders.
Benjamin Mays best described this function on a 1945 radio program
about the meaning of black colleges:

> It will not be sufficient . . . to produce clever grad-
> uates, men fluent in speech and able to argue their
> way through; but rather honest men, men who can be
> trusted in public and private—men who are sensitive
> to the wrongs, the sufferings and the injustices of
> society and who are willing to accept responsibility
> for correcting ills. (Willie 1978, p. 13)

It was extremely clear then, as it still is today, that black
colleges have a broader mission than simply educating students.
That mission is the social one of producing men and women sensitive
to problems and with a burning desire to rectify them. Most black
educators expected that those blacks fortunate enough to go to college would be the leaders of the black community.

In further support for the role of the black leader in the community, take note of what DuBois said of the "college-bred" Negro:

> He is, as he ought to be, the group leader, the man
> who sets the ideals of the community where he lives,
> directs its thoughts, and heads its social movements.
> It need hardly be argued that the Negro people need
> social leadership more than most groups; that they
> have no traditions to fall back upon, no long-established
> customs, no strong family ties, no well-defined social
> classes. All these things must be slowly and painfully
> evolved. (DuBois 1903)

COMPETITION FOR THE FUTURE LEADER

Black colleges have done a good job in the past training black leaders, but the competition for black students is greater today. Predominantly white colleges and universities no longer exclude blacks; more than 40 percent of black students attend two-year colleges; black colleges enroll less than 20 percent of the total number of black students enrolled in postsecondary institutions. In many instances, the better financed, predominantly white schools offer more by way of physical facilities, extracurricular activities, and a greater variety of academic programs than do many black colleges. Competition for students is intense and will continue to be so, as documented in Chapter 12 by Mary Carter-Williams. Yet, although white colleges enroll over 75 percent of the black college students, the 105 black colleges still award almost half the baccalaureate degrees blacks earn nationally.

One of the advantages black colleges seem to have over the predominantly white schools is that they do more than simply educate their students; a spirit of leadership responsibility pervades the black campus. This must be the focus in a world where purpose and commitment seem to be fading, where students are more interested in doing their own thing, rather than righting wrongs or social injustices. Alan Pifer, then president of the Carnegie Corporation of New York, stated in a speech at Atlanta University:

> The next decade will be a critical time for black prog-
> ress. It will require continued vigilance and organized
> pressure by blacks just to sustain the gains of the re-
> cent past. At the same time, attention must be paid to
> that segment of the black population which remains
> totally excluded from the good life and which presents

both a moral and practical danger to the well being of
a society of which we are a part. It is imperative that
we develop the analysis, the language, and the leadership that can arouse once more the sense of collective
and individual responsibility to help those less fortunate
than ourselves that was the hallmark of the 1960's and
to recognize further, that it is in our national self
interest to do so. (Pifer 1980, pp. 100-03).

It is precisely those intangible leadership goals of black colleges that I believe can lure tomorrow's black leaders to these
institutions. Contrary to conventional wisdom, young people have
not totally lost their sense of purpose. Witness the rise of religious
cults, and the thousands of young people who join these movements,
often giving up material possessions to do so. Look at the young
people who cannot find jobs and leave school, and those who are
discouraged as they hopelessly search for purpose and meaning.
Black colleges have been able to give young blacks purpose and
meaning in the past and they can in the future, but they must update
their approach and offer unique programs.

THE UNIQUE CAPABILITIES OF BLACK
COLLEGES AND UNIVERSITIES

Some institutions, such as Morehouse College or Howard University, are well-known as black colleges that have produced leaders, chiefly because of the prominence of a few of their graduates
like Martin Luther King, Jr. or Thurgood Marshall. But the contributions of other black colleges, such as Tougaloo in Tougaloo,
Mississippi, Spelman in Atlanta, Georgia, or Xavier in New
Orleans, Louisiana, are not as well-known nationally, because
their graduates have made outstanding contributions to local communities. Such is the case with a great many black colleges. There
is a need to document these accomplishments more systematically
and to conduct research that attempts to describe the "inner lives"
of these institutions. Charles Willie and Susan Greenblatt's recently completed study, "Characteristics That Contribute to Excellence Among Black Scholars," funded by NIE, may provide a start-
ing point for this kind of analysis.*

---

*Charles V. Willie and Susan L. Greenblatt's 18-month NIE
study (NIE-G-80-0035), which began in March 1980, examined the

Student Involvement

Because black colleges are small, there are obviously more opportunities for students to participate in the activities of their institutions. They can serve in leadership positions in student organizations, student governments, fraternities, sororities, or other extracurricular clubs. Through these involvements, student-support networks are developed and students build a sense of confidence in their ability to lead and a strong measure of self-pride. For many, too, the homogeneity of the student body is an asset, especially for those who have not had the opportunity to attend school with a large majority of blacks. That was not the case 20 years ago when many elementary and secondary schools were segregated.

Faculty Commitment

A great many outstanding graduates of black colleges were trained by faculty who committed themselves totally to these institutions. Take, for example, the fact that for many years there were few institutions where blacks could go to obtain a law, medical, or pharmacy degree. Thus, the law schools of Howard University (Washington, D.C.) and Texas Southern University (Houston), the medical schools of Meharry (Nashville, Tennessee) and Howard, and the pharmacy school of Xavier University provided opportunities to blacks that were not easy to obtain at most other universities and professional schools. The faculties of these schools were men and women who not only dedicated their lives to their institutions but cultivated relationships with students that deeply affected their

----

life histories of five prominent black scholars in the humanities and the social sciences (English, History, Political Science, Psychology, and Economics). The major purpose of the study was to identify those influential characteristics and experiences that contributed to the attainment of academic excellence by these scholars in their respective disciplines. Through interviews with scholars' relatives, friends, professional colleagues, and other significant individuals, Willie and Greenblatt hoped to identify common and salient factors in their family relations, teacher-student ties, and achievement patterns. From these analyses the authors expect to outline additional supportive and nurturing relationships that helped these individuals to become recognized scholars. The completed study will be published in a book, tentatively titled Stages in a Scholar's Life.

career aspirations. This kind of nurturing relationship continues at most black colleges. Thus, black colleges and universities should emphasize this aspect of their educational environments when they recruit students.

BLACK COLLEGES AS RESOURCES FOR PUBLIC OFFICIALS

Black colleges and universities can effectively and realistically address problems facing the leaders of today and those of the future. The role and constituency of any black leader are, by their very nature, more demanding and all-encompassing than those of other leaders. There are so few black leaders that they become central clearinghouses for all the problems of their sectors of black society. A 1980 report by the Joint Center for Political Studies indicated that there were 4,912 black elected officials in the United States in July 1980. This figure represents 1 percent of the 490,200 elective offices in this country. And despite the fact that there were 300 more black elected officials in 1980 than in 1979, blacks still remain grossly underrepresented in elective offices throughout the country: there are roughly 19 black elected officials for every 100,000 blacks compared to 252 nonblack officials for every 100,000 nonblacks in the population. Thus, the leaders find that the expectations of their constituencies cannot always be completely and easily fulfilled. As a result, by serving and leading they are involved with thousands of small problems of everyday life. The net result is that they have little time left to grapple with, analyze, and seek remedies for the larger issues.

Forums at black colleges in which leaders can participate can prescribe comprehensive remedies. Bringing individuals who serve in leadership positions to the various campuses also gives students an opportunity to meet with, discuss, and listen to those blacks who are in influential positions in their community. Recognizing the fact that the black population in the South increased by more than two million between 1970 and 1980, and that 20 of the 32 black majority central cities are projected to be in the South by 1990 (Joint Center for Political Studies 1982), the following suggested activities of involvement by black colleges will be beneficial to both black and white leaders in the years ahead.

Developing Policy Centers

The black colleges can provide "thinking rooms" for leaders in influential positions in government or the private sector. Major universities such as Harvard and Stanford have established policy institutes as a mechanism to bring national and community leaders to their campuses to reflect on their experiences and for inter-changes of information and technical advice. Blacks in leadership positions need this type of service and it can best be provided by the black colleges. Through the development of such policy centers, the colleges can take a more active role in influencing public policy so that they become the hubs of regional or local activities, train future political scientists and other leaders, and establish national reputations for themselves. A college may choose solely to conduct research or to provide policy advice or to take a stance of political activism. Links can be developed with other civic organizations and advocacy groups through coalitions and consortia so that the resulting umbrella organization has some meaningful political clout.

Internship Programs

First and foremost, black colleges must provide a stimulating and competitive curriculum that will not only attract and teach future black leaders but will also mold them into effective and capable leaders. One of the proven approaches to this goal is an internship program which provides avenues for students to work in government, communities, and private industry. The student learns about the operational side of a company or of a division of government, as well as the styles and types of organizational leaders. Through observation and imitation, the student has an opportunity to get a realistic idea of problems and solutions in the field. Most programs also encourage students to develop their skills and abilities by allowing them to work with mentors who have records of proven success.

Training Neighborhood Leaders

Black universities can also assist neighborhood organizations by providing technical assistance and in-service training programs for indigenous neighborhood leaders. Many black leaders get their start in neighborhood organizations, but are not able to attend universities and colleges because of limited finances or an inability to deal with a structured curriculum. Thus, the universities have the potential to assist those community organizations. They can help foster the development of bright, young individuals. The black colleges can provide faculty experienced and trained in community organizations, management, administration, and personnel. These skills are vitally needed for the development of neighborhood organizations. The colleges might also develop special programs which focus on the development of neighborhood leaders.

Securing Necessary Funding

The role of black colleges in developing effective black leadership will be lost unless these institutions have the necessary resources to survive and implement academic and action programs. This is a critical problem. Black colleges receive less than 2 percent of all the foundation money that is dispensed and only a very small percentage of the total amount of monies given to colleges and universities by the federal government. It is imperative that black colleges secure the necessary funding if they are to educate black leaders. Present black leadership must begin to take effective measures to assure proportional funding from foundations and the federal government. In 1981, the United Negro College Fund's Capital Resources Development Program raised more than $60 million for its members, 41 private colleges located primarily throughout the South (Johnson 1981). Blacks must look at these and other funds as investments, not gifts. The funds are there and it is the responsibility of black leadership to obtain them.

Alumni Responsibilities

Alumni of black colleges have an obligation to contribute their fair share to the fundraising drives of their institutions. These colleges cannot continue to produce leaders for the future without the financial support of their graduates. Black leaders and professionals who are alumni of these schools should also use their many speaking engagements to acknowledge the important contributions these institutions have made in their lives. These individuals are in highly visible positions and can best convince many people that black colleges and universities should continue to promote their mission of educating and training black leaders. During these critical times for our society and for higher education, we cannot wait for and expect others to take the lead in this effort.

REFERENCES

Cook, Samuel DuBois. "The socio-ethical role and responsibility of the black college graduate." In Black colleges in America: Challenge, development, survival, edited by Charles V. Willie and Ronald R. Edmonds. New York: Columbia University, Teachers College Press, 1978.

DuBois, W. E. B. The Negro problem. New York: James Pott, 1903.

Hamilton, C. V. "The status of black leadership." New Directions (April 1981).

Hedgepeth, Chester M., Jr., Ronald R. Edmonds, and Ann Craig. Overview, black colleges in America. New York: Columbia University, Teachers College Press, 1979.

Johnson, John H. "Biggest fund-raiser ever for black education." Ebony Magazine 36 (April 1981).

Joint Center for Political Studies. Rosters of black elected officials 1980. Washington, D.C.: Joint Center for Political Studies, 1980.

_____. Blacks on the move: A decade of demographic change. Washington, D.C.: Joint Center for Political Studies, 1982.

Lincoln University, Department of Sociology. Research and learning centers among black colleges in the human services: A feasibility study. Lincoln, PA: Lincoln University, 1972.

Pifer, Alan. "Prospects for black progress in the 1980s." Vital Speeches of the Day 47 (December 1, 1980).

Spearman, Leonard. "Funds lack endangering black colleges." Florida Times Union (May 4, 1975).

Thompson, Daniel C. Private black colleges at the crossroads. Westport, CT: Greenwood Press, 1973.

Washington, Booker T. Up from slavery. In Three Negro classics. New York: Avon Books, 1965.

Willie, Charles V. "Racism, black education, and the sociology of knowledge." In Black colleges in America, edited by Charles V. Willie and Ronald R. Edmonds. New York: Columbia University, Teachers College Press, 1978.

3

Community Service and Development in Historically Black Colleges and Universities

Charles U. Smith

Historically black colleges and universities have been a significant segment of higher education in the United States for many years. Many of these institutions have reached, or are approaching, 100 years of continuous service (see Table 1). The mission of the historically black colleges and universities has been the same as that of institutions of higher education generally, namely, teaching or the transmission of knowledge; research or the acquisition of knowledge; and service or the application of knowledge. The preservation of knowledge through the use of libraries, museums, and archives has also been a universally accepted goal.

Implementation of the specific components of this mission by individual institutions has varied over the years, but the teaching function has been universally emphasized. The development of curricula and courses of study among these schools has paralleled that of all institutions of higher education, particularly at the undergraduate level.

Graduate instruction at the master's degree level is still limited to a relatively small number of the historically black colleges and universities. Only five (Howard, Atlanta, Morgan State, Meharry, and Texas Southern Universities) offer doctoral degrees of any kind. Faculties and administrators at these schools have always been astute enough to recognize that they lacked the professional personnel, financial resources, and other support systems to carry on upper-level graduate work at academically respectable standards. The inability to offer advanced graduate study has seriously hampered these institutions in their efforts to optimally perform research and service functions.

educationally unnecessary to maintain the historically black schools. This problem is often exacerbated in those communities where a traditionally black and a traditionally white college are located in close proximity.

From the standpoint of service delivery, the situation outlined above is paradoxical. On the one hand, federal law has opened up occupational and career opportunities for which blacks and minorities need to be trained. On the other hand, the historically black institutions that customarily filled the higher education needs of blacks are being threatened with abolition and are being forced to allocate scarce resources to fighting for survival.

Despite this and other problems, the historically black institutions have opportunities and face challenges in the arena of community service and development unprecedented in U.S. history. Blacks have increased access to nontraditional careers and they must acquire new knowledge and skills to prepare for scientific and technological changes as well as for developments in international affairs. For example, the historically black colleges must design both long- and short-range courses of study and applied research to ameliorate the massive problems growing out of the scarcity of energy, its production, use, and conservation, and the associated need to readjust lifestyles at all socioeconomic levels.

The extended life expectancy of the population of the United States and the importance of productive activity in the years after age 65 demonstrate the necessity for institutions to provide continuing education programs. The black population in the United States is just beginning to produce visible and increasingly large numbers of retirees, a situation that is both a challenge and an opportunity for the historically black colleges and universities.

The 16 traditionally black land-grant institutions (and Tuskegee Institute) have a special mandate. The federal legislation providing for the operation of the land grants stipulated that they "teach such branches of learning as are related to agriculture and the mechanic arts . . . [and] promote the liberal and practical education of the industrial classes in the several pursuits and professions of life." (American Council on Education, 1973, p. 21). The legislation also recognized the need for trained manpower as an ongoing national concern.

SPECIFIC SERVICE AND DEVELOPMENT AREAS

The populations and the communities served by many historically black colleges and universities often have syndromes of victimization and powerlessness resulting from oppression and unequal opportunities. When one trait of pathology is present in a group it is usually accompanied, and reinforced by, other related pathologies. Thus when a family or neighborhood is poor, it is also likely to have low educational attainment, high morbidity rates, low self-esteem, and restricted social participation. Conversely, if there is low educational attainment, the group is likely also to be poor and to have the other characteristics listed above. This situation is greatly intensified and complicated if the families or communities are black.

Community Service

Another way to understand the complexities and interrelationships of problems and needs of many families and communities served by historically black colleges is by utilizing the "culture of poverty" concept developed by Oscar Lewis (1965) and others. "Culture of poverty" has been used to designate the lifestyle of peoples who share common fatalistic attitudes, beliefs, and values about their existence in the world. The victims of the culture of poverty tend to transmit their limited survival strategies to their children, thereby perpetuating the existence of future generations at the poverty level. Although many social scientists have disavowed the "culture of poverty" concept because it does not adequately take into account the institutional structures and social networks of a true culture, it is nevertheless a useful way of viewing the need for developmental services in economically depressed neighborhoods and communities.

The service and development challenge facing the historically black colleges as they project their programs for the 1980s is that of intervention in the culture of poverty so that they can improve conditions with lasting results. For many persons and institutions in the service professions, community service is viewed as an unending activity in aid of the human condition. Indeed, many social workers perceive the process of service delivery as the end rather than the means to a permanently changed condition in which such service is no longer needed. The view here is that community service is an important function but one that leads to and complements community development, so that persons and groups will achieve the necessary knowledge, skills, strategies, and resources to maintain and enhance their quality of life at positive and meaningful levels. This, of course, is an idealistic model, but one that historically black colleges and universities ought to adopt in their efforts to improve the human condition.

Race Relations and Interethnic Cooperation

Racism victimizes blacks and restricts their ability to gain meaningful access to opportunity—particularly employment opportunity. The U.S. Bureau of Labor Statistics reported in 1975 that the unemployment rates for blacks generally, and for black youth specifically, were 14 percent and 37 percent, respectively (U.S. Bureau of the Census, 1979). These rates were approximately twice as high as those for whites. Because these are long-standing racial differentials, they must be viewed as systemic rather than coincidental. To a significant, but lesser extent, other ethnic groups and women also suffer disproportionately high rates of unemployment. Colleges and universities can provide a significant service to communities by conducting interracial workshops, forums, and projects where facts, opinions, perceptions, and attitudes can be expressed, and strategies to achieve goals and solve problems of mutual concern can be developed and put into operation. Sherif and Sherif (1956) and other students of social psychology have demonstrated the efficacy of bringing divergent or conflicting groups together to work to eliminate common threats and to achieve overriding goals that disparate groups cannot accomplish individually.

Family Assistance Projects

Because the family remains the principal institution of procreation, nurture, protection, and attachment for all age levels, it continues to be an area where historically black colleges and universities can provide conceptual and practical assistance. Conceptually, family relationships may be enhanced through basic and applied research on the functioning of various models of parenting. In 1965, Daniel P. Moynihan critically appraised black families in the United States and concluded that the pathologies associated with low-income black families, in which the mother frequently was the only parent present, were so pervasive as to require remediation by the federal government. Billingsley (1969) and other students of the family subsequently established that single-parent families, including those headed by mothers or other female guardians, had many strengths and filial support networks that belied that "pathology/deviance" concept.

As individuals have recognized the viability of single-parent families and have adopted changes in sexual mores, it has become more acceptable for women to have babies and establish families without being married. This model has gained such popularity and acceptance that adoption agencies now permit single parents to adopt and raise children. Black colleges and universities can contribute in this area by monitoring and researching various familial arrangements so that they can make projections on the probability of success or failure of one or another of these arrangements. From a more practical standpoint, many black and white families need assistance in understanding and utilizing the various state and federal family-support systems. Colleges and universities can render a great service by simplifying and interpreting government documents and guidelines on such programs.

Home Improvement and Safety Assistance

The historically black colleges and universities can also provide home improvement and safety assistance services. Such university-sponsored research and development (R&D) projects will be especially useful in communities where the detached single-family dwelling is the typical residence. Since many of these dwellings are relatively old, modern safety features may not have been installed or, because of age, may have become inoperative or ineffective. Further, in this day of energy scarcity and inflation, R&D programs in weatherization and efficient use of energy and its conservation could be extremely valuable.

Mental Health

In contemporary American society, serious mental health problems increasingly require concerted attention. The incidence of suicide, anxiety, depression, and alienation among youth causes national alarm. Some historically black colleges have begun to deal with this problem by first recognizing the limited availability and prohibitive costs of traditional mental health services. They have followed up by establishing master's level clinical study in school/community psychology. Graduates of such programs are fully recognized by professional associations and licensing bodies and can render preventive health care, referral, and therapeutic services in local schools and communities.

Legal Services

Legal services for the poor and those with moderate incomes are also a necessity. Recently, the case of a black family in Gretna,

Florida received national attention when they lost their homestead for failing to pay property taxes of only $3.06. At the time this happened, Florida law allowed anyone to purchase a delinquent tax certificate, and if the owners did not pay the delinquent taxes and penalties by a specific date, the purchaser of the delinquent certificate could acquire the property at a nominal price. The Kenon family of Gretna claimed that they were not aware that their taxes were delinquent, but to no avail. A white realtor purchased their home and land for $102.31 and offered to sell the property back to them for $10,000. Early in 1980, the Florida legislature in special session passed legislation making such victimization more difficult, but the fact remains that paralegal services are sorely needed in many communities where socioeconomic levels are low. Historically black schools could provide assistance with property transactions, taxes, contracts, civil rights, and the broad spectrum of due process. Instruction in land use, development, and the long-range value of land retention, particularly by blacks and minorities, is a vital component of community development. In colleges and universities without law schools, the resources of the departments of political science, sociology, history, and agriculture can be effectively integrated to deliver this type of service.

Paramedical Services and Health Care

Paramedical services to communities would satisfy important needs by providing essential knowledge, by training community residents to handle medical emergencies, and by reducing the costs of medical assistance and care. Virtually all the historically black colleges have departments of health and physical education and many have schools or programs in nursing and medical technology; a few have schools of pharmacy. Such programs could be coordinated in the delivery of a broad range of paramedical services ranging from hypertension clinics to cardiopulmonary resuscitation, from emergency poison treatment to effective functioning at accident scenes and quick aid for choking victims.

Nutrition counseling is an important adjunct to paramedical services that colleges and universities can offer. The life expectancy of blacks, especially black males, is significantly lower than that of whites. As of 1974, black males and females at birth could expect to live 63 and 71 years, respectively, whereas their white counterparts had life expectancies of 69 and 77 years. Blacks born before 1974 have considerably lower life expectancies than these figures (U.S. Bureau of the Census, 1979).

Much of the reduced life expectancy of blacks can be attributed to nonnutritional and nondietary factors such as occupational hazards, crime, and high rates of maternal and infant mortality, but the impact of poor nutrition and irrational dietary habits on morbidity including hypertension, atherosclerosis, glandular disorder, and coronary disease requires systematic attention. Departments of biology, chemistry, bacteriology, foods and nutrition, generally found at historically black colleges and universities, can provide staff and facilities to fill this community need. Home gardening and energy-efficient cookery could easily be combined in this community service element.

The Humanities

Another important community service component, not often included in the utilitarian services provided by historically black colleges and universities, is in the area of the humanities. Most people think of quality of life as relating primarily to economic status and material possessions. Humanists provide different, refreshing dimensions to life by integrating the arts, literature, dialogue, and introspection into the meaning of human existence.

Many years ago Tuskegee Institute recognized the need to expose people in rural black communities to the humanities and established the "Bucket Theater" in an agricultural area. The name "Bucket Theater" was derived from Booker T. Washington's famous speech in which he advocated that black people "let down their bucket" where they are. Other colleges and universities have provided this community service through touring artistic groups and exhibitions. In the late 1960s, Florida A&M University, in connection with its community service center in Tampa, initiated street theater in an area of that city that had recently suffered a riot (Robertson 1972). Many such programs in the humanities have been discontinued or limited because of funding difficulties. The need for and value of these programs still merit attention by colleges and universities and possibilities for federal financial support for them are outlined later in this chapter.

Political Participation

For communities to develop positively and to endure, it is imperative that they gain access to private and public economic programs and support systems and participate in the decisionmaking that impacts on their welfare. This requires community organization, understanding of governmental structures and operation, and active political participation by the citizens.

Approximately 4,500 blacks hold elected political offices in the United States at the present time (Newspaper Enterprise Association 1980, p. 365). This number represents a tremendous increase over the years since the passage of the 1964 Civil Rights Act and the Voting Rights Act of 1965. Thousands of communities with significant black populations have been affected by this legislation. The great need is to increase and broaden political participation by blacks and other minorities at the local and county political party level with centrifugal impacts at the state and national levels.

Historically black colleges and universities have played key roles in bringing their constituencies into the infrastructure of political parties. In the Democratic Party, the process of involvement has been facilitated by its national policy of nondiscrimination on the basis of race, age, sex, religion, or physical handicap, and its affirmative action programs. Universities such as Southern (Baton Rouge, Louisiana); Tennessee State (Nashville); Alabama State (Montgomery); Jackson State (Mississippi); Atlanta University (Georgia); Kentucky State (Frankfort); Lincoln of Missouri (Jefferson City); and Florida A&M (Tallahassee) have unusual opportunities for political and governmental participation since they are all located in state capitals. Legislative internships, committee staff appointments, and local patronage are manifest areas of potential involvement. Departments of political science could serve as spearheads for this essential community development process. (See Chapter 2 by Sidney J. Barthelemy for more on this topic).

Possible Consortial Arrangements

As indicated earlier, the historically black colleges and universities generally share a common educational mission, but differ in size, resources, emphases, and delivery capabilities. This immediately suggests the possibility of their sharing information about their strengths, weaknesses, and priorities so that consortia may be formed to support effective community service and development.

A significant number of historically black institutions are located close enough to each other to make cooperation feasible (see Table 2). Some of these schools are already working together on various academic programs, as in the Atlanta University Center. Even so, it would probably be worthwhile for them to reevaluate their cooperative arrangements in light of continuing and emerging public service needs.

TABLE 2

Possible Consortia of Historically Black Institutions

State	Institutions
Alabama	Alabama State Talladega Tuskegee
Florida	Bethune-Cookman Edward Waters Florida A&M
Georgia	Albany State Fort Valley Savannah State
Louisiana	Dillard Southern (N.O.) Xavier
Mississippi	Jackson State Mississippi Valley Tougaloo
North Carolina	Bennett North Carolina A&T Shaw
Tennessee	Fisk Meharry Tennessee State

Historically black institutions also might well explore developing cooperative relationships with neighboring historically white schools. Table 3 shows some typical examples of black and white schools in the same cities. Cooperative arrangements of this kind should be approached with the greatest caution, lest legislatures and governing boards view the joint activity as a demonstration of how a merger might begin; the result might be the ultimate submergence of the historically black college.

TABLE 3

Black and White State-Supported College or
University in the Same Cities

Location	Black Institution	White Institution
Montgomery, Ala.	Alabama State University	Auburn University
Tallahassee, Fla.	Florida A&M University	Florida State University
Savannah, Ga.	Savannah State College	Armstrong State College
Baton Rouge, La.	Southern University	Louisiana State University and A&M College
Greensboro, N.C.	North Carolina A&T State University	University of North Carolina at Greensboro
Nashville, Tenn.	Tennessee State University	University of Tennessee
Houston, Tex.	Texas Southern University	University of Houston
Norfolk, Va.	Norfolk State College	Old Dominion University

Student Internships

Formal internships with academic credit are an important means for students to render service to communities. Traditionally, such field or laboratory experiences were reserved for graduate students attached to a governmental service agency. Although it encountered massive resistance in the beginning, Florida A&M University (FAMU) was able to pioneer undergraduate internships with state agencies for black students in the 1960s.

FAMU was also able to provide more direct training and service functions by sending interns to community-based public and private organizations. In selecting such local organizations, a college or university must be careful to insure against "fly-by-night," underfunded, poorly staffed, ineffectual agencies that have no real service or training legitimacy. The historically black institution must constantly monitor and evaluate its internship arrangements to insure that agency supervisors are appropriately qualified so that the academic integrity and respectability of such service and training programs will be maintained.

Volunteer Service

Volunteer service is a preliminary kind of experience for undergraduate students and may be a corollary to formal credit-earning internships. FAMU's Department of Sociology makes volunteer community service mandatory for sociology majors minoring in either social welfare or corrections. Prior to going out on a formal internship for credit, each student has to accumulate a minimum of 120 hours of donated, uncompensated service to a community organization or agency. Students are allowed to choose their service agencies from an approved list compiled by students and faculty, with the whole process coordinated and monitored by a faculty member. Such a student volunteer program has some obvious benefits including: raising social consciousness, recognizing social responsibility, developing service skills, and delivering needed services. The FAMU model may not be appropriate for all schools, but student volunteering is an outstanding way to provide needed community services in an economical fashion.

Interdisciplinary Alliances

The delivery of certain community services and developmental programs can be optimized through interdisciplinary alliances among the departments and schools of historically black colleges and universities. Clearly health-service programs would benefit from the shared expertise of pharmacy, nursing, nutrition, and the biological sciences. Similarly, joint efforts by departments of business, consumer affairs, economics, and sociology could significantly improve the socioeconomic level and income maintenance of families. The integrated activities of political science, sociology, and urban and rural studies could also increase political participation and community self-development.

These and other interdisciplinary alliances may be difficult to establish because of the traditional jealousies, competition, and rivalries that often exist among departments. To give effective service, the colleges and universities must make a commitment that supersedes their often parochial and provincial notions of disciplines, integrity, and autonomy.

Applied Research and Action Institutes

Finally, historically black colleges and universities need to establish permanent applied research and action institutes or centers. Too often, well-designed programs of applied research and community development operate for a few years and then are lost, because the funding that supported them vanishes.

For instance, FAMU established a service-action branch in a riot-torn area of Tampa, shortly after the 1968 riot. The university provided a variety of service/development functions for the community, including voter registration, vocational and career counseling, college recruitment, transportation, community/welfare agency articulation, skill development, mediation, conflict resolution, and street theater. For several years, the program operated effectively and received national acclaim. Unfortunately, this program was supported by Model Cities monies, Title I funds of the Higher Education Act of 1965, and in-kind staff service contributions by the university. Political changes and modifications of funding priorities contributed to the demise of this center in 1973 after only five years of highly successful operation. Despite its demonstrated value to the City of Tampa, the Board of Regents of the State University System of Florida declined to provide continued funding.

Funding for such centers is often difficult to obtain from such governing boards because their work is perceived as neither related to postsecondary education nor leading to a degree. Thus such work is not considered appropriate to colleges and universities. (At least one source of external funding for such projects, the SEA/CR Program at land-grant institutions, will be discussed later in this chapter.)

OPERATION AND USE OF SUPPORT SYSTEMS

One of the obstacles black colleges and universities have faced in performing their community service functions over the years has been their inability to utilize the media effectively. In some instances, the institutions have not aggressively sought media coverage. For the most part, however, the racial attitudes of the white-dominated media, together with the relatively small size of

traditionally black colleges vis-à-vis that of their white counterparts, have resulted in unsystematic and abbreviated presentations
of academic and community service programs and athletic notices.

In recent years, attitudes have changed tremendously in many
communities and access to the media by minority institutions has
been facilitated by federal policies. The Federal Communications
Commission's regulations now require that privately owned radio
and television outlets make available, free of charge, a certain proportion of their programming time for public service functions, announcements, and programs. In addition, stations must conduct
periodic surveys to determine public reaction to their programming.
These developments have helped make it easier for historically
black institutions to utilize existing electronic media resources.
With planning and perseverance, virtually all these schools can organize, produce, and disseminate continuing programs of community service through these media. Even the cable television networks are mandated to maintain and operate a public-access chan-
nel, at no charge to the user.

Mass Media

Public-broadcasting television channels are often located in
the communities and regions served by historically black colleges
and universities. Most often these outlets are housed at a predominantly white institution or agency. It is highly unlikely that the black
colleges and universities can operate additional public-television
stations under these conditions, but here again, regular programming time and technical production assistance can be obtained from
the existing outlets.

Though television appears to be the most widely used medium,
it is a well-established fact that far more people listen to radio than
view television. The opportunity does exist for traditionally black
colleges and universities to obtain and operate their own radio stations. A university-owned and operated radio station can be an invaluable educational device, and insures the ready availability of a
community service programming outlet.

Clearly, there are many uses of the electronic media in community service and development programs. They can range from
simple consumer-interest "how to" programs to sophisticated
humanistic dramatizations. They can present demonstrations of
energy conservation and efficiency as well as ways to cope with
personal problems and strategies for improving intergroup relations.

This is not to imply that newspapers and other print media
should be overlooked. Here too, access by minority colleges and

universities has improved. The print media have the additional advantage of providing written documents for permanent retention. It is not difficult for this writer to visualize regular newspaper columns modeled after "Ann Landers" or "Dear Abby" written by faculty members at predominantly black institutions and focusing on community service and development.

Computers

Computers can be an invaluable tool in community service and development programs. Until recently, computers were bulky, expensive, and could be programmed and operated by only a small number of highly trained persons. Today a comprehensive computer system with multiple terminals can be purchased within the $150,000-$200,000 range. If this price range is prohibitive, microcomputers offer read-out, print-out, storage, and diversity of applications in free-standing models at prices that almost any institution can afford. Some microcomputers are available now for less than $3,000. The reduction in cost and simplification of accompanying software make computers available to the most modestly financed school and they can be operated by anyone with very little training. Software components such as the Statistical Packages for the Social Sciences (SPSS) also make computer language programming and application accessible for almost anyone.

Computer applications for community service and development programs are flexible and varied. They range from the reduction, summarization, and interpretation of data such as census information and vital statistics to sophisticated modeling and simulation of community characteristics and needs. Their uses in applied research are not discipline-bound, but are applicable to both the social and natural sciences. Freestanding portable systems have been developed that can provide color-coded pictorials of land-use patterns that will be extremely effective and cost-efficient for community planners. One system uses earth-satellite photography in its preparation of computer video discs that can show color overlays of changes in land use. The potential for this kind of system in community service and development programs can hardly be fully appreciated at this time.

Other Community Activities

Finally, the community service and development mission of minority colleges and universities can be additionally enhanced and effectively carried out through the following activities and programs:

- Newsletters and reports
- University research journals
- Off-campus credit and noncredit offerings
- Evening and weekend colleges
- Mobile informational and service units
- Community service centers
- Voter education and registration
- Surveys of community services
- Individual and group counseling
- Agency and program evaluation
- Adult basic literacy training
- Graduate theses in applied research

OUTSIDE FUNDING SUPPORTS

Since many boards of trustees, or other governing bodies, feel that the limited funds regularly available to historically black colleges and universities must be concentrated on traditional academic pursuits, the community service and development function is often marginally financed, if at all. This means that vigorous, systematic, continuing efforts must be made for outside funding support. Permanent offices of sponsored research and grants are indispensable for successful community service and development programs.

A significant number of black colleges and universities already have well-established research and grants offices and staffs. The relative success in grantsmanship of such schools as North Carolina A&T University, Tuskegee Institute, Florida A&M University, Howard University, Southern University at Baton Rouge, and others documents the importance of such offices. Sponsored research and grants offices should provide faculty and staff with information on the sources and availability of funds, and on guidelines and deadlines for submitting proposals. In addition, these offices should: (1) maintain up-to-date files of statistical, procedural, and structural data about the institution; (2) establish and maintain contacts with federal bureau officials and congressional delegations; (3) conduct on-campus proposal writing and grantsmanship training programs for faculty, staff, and administrators; (4) identify and establish liaison with private consulting firms and area prime sponsors of comprehensive federal programs; and (5) provide technical assistance in writing proposals and preparing final drafts for submission.

Federal Programs

There is a wide range and diversity of federal programs that aid higher education, including community service activities. <u>The Catalog of Federal Assistance Programs</u> (1974) lists over 300 different funding opportunities and may be obtained from the U.S. Department of Education in Washington. This catalog includes all programs administered by the Department of Education, "as well as programs administered by other Federal agencies in support of educational services, professional training, or library services. . . ." The Departments of Commerce, Transportation, Housing and Urban Development, Labor, Energy, Health and Human Services, Defense, Agriculture, and State offer a variety of other opportunities for community-service grants. In addition, the great number of other federal boards, commissions, and advisory panels can be explored as funding sources. Many federal programs that support community-service and development activities require some level of proportional matching by the institution, state or local governing bodies. Colleges and universities should become familiar with state and local government officials, maintain communication with them, and enlist their cooperation in the delivery of community service programs. The public historically black colleges and universities are generally in a much better position to obtain federal funds for this type of program.

Programs Available to Land-Grant Institutions

The 1890 land-grant institutions are fortunate in that the Scientific Educational and Administration/Cooperative Research (SEA/CR) Program of the U.S. Department of Agriculture (P.L. 95-113) provides renewable funding for a wide range of research and applied service projects. An average of nearly $1 million per year is available to each of the historically black land-grant schools, and to Tuskegee. Traditionally, these funds have been restricted, either by misunderstanding of the legislation or by deliberate intramural design, to projects in agriculture and home economics. SEA/CR monies may be used by any academic unit in a land-grant institution. Each institution is required by law to present, and have approved, a general plan for the use of its funds. Faculty members from all academic units may submit proposals for grants from the institutional allocation. Community-service and development projects such as those described earlier in this chapter are appropriate for SEA/CR funding. In fact, the experiment in the amelioration of rural poverty was funded over several years from this source.

Each historically black land-grant institution has an SEA/CR co-ordinator who can provide specific information about access to these funds for those wishing to initiate community-service projects.

Another little-known but long-standing vehicle of community-service and development activities for the 1890 land-grant universities is the Cooperative Extension program of the Department of Agriculture, funded under the Smith-Lever Act. This program, targeted mainly for low-income agricultural populations, supports extension work in such areas as:

— Four-H (4-H) and youth development
— Consumer competence
— Community resource development
— Commercial agriculture management assistance to low-income families
— Food and nutrition
— Safety
— Housing and home environment
— Leadership development
— Comprehensive community planning
— Community service and facilities
— Economic manpower and career development
— Leisure and cultural education

Traditional institutional structures and perceptions have done little to encourage planning, articulation, and service delivery of cooperative extension programs utilizing the interdisciplinary resources of the 1890 land-grant schools. If these institutions are to optimize their community service and development potentials, they must no longer be isolated. Indeed, Dr. Beverly Archer, Director of Cooperative Extension at FAMU, states: "An important key to the future survival of the 1890 Land-Grant Universities is the extent to which the various academic resources can be marshalled in unified community service thrusts with programs such as Cooperative Extension." (Archer 1980)

Under the federal revenue sharing program, many municipalities receive community block grants provided by the U.S. Department of Housing and Urban Development. Frequently these are substantial funds that can be used in discretionary fashion for a broad range of community-service and improvement projects. Historically black colleges could monitor the block-grant awards, participate in the mandated public hearings on the use of the funds, and submit proposals for regrants for specific service and development components. Following this procedure some historically black institutions have been able to assist minority communities in getting much needed facilities, services, and programs.

Title I of the Higher Education Act is still a viable funding source. Under the heading, "Community Service and Continuing Education Program," this title has funds available for projects such as ". . . an educational program, activity, or service, including a research program and a university extension or continuing education offering, which is designed to assist in the solution of community problems in rural, urban, or sub-urban areas . . ." (Higher Education Act of 1965).

The National Science Foundation (NSF) through its division of Applied Social and Behavioral Sciences has for a number of years awarded grants for research projects designed to impact positively on important social and behavioral problems. Most of these research grants have gone to "established scholar/researchers" at "major" (nonblack) universities. In fact, during the two years (1978-80) this writer served on the Advisory Subcommittee to review proposals and make recommendations on funding, not a single proposal from a historically black college or university reached the subcommittee for consideration. Inquiries of the NSF staff revealed that although program announcements are systematically sent to the black schools, very few if any had submitted a proposal.

In 1980, NSF's Applied Social and Behavioral Sciences division started a grant program for lesser known and beginning applied science researchers. These new "Research Initiation Grants" provide funding for applied research projects in the $25,000-$35,000 range. Assurances have been given to this writer that proposals submitted by researchers at predominantly black institutions will be welcomed, provided, of course, that the program continues.

Another potential source of federal support for community services and development projects became known to this writer only after he was appointed to the Environmental Affairs Advisory Committee of the Coastal Plains Regional Commission. Under the aegis of the U.S. Department of Commerce there are nine regional commissions. Each of these commissions has funds for grants to eligible institutions, agencies, and private industry in support of community and regional service and development projects. The total funding requested for the nine regional commissions for fiscal year 1981 was $175 million.

Finally, one community-service and development area not often included under this rubric relates to the quality of life enhanced by awareness and understanding of, and participation in the humanities. The National Endowment for the Humanities (NEH) coordinates a wide assortment of humanistic programs for which it provides financial support. A partial listing includes: projects in social sciences, the arts, education, research grants, state programs, special programs, youth programs, and public programs. The funds most readily available to historically black institutions are in the state programs. In 1979, a total of $22.1 million was made available to the states; the average state grant was $393,000.

Each state has an administering body such as a committee, council, commission, or board of directors that makes continuation grants to eligible institutions, groups, or agencies for projects that coincide with established guidelines. As a past vice-chairman of the Board of Directors of the Florida Endowment for the Humanities, this writer can attest to the fact that although the continuation grants may not be large, these monies are among the easiest for historically black schools to obtain, at least in Florida. Information about the NEH state program can usually be obtained from the governor's office.

CONCLUSION

Historically, community service has been a key mission of black colleges. Because most are located in communities where a sizable proportion of the population is black and low income, there are numerous opportunities and challenges for these institutions, their faculty, students, and alumni to initiate activities that will improve the social and economic well-being of the entire community. Several examples of community service activities have been outlined in this chapter with the hope that some black colleges will pursue one or several of these projects. Unlike in the early days when black colleges financially supported service activities with their own resources, funding for these efforts are now provided through federal, state, and local governments; private foundations and corporations; as well as local and national businesses. Consortial arrangements between institutions are possible and so are joint efforts between institutions and local community service agencies. Black colleges must, therefore, give this mission a priority equal to the institution's objectives of teaching and research. Community service must be enhanced, expanded, and more actively encouraged. But the translation of commitment to community service into effective action will be almost totally determined by the ability of faculty and administrators to rise above parochial rivalries among the disciplines to serve as a united force for the common good.

REFERENCES

American Council on Education. American universities and colleges. 11th ed. Washington, D.C.: American Council on Education, 1973.

Archer, Beverly. Personal interview. 1980.

Billingsley, Andrew. Black families in white America. Englewood Cliffs, NJ: Prentice-Hall, 1969.

Jencks, Christopher, and David Riesman. "The American Negro college." Harvard Educational Review 37 (1967).

Lewis, Oscar. La Vida: A Puerto Rican family in the culture of poverty. NY: Random House, 1965.

Moynihan, Daniel Patrick. The Negro family: The case for national action. Washington, D.C.: U.S. Government Printing Office, 1965.

Newspaper Enterprise Association. World almanac and book of facts. NY: Newspaper Enterprise Association, 1980.

Higher Education Act of 1965. Public Law 89-329, amended in 1974.

Robertson, Warren. "The theatre as a vehicle for community action." Doctoral dissertation, Florida State University, Tallahassee, 1972.

Sherif, M., and C. W. Sherif. Outline of social psychology. NY: Harper & Row, 1956.

Smith, Charles U. "Teaching and learning the social sciences at predominantly black colleges and universities." In Black colleges in America, edited by Charles V. Willie and Ronald R. Edmonds. NY: Columbia University, Teacher's College Press, 1978.

U.S. Bureau of the Census. The social and economic status of the black population in the United States: 1970-1978: Current population reports. Washington, D.C.: U.S. Government Printing Office, 1979.

U.S. Department of Education. Catalog of federal education assistance programs. Washington, D.C.: U.S. Government Printing Office, 1974.

PART III

STRENGTHENING AND EXPANDING THE ROLE OF BLACK COLLEGES IN U.S. HIGHER EDUCATION

This section of the book considers three less traditional roles that some black colleges might be able and willing to assume in the next several years. Since blacks are underrepresented in the natural sciences, engineering, and graduate education, the first two papers by William Jackson and Jewel Prestage urge the expansion of programs in these areas by black colleges. The final paper by Madelon Delany Stent explores a more innovative and unconventional role for black colleges. Stent suggests the establishment of more formal alliances between black colleges and other countries, especially those that now send or have sent large numbers of students to black colleges.

The three authors offer a variety of strategies and recommendations in the event that some black colleges will see these as meaningful and feasible roles they wish to pursue. Much recent data is cited on enrollment and graduate production of black students, as well as indications of a significant foreign student population on black college campuses. Because of the tremendous national underrepresentation of black scientists and engineers, black graduate students, and the large numbers of foreign students in this country, the authors believe that there are opportunities for black colleges to develop or expand their roles in the sciences and graduate education.

The Role of Black Colleges
and Universities
in Graduate Education

Jewel L. Prestage

The historically black college has traditionally been the major source of education for black Americans. Frank Bowles and Frank DeCosta wrote in 1971: "Whatever the Negro has achieved in terms of professional entry has been achieved through the Negro colleges." Horace Mann Bond in his 1972 volume on black academicians estimated that nearly two-thirds of those with doctorates received their undergraduate degrees from black colleges. In a 1956 study focusing on black women college graduates, Jeanne Noble observed that graduates of historically black colleges were more consious of professional goals than those who graduated from historically white institutions. Gilford and Snyder (1977) found that 22 of the 25 leading undergraduate institutions of blacks who received PhDs in the period from 1973 to 1976 were historically black colleges located in the South.

This chapter is concerned with the role of the black college in an era when its mission is no longer restricted to undergraduate education of blacks. The major premise here is that the historically black institutions should provide viable options for individuals seeking quality graduate education.

A great deal of data from a variety of sources has been cited in the first section of this chapter, and a few general comments are necessary when reading this material. The first has to do with the race of degree recipients, particularly of those who are black. For example, in the annual Summary Reports of Doctorate Recipients from U.S. Universities of the National Academy of Sciences (Gilford and Syverson 1978, 1979; and Syverson 1980, 1981), figures for blacks are broken down according to citizenship into those of black U.S. citizens, and black non-U.S. citizens with permanent and temporary visas. These distinctions make it possible to exclude foreign blacks, who usually tend to inflate the data, from most of the analyses focusing on black U.S. citizens. Not all sources and reports make these distinctions, however, and I have attempted to point out citizenship status where it seems appropriate and if it is known.

Another issue involves periodic changes in the reporting of racial or ethnic status on the U.S. government's questionnaire for doctorate recipients as the Office of Management and Budget has modified these definitions. In 1977, for example, the exclusion from the Hispanic group of individuals from Brazil, Guyana, Surinam, Trinidad, and Belize may have moved some individuals into the black group. Changes in the total number of black PhDs from one year to another may, therefore, reflect changes in the composition of the group, rather than changes in the rate at which doctorates are earned by group members.

The final consideration relates to total PhDs received by all students, but particularly blacks, over the last few years. Just because the numbers of PhDs have not been rising steadily may not be a sign that fewer students are pursuing advanced degrees. Rather, it may suggest that professional fields such as law and medicine are making up for the decreases. More detailed analyses of the various professions are needed, but this paper deals solely with graduate education.

CURRENT STATUS OF BLACK PhDs IN HIGHER EDUCATION

The first black Americans to be awarded the Doctor of Philosophy degree were: Edward Bouchet, Yale University (physics), 1876; John W. Bowen, Boston University (religion), 1887; William L. Bulkey, Syracuse University (Latin), 1893; and W. E. B. DuBois, Harvard University (history), 1895 (Greene 1946). It was not until 1921 that the first black woman received a doctorate—Sadie T. Alexander, in economics from the University of Pennsylvania. There is only limited information on graduate education of blacks prior to 1954, especially on doctoral training in specific fields. Isolated bits of information do illustrate the delayed access of blacks to advanced training in most academic disciplines. For example, blacks received the first two PhDs in accounting in 1950 and 1953 from the University of Illinois and Ohio State University, respectively. The University of Iowa awarded the first PhD in music to a black in 1942 and the first PhD in history to a black woman in 1941 (Bergman 1976). Ralph Bunche had received the first PhD for a black in political science from Harvard University in 1934;

Thomas R. Solomon received the second from the University of
Michigan in 1939; and the University of Iowa awarded the first PhD
to a black woman in political science in 1954.

Studies on Black Doctorates

A study by Earl McGrath in 1965 gave an indication of the
dearth of PhDs among blacks. He observed that about 30 percent of
the faculty at black colleges held doctorates compared to about 51
percent of all college faculty members nationwide (McGrath 1965,
p. 118). Since faculties at black colleges included whites, it is
reasonable to assume that PhD holders at such colleges included
some whites. At the same time, very few blacks were on faculties
of predominantly white institutions. Thus, while there is not a
direct match between PhD holding by blacks and the presence of
black PhDs on the faculties of predominantly black institutions,
McGrath's findings are suggestive. Later, a study of a sample of
PhD scientists and engineers who had obtained their degrees between
1930 and 1972 yielded an estimate that blacks had received 1,860
(or less than 1 percent) of the 244,829 doctorates awarded in these
fields (National Research Council 1974, p. 19).

Systematic efforts to assemble data on doctorates awarded to
blacks were not undertaken until the 1960s. The Ford Foundation
initiated one such effort in 1969 when it sponsored a series of conferences on the status of blacks in selected disciplines, which produced some information about the distribution of degrees (Bryant
1970). Specifically, 65 blacks held PhDs in political science and
129 in sociology (Ford Foundation 1969). A study of the natural
sciences indicated that between 1876 and 1969 blacks earned only
587 doctorates or .36 percent of all degrees in the natural sciences
conferred during that period (Jay 1969). Moreover, the most recent data on doctorate recipients in the United States indicate that
in 1980 blacks (U.S. citizens and non-U.S. citizens with permanent
visas) received only .1 percent of the total PhDs awarded in the
physical and life sciences and less than .2 percent of those in the
humanities (Syverson 1981).

More recent studies show that although the actual number of
doctorates awarded to blacks has increased, they still receive only
a small percentage of the total number conferred by U.S. universities each year. Of all doctorates awarded in 1971-73, 2.8
percent went to native-born blacks (National Board of Graduate
Education [NBGE] 1976, p. 241). Gilford and Snyder state that of
the U.S. native-born doctorate recipients from 1973 to 1976, only
3.7 percent were black (1977, p. 125). For the four-year period

1977-80, the figures were 4.5, 4.3, 4.4, and 4.1 percent (Gilford and Syverson 1978, 1979; Syverson 1980, 1981). The figures have risen slightly in recent years, but they are still quite low.

Within the total number of doctorates earned by blacks, there are significant variations with respect to institutions at which recipients received undergraduate degrees, institutions granting the doctorate, region, fields of specialization, median age, and sex of recipients. For example, blacks received 833 or more of a total of more than 24,000 doctorates awarded to native-born citizens in 1973-74. Over half of the 833 came from only 24 of the PhD-granting institutions in the United States, and 110 institutions did not award a single degree to a black that year (NBGE 1976, p. 71). Only 15 institutions granted more than ten degrees to blacks.

Doctorate Production in the South

Data for 1975-76 show that 1,213 doctorates went to blacks across the nation, and universities in the South conferred 320 of these. Table 1 lists southern states in rank order according to percentage of total doctorates awarded to blacks in 1975-76. The number of doctorates per state ranged from 120, or 8.5 percent of the state's total, in Florida, to none in Kentucky.

Figures for the 1976-77 period show blacks received 1,253 doctorates, or 3.8 percent of all those awarded by U.S. institutions. Approximately one-fourth of these, 322, came from universities in the South (Mingle 1979, p. 9). At the time, blacks represented an estimated 18.8 percent of the population of the South and 11.5 percent nationwide. Thus, southern universities exceeded the rest of the nation in the percent of total degrees (15 percent) to blacks, but not in proportion to the South's population advantage (63 percent). This is especially significant since the historically black colleges and universities, which award the majority of all bachelor's degrees to southern blacks and to blacks nationwide, are almost all located in the South. Obviously, graduate schools in the region are not fully exploiting this potential source of students.

Age of Doctorate Recipients

Another interesting breakdown of the PhD population is by age. In the main, blacks are older than whites when they receive PhDs. One study shows that overall they are about five and one-half years older than whites, 36.7 to 31.2 years (NBGE 1976, pp. 54-55). But the difference is reduced if the analysis is limited to noneducation

TABLE 1

Doctorates Awarded by Southern Institutions by State, 1975-76

State	Percentage of Total Doctorates to Whites	Percentage of Total Doctorates to Blacks	Percentage of Total Degrees to Others	Number of Doctorates to Blacks
Florida	82.7	8.5	8.7	120
Georgia	88.5	8.3	3.1	47
Mississippi	81.42	7.5	11.07	21
Arkansas	90.0	4.2	5.8	5
Louisiana	81.3	3.9	14.8	13
Tennessee	87.3	3.6	9.0	21
Virginia	91.9	3.6	4.5	19
Alabama	91.5	3.5	4.9	8
Maryland	81.6	3.3	15.0	20
Texas	83.8	2.1	14.0	31
South Carolina	93.0	2.0	5.0	4
North Carolina	89.9	1.4	8.7	10
West Virginia	91.7	0.8	7.4	1
Kentucky	90.1	0.0	9.8	0

Source: James R. Mingle, Degree output in the south, 1975-76: Distribution by race. (Atlanta: Southern Regional Education Board, 1978).

majors. For the period 1973-76, figures on native-born U.S. citizens show that the median age for white men receiving the doctorate was 31 and for black men 36, while the median age for white women was 32.3 and for black women, 37.2 (Gilford and Snyder 1977, p. 34). The time actually enrolled in school is about the same for both races, so the age difference can be attributed to factors other than academic requirements. Lower family incomes and few employment possibilities are probably causes that contribute to delayed entry into graduate school and more interruptions once graduate study is begun. Table 2 indicates that 70 percent of white male doctorate recipients entered graduate school immediately after receiving their bachelor's degree, while only 46.4 percent of black male recipients, 57.5 percent of white females, and 34 percent of black females did so. The table also shows that only 1.9 percent of white males, but 7.2 percent of black males, 7.6 percent of white women, and 12.1 percent of the black women recipients reported delays of nine years or more. Figures for 1976 doctorate recipients reflect some changes: 67.5 percent of the white males, 41.1 percent of the black males, 57.2 percent of the white females, and 42.5 percent of black females reported immediate entry into graduate school. The only improvement seems to have been for black females. On the other hand, delays of nine years or more were characteristic of 1.6 percent of the white men, 4.2 percent of the black men, 6.3 percent of white women and 8.2 percent of the black women. However, while these figures tell a great deal about aggregate patterns of matriculation for men and women and blacks and whites through graduate school, it is imperative to note that there are differences in entry and delays in graduation by fields of study and those factors should be controlled for in analyses of this type.

Fields of Specialization

A factor which contributes to the age differential between black and white doctorate recipients is the heavy concentration of blacks in education. In that field, students of all races take more time between the bachelor's degree and the doctorate than do noneducation majors. Eliminating education doctorates from the analysis of 1973-74 PhDs reduces the median age for receipt of the degree for whites and blacks to 30.3 and 33.5, respectively (NBGE 1976, p. 55).
There are interesting constant patterns revealed in the fields of doctoral study pursued. Reasons for this distribution are complex and impossible to identify and explain definitively in the absence of empirical data. The historical context in which higher education for blacks exists suggests several possibilities:

58 / Jewel L. Prestage

TABLE 2

Elapsed Time between BA and Graduate School Entry for
U.S. Native Born Doctorate Recipients, by Race and
Sex, 1973 and 1976

Time Lapse	White Men		Black Men		White Women		Black Women	
	1973	1976	1973	1976	1973	1976	1973	1976
0	70.0	67.5	46.4	41.1	57.5	57.2	34.0	42.5
1-2 years	17.0	18.9	20.4	25.2	20.7	22.6	31.9	25.7
3-8 years	11.1	12.0	26.0	29.5	14.2	13.9	22.0	23.6
9 or more	1.9	1.6	7.2	4.2	7.6	6.3	12.1	8.2

Source: Dorothy M. Gilford and Joan Snyder, Women and minority PhDs in the 1970's: A data book (Washington, D.C.: National Academy of Sciences, 1977), p. 52.

● Science and engineering undergraduate programs require greater institutional financial outlay for equipment and instructional materials than do programs in the social sciences and arts and humanities. Financial resources have always been at a minimum in institutions enrolling the overwhelming majority of black students.

● The absence of a large cadre of black faculty members with training in the sciences and engineering makes recruitment extremely difficult. (See Chapter 5 for more on this topic.)

● Strong degree-granting programs cannot be developed and maintained without qualified faculty.

● Until recently, career opportunities for blacks in the sciences had been extremely limited. Black students, like students generally, usually select majors in those areas they perceive as offering optimum job possibilities. Education has been perceived as one such field for blacks and has been a major offering at historically black institutions.

● Education and social sciences are attractive majors for black students who are socially conscious and who regard the quest for solutions to social problems as intellectually stimulating.

● Undergraduate offerings in science and engineering have been greatly expanded at historically black institutions, and salaries and other benefits for bachelor's degree holders are sufficiently attractive to discourage pursuit of advanced degrees.

• Since blacks account for less than 5 percent of the doctorate holders in America, no field, not even education, has an oversupply. The expanding subfields in education and the shortages of qualified faculty in these newer areas demand an increased supply of black expertise at all levels. Adequate response to the problems in areas like urban education and learning disabilities, for example, will require black scholars capable of sensitive but rigorous research and scholarly output. The emphasis should be on increasing the total output of black doctorates in all fields.

The fact that a large percentage of blacks seeking doctorates choose education as their preferred field of specialization is not, in my opinion, a reason for extreme concern, but the transfer of a substantial number of black doctoral students from other fields to education at the postbaccalaureate level suggests problems of access that require further investigation (Harmon 1978, pp. 60-67). The National Board on Graduate Education reported that one-third of blacks who received the bachelor's degree in the physical sciences and engineering and continued to the doctorate switched from the physical sciences to education. Only 44 percent of the black doctorates (1972-74) who received the bachelor's degree in the physical sciences continued in those fields for doctoral work, while one-third switched to education (NBGE 1976, p. 51). In contrast, 68 percent of the white doctorates with undergraduate degrees in the physical sciences earned a doctorate in the same field and only 8 percent shifted to education. This might well suggest that education is the field of last resort rather than the preferred field of doctoral study for a significant number of blacks.

Some additional statistics further reveal the imbalance between fields. In 1972-73, native-born blacks received only 1 percent of all doctorates conferred in the physical sciences and mathematics, 1.1 percent of those in engineering, 1.7 percent in life sciences, 0.4 percent in the arts and humanities, 1.6 percent in social sciences, and 6.9 percent in education. Data for 1973-76 (see Table 3) indicate that no marked changes were occurring in the established patterns (NBGE 1976, pp. 239-41; Gilford and Snyder 1977, p. 40). For the 1976-77 group of 1,253 black doctorate recipients, including foreigners, education accounted for over half (54.7 percent) of the degrees awarded to blacks; the social sciences for 9.3 percent; psychology for 8.4 percent; the humanities, 4.8 percent; biological sciences, 4.2 percent; physical sciences, 3.6 percent; and engineering 1.8 percent (Mingle 1979, p. 14).

TABLE 3

Field Distribution of Black and White Doctorate Recipients,*
1973-76, by Sex and Race

Subject Matter Field	Race	Male	Female
Mathematics	White	3.7	1.5
	Black	1.4	0.4
Physics and astronomy	White	4.5	0.6
	Black	0.9	0.3
Chemistry	White	6.1	2.2
	Black	3.3	0.5
Earth sciences	White	2.4	0.6
	Black	0.2	0.3
Engineering	White	8.1	0.4
	Black	2.3	—
Biosciences	White	14.7	12.7
	Black	6.8	6.0
Psychology	White	8.3	13.3
	Black	6.5	7.3
Social sciences	White	10.7	10.2
	Black	8.3	5.8
Arts and humanities	White	14.5	23.3
	Black	8.5	9.1
Professional fields	White	4.8	3.2
	Black	3.5	4.5
Education	White	22.1	31.8
	Black	58.4	65.8

*U.S. native born citizens.
Source: Dorothy M. Gilford and Joan Snyder, Women and minority PhDs in the 1970's: A data book (Washington, D.C.: National Academy of Sciences, 1977).

Sex Distribution of Black Doctorates

Up to 1980, black women received a minority of the total number of doctorates conferred on blacks as did white women of the total number of doctorates conferred on whites. Black women, however, have received a larger share of the doctorates awarded to blacks than have white women and other minority women in their respective groups. Among black U.S. citizens in 1980, black women received 51.5 percent of the doctorates awarded compared to 48.5 percent black men; white women received 33.1 percent of the PhDs among white U.S. citizens (Syverson 1981). And women outranked men 57 to 43 percent among black bachelor's degree earners. White women received only 44 percent of the total undergraduate degrees awarded to whites (NBGE 1976, p. 63). In 1973-76, black women received 34.3 percent of the doctorates conferred on blacks, while white women received 21.8 percent of those conferred on whites (Gilford and Snyder 1977, p. 26). Whatever advantages black women have at the undergraduate level seem to dissipate at the graduate level even though they fare well in relationship to women in other racial/ethnic groups. Literature on women in higher education suggests that women earning the doctorate are older than men receiving it and that women, more often than men, find it necessary to work while pursuing the degree. Further, except perhaps for education, women are less apt than men to have predoctoral employment that is suitable for continuation after the doctorate (Centra 1974). The extent to which black women face special barriers in pursuit of the doctorate is of special concern. Given the disproportionate share of undergraduate degrees they have received in recent years, black women provide the greatest potential source for expanding the pool of black doctorates in the short run. It is interesting to note that two predominantly black PhD-granting institutions are "above average" in the proportion of doctorates granted to women (Gilford and Snyder 1977, pp. 130-33). Over the long run, however, any commitment to educational equity would seem to dictate that priority be given to increasing the number of young black men completing undergraduate education and becoming eligible for graduate study. Among black undergraduates and graduates, females traditionally outnumber males. Most recent available data of college enrollment of black men and women at the undergraduate and graduate levels, respectively, for the 1980-81 academic year were: males, 388,389; females, 538,321; males 22,780; females, 37,198 (Hill, 1983). Black women also graduated in larger numbers than black men in 1981 at the BA and MA levels while black men surpassed black females in doctorates and first-professional degrees: BAs—men, 24,500 compared to 36,200 women; MAs—men, 6,200 versus 11,000 women; doctorates—men, 700 compared to 600 women; and first-professional degrees—men, 1,800 versus 1,200 women (Hill, 1983).

Black Doctorates in 1979-80

U.S. universities awarded 30,892 doctorates in the period July 1, 1979 to June 30, 1980 (Syverson 1981). Of these,

25,108 went to U.S. citizens, 1,021 of whom were black, or 4.1 percent of the total. Black women represented 51.5 percent of the black recipients, but overall women represented only 30.3 percent of the total degrees awarded to U.S. citizens. The median age for all 1980 degree recipients was 32.2; for blacks, 36.9 years, for whites, 32.1 years (Syverson 1981, pp. 38-39). Of all doctorates awarded to U.S. citizens, education degrees constituted 26.8 percent. Of all doctorates awarded to black U.S. citizens, 57.4 percent were in education compared to only 25.4 percent of all doctorates received by whites. In the main, it seems that patterns that have been characteristic of black doctorates over time continue to prevail.

The data for 1979-80 also include information on financial support for graduate study. It is striking to note that while 47.3 percent of white doctorates who were U.S. citizens had held teaching assistantships, only 24.8 percent of the blacks had. Also, 18.8 percent of the black recipients had national direct student loans and 16 percent had other loans as compared to 11.1 percent of the whites on national direct loans and 10.7 percent on other loans (Syverson 1981, pp. 38-39).

Another dimension of the 1979-80 data, postdoctoral employment plans, is relevant to this article. Black doctorate recipients, particularly those in the physical sciences, engineering, biological sciences, and education, plan to seek employment in government in greater proportions than any of the other racial/ethnic groups (Syverson 1981, pp. 38-39). The proportion of blacks planning to work in academe is nearly the same as for other groups.

HISTORICALLY BLACK COLLEGES AND BLACK GRADUATE PRODUCTION

The potential of the existing doctoral programs at predominantly black institutions to produce more black doctorates is of special concern. Graduate education on a continuous basis as we know it today began in black universities about 1927 with Fisk University leading the way. By 1934, Hampton Institute, Xavier University, Atlanta University, and Howard University developed graduate programs (Dyson 1941). Currently over 30 black institutions offer graduate degrees. As of the 1980-81 school year, six historically black institutions were authorized to offer doctoral training (see Table 4).

In 1975-76, historically black institutions awarded 50 doctorates to blacks or 4.1 percent of the total of 1,213 doctorates awarded to blacks that year. In the South, the percentage was 8.1

TABLE 4

Graduate Degrees Authorized at Historically Black Institutions, 1980–81

| Institution | Degrees Offered | |
	Masters	Doctorate
1. Alabama A & M University	X	
2. Alabama State University	X	
3. Tuskegee Institute (Alabama)	X	
4. Howard University (District of Columbia)	X	X
5. Florida A & M University	X	
6. Atlanta University	X	X
7. Fort Valley State (Georgia)	X	
8. Interdenominational Theological Center		X
9. Savannah State College	X	
10. Kentucky State University	X	
11. Grambling State University (Louisiana)	X	
12. Southern University—Baton Rouge	X	
13. Xavier University (Louisiana)	X	
14. Bowie State University (Maryland)	X	
15. Coppin State University (Maryland)	X	
16. Morgan State University (Maryland)	X	X
17. University of Maryland—Eastern Shore	X	
18. Alcorn State University (Mississippi)	X	
19. Jackson State University (Mississippi)	X	
20. Mississippi Valley State University	X	
21. North Carolina A & T State University	X	
22. North Carolina Central University	X	
23. Cheyney State College (Pennsylvania)	X	
24. Lincoln University (Pennsylvania)	X	
25. South Carolina State College	X	
26. Fisk University (Tennessee)	X	
27. Meharry Medical College	X	X
28. Tennessee State University	X	
29. Prairie View A & M University (Texas)	X	
30. Texas Southern University	X	X
31. Hampton Institute (Virginia)	X	
32. Norfolk State College	X	
33. Virginia State College—Petersburg	X	

Source: Target date, 2000 A.D.: Goals for achieving higher education equity for black Americans, Volume I (Washington, D.C.: National Advisory Committee for Black Higher Education and Black Colleges and Universities, September 1980), Appendix A.

or 26 out of 320 degrees awarded (Mingle 1978, pp. 41-56). Further, black institutions conferred 22 percent of all master's degrees awarded to blacks in 1976 (NACBHEBCU 1979, p. xiv). These figures emphasize the importance of predominantly black institutions in the provision of master's level graduate education to blacks and in expanded graduate educational opportunities.

Enrollment in Graduate Programs

The irony of the "search" for black faculty members by leading U.S. universities during the past decade is that the institutions that are searching are themselves the primary source of such faculty. According to a study by the American Council on Education, black faculty represented 2.2 percent of all university faculty members in 1968-69 and 2.9 percent in 1972-73 (Weidlein 1972). Availability of faculty in the future will largely depend on the status of black enrollment in programs leading to the doctorate in the various disciplines.

In 1973-74 it was estimated that blacks made up 4 to 5 percent of enrollees in graduate programs nationwide (NBGE 1976, p. 44). For 1976, the percentage was 6.0 for the nation and 10.1 for the South (Mingle 1978, p. 1). In the predominantly black institutions, where 43 percent of all blacks were enrolled in 1976, graduate students comprised 8 percent of the total enrollment (Mingle 1978, p. 3). Two years later, in 1978, blacks constituted only 5.7 percent of all graduate students in the United States and only 4.9 percent of those studying fulltime (NACBHEBCU 1980, p. 1).

Predominantly black institutions accounted for 17.8 percent of all black graduate students in 1978, although these institutions represented less than 3 percent of the country's graduate schools (NACBHEBCU 1980, p. 2). Further, in 1976-77, blacks received 21,028 master's degrees, or 6.6 percent of the 316,737 awarded nationwide. Of all master's degrees earned by blacks that year, historically black schools awarded 21.6 percent, or 43.9 percent in the states where those institutions are located (NACBHEBCU 1980, p. 2). This is interesting because a higher proportion of blacks than whites have earned master's degrees before taking their doctorates, especially in the physical and life sciences (NACBHEBCU 1980). Receiving a master's degree tends to be an important juncture in the educational career of black doctorate recipients. The fact that historically black institutions contribute disproportionately to master's level education in a number of fields suggests that they may also be effective in increasing the output of black doctorates.

Distribution of black graduate students among the academic
fields and patterns of financial support continue to be causes for
concern. Low representation in agriculture, engineering, and the
physical sciences at both the master's and doctoral levels and the
relatively high representation in education suggest that existing
imbalances will extend into the future. Yet, predominantly black
institutions have tended to produce an unusually large share of
master's degrees in those areas in which blacks are most sparsely
represented (NACBHEBCU 1980, p. 2).

Financial support is a critical factor in the decision to pursue
graduate education. Black students have not fared well in this regard. Among 1978 recipients of the doctorate, blacks received
two of 422 National Science Foundation traineeship awards, 16 of
725 National Science Foundation fellowship awards, 243 of 13,193
institutional teaching assistantships, and 156 of 10,206 institutional
research assistantships (NACBHEBCU 1980, p. 42). In 1978 black
doctorate recipients in engineering or the physical and life sciences
were given virtually no federal nor institutional support. They
received only four National Science Foundation awards compared
to 629 to whites and 133 to other minorities and non-U.S. citizens;
37 research assistantships, compared to 4,049 to whites and 2,232
to foreign students and other minorities (NACBHEBCU 1980, p. 44).
If there is a substantial increase in the attainment of the PhD by
blacks it must be accompanied by a change in patterns of distribut-
ing financial aid for graduate study and in distribution of enrollment
by field.

As with other population groups, black graduate enrollment
exceeds black doctoral degree output. But even if all of those currently enrolled were to receive the doctorate, the supply would still
fall critically short of existing demand, assuming equity in representation as a reflection of the presence of blacks in the general
population. More realistically, the number will probably remain
far less than current enrollment.

POLITICAL SCIENCE: A CASE STUDY

The status of political science as an academic profession can
be traced to the founding of the American Political Science Association (APSA) in 1903. From just over 200 members in 1903, the
Association grew to nearly 12,000 members by 1968 and about
14,000 in 1976, then declined to 12,377 in July 1980. The discipline
is overwhelmingly male, overwhelmingly white, overwhelmingly
youthful, and overwhelmingly U.S. citizens. In his presidential address in 1966, Gabriel Almond estimated that two of every three

political scientists who ever lived were alive and practicing (Almond 1966, p. 869). The APSA estimated that the profession was about 3 percent black in 1973, and that black fulltime faculty was 3.2 percent of all faculty in 1979 (PS Summer 1979, p. 334). Political science has proliferated in American higher education generally but this has not been the case with predominantly black institutions or with black students and faculty.

Early Development in Black Institutions

Howard University in Washington, D.C., Morehouse College in the Atlanta University Center, and Southern University in Baton Rouge, Louisiana were major sites for the early development of political science departments. This development seems to have been associated with the employment of a black with a doctorate in political science. Some students who received bachelor's degrees went on to receive graduate degrees, then returned to serve on the faculty. A significant number of students who received their master's degrees from Atlanta University followed this pattern. Typically, they took time out to teach at predominantly black institutions and later went on to predominantly white institutions in pursuit of doctorates. From 1956–66, Samuel D. Cook served as chairperson of the Atlanta University Political Science program, succeeding William Boyd. During that decade, 38 students received master's degrees in political science at Atlanta University. Several of the scholars, who later earned the doctorate, have credited the Atlanta University experience with facilitating the transfer from undergraduate to PhD study in an era of very limited access to graduate study opportunities in the South. As of 1981, 11 of the 38 master's degree holders are known to have earned the doctorate.

Development of the field at Howard University is generally associated with the tenure of Ralph Bunche, beginning in 1928. A separate department with a bachelor's degree was established in 1929; the master's program followed in the 1930s and the first PhD was awarded in 1967. A 1971 Ford Foundation grant to Howard to enhance its PhD program in political science provided funds to increase the faculty by over 100 percent and to expand the number of graduate assistantships (Browne 1977).

A number of scholars were instrumental in the emergence of Howard University's political science program. Emmett Dorsey, who joined the faculty in 1929, became chairperson when Bunche took a leave of absence in 1941. William P. Robinson, a Howard graduate who later received a PhD from New York University in 1952, taught at Howard from 1935 to 1939, and John Syphax served

for a brief period. One of Ralph Bunche's early students, Vincent
Browne, a 1946 Harvard PhD, who is currently department chairperson, began his tenure in 1946. Others who contributed to the
development of Howard's political science department include John
Herz, Wolfgang Kraft, Glendon Schubert, Anthony Dexter Lewis,
Bernard Fall, Harold Gosnell, and Earl M. Lewis who served for
varying periods in the 1940s and 1950s. Another Bunche protégé,
Robert Martin, a 1947 University of Chicago PhD, served from 1960
until his retirement in 1979. As of May 1980, the Department had
awarded 186 masters and 56 PhDs (Browne 1979).

Morehouse's political science program emerged in a formal
sense about 1948 with the arrival of Robert Brisbane, but separate
departmental status was not accorded until 1964. In 1949, William
Boyd joined the political science faculty at Atlanta University, the
graduate study component of the Atlanta University Center. Boyd,
holder of a University of Michigan doctorate, began the master's
program in political science, served as Georgia State president of
the NAACP, and worked closely with Morehouse and Brisbane. A
Harvard University PhD, Brisbane taught all political science
courses at Morehouse until 1960. At that time he was joined by
Arthur Banks, who had been his undergraduate classmate at
St. Johns University in New York City and had received a PhD from
Johns Hopkins. In 1962, Tobe Johnson, a Morehouse alumnus and
holder of a PhD from Columbia University, began a period of continuous service; in 1969 Abraham Davis, a Morehouse alumnus with
an Ohio State doctorate, joined the faculty. Arthur Banks left in
1967 to become a college president. Brisbane reported that graduates of the department included six PhDs, the mayor of Atlanta,
outstanding lawyers and journalists, and leaders in business and
civic affairs (Brisbane 1977; APSA 1948, 1961, 1968). Development
of the program at Morehouse was a herculean task by today's
standards. Brisbane taught 18 hours per semester for four years,
at times had as many as six courses per semester, served as advisor for some master's degree students in the Atlanta University
program and, in 1964, assumed the responsibilities of departmental
chairperson. In 1969, the department had a faculty of four. Based
on available information, ten of its bachelor's degree holders had
earned the doctorate in political science as of May 1981 (Brisbane
1981).

Southern University awarded its first bachelor's degrees with
a major in political science in 1948. Development of the discipline
evolved around Rodney G. Higgins, a University of Iowa PhD, who
joined the faculty as chairperson in 1946 and served in that capacity
until his death in 1964. A separate department was established that
same year and was called the Department of Social Science until

about 1956. Between 1948 and 1980, there were 573 undergraduate degrees awarded to students with majors in political science (Southern University 1980). In 1968, Southern University initiated an interdisciplinary program leading to the Master's of Arts in Social Sciences, with a concentration in either history, political science or sociology. As of May 1981, some 33 master's degrees had been awarded to students with a concentration in political science (Southern University 1980).

Political science faculty members at Southern University between 1940 and 1969 included 17 of the 65 blacks who held PhDs in the discipline. In addition, four of these 65 doctorate recipients had received their undergraduate training at Southern University, six at Morehouse, and six at Howard University. Only two other predominantly black institutions were responsible for undergraduate training of more than one of the 65 doctorate holders—Florida A&M University, two, and Huston-Tillotson, two. Among nonblack institutions, two each were from Oberlin, St. John's, Southern Illinois, Tufts, UCLA, and Wayne State, while three had undergraduate degrees from Roosevelt University. Overall, 38 had undergraduate degrees from black institutions and 27 from white universities.

Twiley W. Barker, a Southern alumnus who earned his doctorate at the University of Illinois, played a significant role among faculty members at Southern University in helping to build the curricula. His tenure on the faculty extended from 1949 to 1962. During the last year of his tenure, 1964-65, T. E. McKinney, Jr., was the first chairperson of the separate department. Alfred Robertson, William Johnson, Thomas E. Smith, Arthur J. Penson, and this author, all of whom remain on the faculty, have four to ten years of continuous service. This author, the first black American woman to receive the PhD in political science, has been chairperson of the department since 1965.

As of May 1981, 17 graduates of the Southern University political science department are known to have received the PhD in political science. Another earned a combination education-political science doctorate and at least two have earned degrees in related social science fields.

Political science course offerings were also available at other black colleges and universities where there were black faculty members with advanced training in the discipline (Barker 1959, pp. 139-48; Jackson and Prestage 1969). The mainstays of each college or university faculty seemed to have been one or two holders of the doctorate in the field. For example, in 1950, 13 blacks held the PhD in political science. Eleven of them spent their academic careers almost exclusively in black institutions. The sources of their doctorates were as follows:

Harvard University	3—Robert Brisbane, Vincent Browne, Ralph Bunche
University of Michigan	3—William Boyd, Robert Gill, Thomas Solomon
University of Iowa	2—Rodney Higgins, Alexander Walker
University of Pennsylvania	2—G. James Fleming, J. Erroll Miller
University of Chicago	1—Robert Martin
Columbia University	1—John Davis
Ohio State University	1—William Nowlin

Five of these PhD recipients held undergraduate degrees from predominantly black schools and eight from predominantly white schools. Three of the five were from Howard. The 11 who spent their careers at black institutions were at Howard, two; Morehouse, one; Southern University, one; Prairie View, one; Morgan State, three; Atlanta University, one; Lincoln (Missouri), one; and Bluefield State, one.

By 1954, the year of the Brown v. Board of Education decision, the number of black doctorates in political science had increased to 21. The eight additional degrees were one each from:

American University	Emmett Dorsey
University of Chicago	Earl M. Lewis
University of Illinois	Lucius J. Barker
University of Iowa	Jewel L. Prestage
University of Minnesota	William McIntosh
New York University	William P. Robinson
Ohio State University	Samuel D. Cook
University of Pittsburgh	George Davis

During the 1954-55 school year, seven of this group were employed by predominantly black institutions and one was in military service. Of the 65 living black political science doctorate holders in 1969 who were teaching, 25 were at black institutions and 24 at predominantly white ones.

The final report of the 1969 "Conference on the Political Science Curriculum at Predominantly Black Institutions" indicated that black participation in the association had been limited to a president of the association (Ralph Bunche), eight persons who appeared 16 times on panels at annual meetings, three members of the executive council, and seven members of various association committees (Prestage 1979, pp. 763-83). There was considerable overlap in this involvement. Overall, the conferees found that:

— The APSA in the past had, for the most part, failed to include blacks in its deliberations.

— Such failure deprived the association of a source of information and assistance, especially in the promotion of political science as a discipline.

— Blacks, up to that point, felt "alienated" from their white colleagues.

— Future participation by blacks should be on a larger scale and embrace a wider and more representative sample of the predominately black schools served by most of the black members of the profession (PS Summer 1979).

The APSA compiled some records on black participation in the profession in conjunction with the "Conference on the Political Science Curriculum at Predominantly Black Institutions" held at Southern University in April 1969. Since 1969 a number of studies and special reports on blacks have appeared and provide valuable information about blacks in the discipline (Woodard 1977).

Holders of the Doctorate

According to estimates in issues of the APSA's Guide to Graduate Study between 1969 and 1973, blacks received 43 doctorates and 87 more between 1974 and 1976. Collectively then, APSA records showed that about 195 blacks held doctorates in political science in 1976, 130 of which were awarded after 1969 (APSA 1976). There were 115 PhD-granting institutions listed in the APSA Guide in 1976. Nearly half, 55, had not awarded a single terminal degree to a black. When the focus was narrowed to the South, the picture was even more bleak in light of the density of the black population and the concentration of black colleges. The 31 PhD-granting institutions in the South estimated that they had awarded approximately 430 degrees between 1972-73 and 1975-76—only 16 of these to blacks. Twenty of the southern institutions had never conferred a PhD on a black, although 13 of them are public universities. Obviously, blacks who received doctorates in political science in the 1970s were not distributed throughout the nation in proportion to their population.

There have been a number of positive developments for blacks in political science over the last decade. In 1969-70, the National Conference of Black Political Scientists was established; and between 1975 and 1978, 142 PhD degrees were awarded to blacks, although citizenship status of that group of recipients was not known (APSA 1979). Among 522 PhD recipients in 1979 were 24 blacks (U.S. citizens or noncitizens on permanent visas) and in 1980 16 blacks received the PhD in political science out of a total of 505 (Syverson 1980, 1981). The cumulative impact of these accomplishments has been to facilitate minimal growth in the numerical representation of blacks as doctoral degree holders, most significantly through the expansion of offerings at the black universities, and an increase in the involvement of blacks in the scholarly exchange that characterizes the learned disciplines throughout academia. If the experience of political science as a fledgling discipline can be regarded as a model, then developments at black institutions, such as Atlanta and Howard, hold the greatest potential for increasing both the pool of doctorates and the level of professionalism among blacks.

RECOMMENDATIONS FOR BLACK COLLEGES AND UNIVERSITIES

Efforts to increase the number of blacks in graduate education will necessitate adoption of a multifaceted strategy by black colleges and universities. At a minimum, this strategy entails maximizing the potential for access to traditionally white universities, especially for programs not currently available at black colleges, and the addition of graduate and professional programs at black institutions.

Black institutions of higher education must continue to give priority to providing educational access for as many students as possible, creating the largest possible eligible pool from which to draw candidates for graduate and professional study. According to some mainstream criteria for predicting academic success, the bulk of the students entering black universities as freshmen are "exceedingly bad risks." Black institutions, however, have been able to take these students and "defy statistics" by offering them the kind of educational experiences that have enabled them to compete successfully with students in graduate and professional schools across the nation. History has taught us that the potential is there, the challenge is to discover and develop it. Therefore, priority should be given to the recruitment of students of all ability levels with the view that it is possible for them, in the appropriate educational environment, to develop whatever intellectual capacity they possess. Once students are enrolled, black universities must consider it a moral responsibility to provide each with the best possible education. Creation of new pedagogical techniques and subject matter priorities are mandatory if this responsibility is to be effectively met. Changes designed to enhance performance on standard-

ized tests which are required for gaining entry to graduate schools
and for receiving financial aid would be especially significant.
This must be achieved without sacrificing the quality of education
offered or making test preparation, rather than the transmission
of relevant meaningful information, the major goal.

Just as historically black colleges have been the prime source
of black undergraduate degrees, they may hold the greatest potential for coming to grips with the flagrant underrepresentation of
blacks among graduate and professional degree holders. For whatever reason, white institutions have failed to provide adequate
undergraduate education for blacks. For example, one major
urban university in the South recently enrolled more than 1,200
freshmen in a fall entering class. Less than 350 returned to
register for the sophomore year. The figures were released by
the research office of the institution with the explanation that the
concerned administrators were hard pressed to find a reason for
the high failure rate among black students. The enrollment and
degree-awarding patterns in political science suggest that black
institutions might provide more supportive settings for black
graduate students.

Doctoral dissertations completed and the performance of PhD
graduates serve as measures of quality control for these programs
in the same way they do for PhD programs generally. Graduates
of the programs have done well in the academic marketplace as reflected by the types of positions they hold. Master's level programs
at black universities have been especially effective in facilitating
the transition from bachelor's degrees at historically black universities to doctoral programs at large universities outside of the
South, especially in fields like political science and social work.
Atlanta University and Howard University fulfilled this purpose for
many years, prior to the expansion of MA programs at other black
universities.

Increasing black enrollment in areas where blacks hold the
smallest percentage of the doctorates is a laudable goal. Since
blacks hold less than 1 percent of all doctorates, however, no area
should be slighted for upgrading black output. In spite of the
prominence of education among fields in which blacks hold doctorates, in my view, blacks do not hold faculty positions in education
to any marked degree. Further, new subfields in education are
evolving and blacks are not well represented in these newer areas.
Education in the United States is in a state of crisis and much of
the crisis is due to the failure to educate blacks at the elementary
and secondary levels. Competent, well-trained black scholars
are needed if the resolution of the crisis is to occur without ir-
reparable damage to black children. Rather than directing students

away from education, a more efficacious strategy might be simply to increase the overall level of student interest in pursuing advanced degrees.

Bidding for increased doctoral level programs at black universities should emphasize the areas in which the greatest needs for additional black doctorates exist, in terms of absolute and relative shortages and of relevant conditions in the black community. In short, the most pressing skill needs of the black community should weigh as heavily as the shortage of blacks holding doctorates in an area. In my opinion, expansion of PhD programs at black institutions is essential if the production of black doctorates is to increase.

Black institutions must move toward effecting fundamental changes in the U.S. system of higher education by exerting, collectively and individually, greater impact on what is contained under the rubric of "American higher education." For example, black institutions must press for the legitimation of their experiences as institutions of higher learning, with universal implications and significance.

Professional organizations can be extremely useful in efforts to bring about changes in opportunities for graduate study in particular disciplines. Through their journals and annual meetings, they help to introduce their members to the need for change as articulated by the affected groups. The efforts of the American Political Science Association provide some indication of this kind of leadership role.

The presence of a selected group of well-trained, highly motivated scholars, committed to long tenure at black universities, served as the impetus to political science program development at the undergraduate level during the 1940s and 1950s especially. These scholars provided instruction, but they also served as role models for young blacks. This black faculty presence must be expanded to white institutions as well.

The establishment of special financial assistance programs for black students to pursue the PhD is crucial to increase the number of black doctorates. The information about existing programs and other types of federal student support programs indicates that blacks have received little assistance. Again, the APSA's Fellowships for Black Students program is an example of one type of nongovernmental aid.

Cooperative programs between black graduate schools and selected departments at predominantly white institutions and at selected historically black institutions provide one means for enhancing the prospect for successful achievement of the doctorate.

Finally, more basic research on black colleges and universities is needed, and black scholars should lead the way.

74 / Jewel L. Prestage

REFERENCES

Almond, Gabriel. "Political theory and political science." American Political Science Review 60 (December 1966):869.

American Political Science Association (APSA). Guide to graduate study in political science, 1976. Washington, D.C.: APSA, 1976.

_____. Guide to graduate study in political science, 1979. Washington, D.C.: APSA, 1979.

_____. Roster of black women political scientists. Washington, D.C.: APSA, 1980.

Barker, Twiley W., Jr. "Political science in institutions of higher learning for Negroes; Some observations on departmental organization and curriculum." Quarterly Review of Higher Education among Negroes 27 (July 1959):139-48.

Bayer, Alan. "Teaching faculty in academe: 1972-1973." In Minority group participation in graduate education. Washington, D.C.: National Board on Graduate Education, 1976.

Bergman, Nancy. Negroes in Iowa. Iowa City, IA: Iowa State Historical Society, 1976.

Bond, Horace Mann. Black American scholars: A study of their beginnings. Detroit, MI: Balamp, 1972.

Bowles, Frank, and Frank A. DeCosta. Between two worlds: A profile of Negro higher education. New York: McGraw-Hill, 1971.

Brisbane, Robert. Telephone interview at National Conference of Black Political Scientists meeting. Atlanta, Georgia, March 1977.

_____. Telephone interview. August 28, 1981.

Browne, Vincent. Telephone interview. August 1979.

_____. "The black political scientist: Historic and contemporary." Statement on panel at 76th Annual Meeting of American Political Science Association. Washington, D.C., August 29, 1980.

Bryant, James W. _A survey of black American doctorates_. New York: Ford Foundation, 1970.

Centra, John. _Women, men and the doctorate_. Princeton, NJ: Educational Testing Service, 1974.

Crossland, Fred. E. "Graduate education and black Americans." The Ford Foundation, November 25, 1968. Unpublished paper cited in _Minority group participation in graduate education_. Washington, D.C.: National Board on Graduate Education, 1976.

Dyson, Walter. _Howard University_. Washington, D.C.: Howard University, 1941.

Ford Foundation. "Roster of black doctorates in political science and roster of black doctorates in sociology." Unpublished mimeographed papers, 1969.

Galambos, Eva C. _Racial composition of faculties in public colleges and universities of the south_. Atlanta, GA: Southern Regional Education Board, 1979.

Gilford, Dorothy, M., and Joan Snyder. _Women and minority Ph.Ds in the 1970s: A data book_. Washington, D.C.: National Academy of Sciences, 1977.

Gilford, Dorothy M., and Peter D. Syverson. _Doctorate recipients from United States universities: Summary report 1977_. Washington, D.C.: National Academy of Sciences, 1978.

_____. _Doctorate recipients from United States universities: Summary report 1978_. Washington, D.C.: National Academy of Sciences, 1979.

Greene, Henry W. _Holders of doctorates among American Negroes_. Boston, MA: Meador, 1946.

Harmon, Lindsay. _Doctorate recipients from United States universities, 1958-1966_. Washington, D.C.: National Academy of Sciences, 1967.

_____. _A century of doctorates: Data analyses of growth and change_. Washington, D.C.: National Academy of Sciences, 1978.

76 / Jewel L. Prestage

Hill, Susan. "Participation of black students in higher education: A statistical profile 1970-71—1980-81." Washington, D.C.: National Center for Education Statistics, October 1983.

Jay, James. Negroes in science; Natural science doctorates, 1876-1969. Detroit, MI: Balamp, 1971.

Jones, Mack H. Interview at Southern University, Baton Rouge, Louisiana, July 16, 1981.

Ladd, Everett C., Jr., and Seymour M. Lipsett. "The politics of American political scientists." PS IV (Spring 1971):140.

McGrath, Earl. The predominantly Negro colleges and universities in transition. New York: Columbia University, Teachers College Press, 1965.

Mingle, James R. Black enrollment in higher education. Atlanta, GA: Southern Regional Education Board, 1978.

_____. Degree output in the south, 1975-76: Distribution by race. Atlanta, GA: Southern Regional Education Board, 1978.

_____. Degrees awarded in the nation and in the south, 1976-77. Atlanta, GA: Southern Regional Education Board, 1979.

National Advisory Committee on Black Higher Education and Black Colleges and Universities (NACBHEBCU). Access of black Americans to higher education: How open is the door? Washington, D.C.: NACBHEBCU, 1979.

_____. A losing battle: The decline in black participation in graduate and professional education. Washington, D.C.: NACBHEBCU, 1980.

National Board on Graduate Education (NBGE). Minority group participation in graduate education. Washington, D.C.: NBGE, 1976.

National Research Council. Minority groups among United States doctorate-level scientists, engineers and scholars. Washington, D.C.: National Academy of Sciences, 1974.

Noble, Jeanne L. The Negro woman's college education. New York: Columbia University, Teachers College Press, 1956.

"Pace seen slow for women and minorities in gaining places on nation's faculties." The Chronicle of Higher Education, October 9, 1973.

Prestage, Jewel L. "Quelling the mythical revolution in higher education: Retreat from the affirmative action concept." Journal of Politics 41 (August 1979):763-83.

Prestage, Jewel L., and Edwin R. Jackson. "Political science in the black colleges." Paper presented at the Forty-first Annual Convention of Southern Political Science Association, November 1969.

PS VI Summer 1973.

PS XII Summer 1979.

"Report of the conference on the political science curriculum at predominantly black institutions." PS II (Summer 1969).

Southern University. A report of the graduate program in social science to the Louisiana board of regents. Baton Rouge, LA: Department of Political Science, Southern University, October 1, 1980.

Syverson, Peter D. Doctorate recipients from United States universities: Summary report 1979. Washington, D.C.: National Academy of Sciences, 1980.

_____. Doctorate recipients from the United States universities: Summary report 1980. Washington, D.C.: National Academy of Sciences, 1981.

Weidlein, Edward R. "Affirmative action has little impact on faculty hiring, study shows." The Chronicle of Higher Education 7, 41 (August 27, 1972):1.

Who's who among black Americans, 1980-81. Afro-American Encyclopedia, Volume 1. North Miami, FL: Educational Book Publishing, 1974.

Woodward, Maurice C., ed. Blacks and political science. Washington, D.C.: American Political Science Association, 1977.

5

Black Colleges
and Universities:
A National Resource
for Black Science
and Engineering Manpower

William M. Jackson

Many demands are made on black colleges and universities, so it is important to identify and define the relative importance of those demands and to set priorities. Education in science and engineering is one of the most expensive endeavors that an educational institution can undertake. What then is the importance of science and engineering training in the black colleges compared to the other demands on them?

TECHNOLOGY'S ROLE IN TODAY'S SOCIETY

Science and engineering play essential roles in Western civilization. And, in the 1980s, more than ever before, the accelerating drive by major businesses to develop, for example, new and alternative sources of energy for homes, cars, and appliances has spawned intense competition among companies and nations in the high-technology market. Thus, it is not surprising to discover that the majority of the largest companies on the Fortune Five Hundred list are heavily concentrated in advanced technology. Computers, "intelligent" appliances, and even toys operated by miniature processors and integrated circuits have not only improved our standard of living but have also changed our way of life.

With this technology, the Western industrialized countries and Japan have been able to supply their citizens with a standard of living that is the highest in the history of the world. Many of these scientific and technical activities have put pressure on our environment, a trend that will continue in the future. The challenge of the future will be to provide a decent standard of living for all the citizens of the world, using the available resources, without damaging the environment. To bring this about, we cannot turn back the clock but must understand the complex technical factors that control our society.

SCIENCE AND THE BLACK COMMUNITY

If science is important to the entire society, it is equally or even more important to the black community. There are several reasons for this. First, if blacks are to be full participants in the solution of our society's problems, they will have to have the scientific and technical expertise to solve them. The development of the full economic potential of the black community will require black workers to gain skills that are marketable and beneficial to the entire society. While it is important to address the social ills of the black community, it is clear that this is primarily the concern of the black community rather than of society as a whole. Blacks will participate fully in the economy only when they have the skills and expertise to negotiate with the larger society.

Development of black scientific and technical expertise is also important in our relationships with African and Caribbean countries. Many of the leaders of these countries have been trained in the black colleges, have developed very special relationships with this country, and understand our culture. The sensitivity that black technical experts can bring to our foreign aid and development programs should not be discounted. Certainly, our diplomatic relationships with these countries substantially improved during the recent tenures of Andrew Young and Donald McHenry at the United Nations. Yet it appears that the black world overseas pays more attention to the United States than vice versa. Much of that is changing, however, as the United States recognizes the importance of Nigeria's one million barrels of oil each day, Zaire's supply of one-third of the United States' cobalt needs, and Jamaica's supply of one half of this country's bauxite that is refined into aluminum (Barry 1981).

Finally, the negative and inferior stereotypes through which the white majority views blacks will persist until blacks are represented in the scientific and technical areas in proportion to their percentage in the population. The fact that the numbers of blacks in the natural sciences and in engineering are so low has even led some critics to suggest that blacks cannot succeed in mathematics or in other difficult technical subjects.

CONDITION OF BLACK SCIENCE AND
ENGINEERING MANPOWER TODAY

Table 1 shows the percentages of blacks in the total composition of scientists and engineers by field in 1974, 1976, and 1978, and the highest degree held. Blacks represent 11.7 percent of the nation's population, but less than 2 percent of the total number of scientists and engineers at all degree levels. Significantly, between 1974 and 1978, there was no percentage increase in the total number of black scientists and engineers. The highest percentages among the fields listed in Table 1 are in the social sciences and, even though those are disciplines in which blacks are often reported to be represented in large numbers, the percentages are still less than half their percentage of the total population. Furthermore, the fact that the percentages in the social sciences are at least twice those in the other fields obviously increases the total percentages in each of the three years.

TABLE 1

Percentages of Black Scientists and Engineers:
1974, 1976, and 1978

Fields	1974	1976	1978
Physical sciences	1.7	1.6	1.5
Mathematics	2.5	2.5	2.8
Computer science	1.9	2.1	0.59
Environmental science	0.25	0.12	0.87
Engineering	0.91	0.92	0.82
Life sciences	1.2	1.1	2.0
Psychology	1.6	1.3	2.8
Social sciences	5.3	4.9	5.4
Total	1.6	1.5	1.6

Source: National Science Foundation, National Patterns of Science and Technology Resources 1980. NSF 80-308, Table 70. (Washington, D.C.: National Science Foundation, 1980), p. 65.

Table 2 gives the distribution of blacks and whites who received PhDs in the sciences, engineering, the humanities, education, and other professional fields in each of the years between 1974 and 1979. The percentages in this table show the distribution of blacks and whites across fields within their respective racial groups as compared to Table 1 which showed the representation of blacks in entire disciplines. Thus Table 2 demonstrates that in 1974, of all doctorates awarded to black students, 8.2 percent received degrees in the life sciences compared to 14 percent of whites. The percentages in many fields are obviously higher than those cited earlier but the actual numbers are quite small. For example, 8.2 percent of black doctorates in the life sciences corresponds to only about 95 individuals who received those degrees in 1974. Looking across the years in many of the fields, it is easy to see that the percentages have not risen substantially, although the total number of doctorates has increased slightly. For example, in 1979, 5 percent of blacks who received PhDs in that year received them in the life sciences. This small percentage corresponds to approximately 53 PhDs awarded, although more than 1,000 blacks received doctorates that year. And, once again, the social sciences and education together account for almost three-fourths of all black PhDs received. In order to achieve anything near parity with the general population, the numbers of black baccalaureate degrees in the sciences and engineering would have to increase two to four times. Even more, the percentages of doctorates would have to increase by nearly a factor of ten just to achieve parity with the majority. Larger increases, especially in the numbers of science and engineering baccalaureate degrees awarded, would be required to compensate for the accumulated long-term deficiencies. Higher rates of enrollment would also be necessary to offset the usually significant attrition rates and normal patterns of students switching fields from the natural sciences to the social sciences and education.

Given the disparities between blacks and whites in the number and rate of production of degrees in science and engineering, how can the situation be improved? To answer this question, we need additional information: enrollment data for blacks at the graduate and undergraduate level and data on college freshmen preferences for these fields.

Table 3 summarizes fall 1978 enrollment data for blacks in the biological and physical sciences and engineering. There are clearly sex differences in enrollment in the different fields (not shown on the table). Forty percent of all blacks enrolled in the physical sciences in 1975-76 were women. In the biological sciences in the same year, black women accounted for 58 percent of

TABLE 2

Distribution of Black and White PhDs, 1974–79 (Black/White)*

	1974	1975	1976	1977	1978	1979
Total	846/23,442	989/24,183	1,085/24,204	1,109/22,824	1,029/21,601	1,050/21,750
Percent male	68.6/79.4	64.9/76.5	59.6/75.4	61.4/73.7	56.5/71.5	52.2/69.7
Percent female	31.4/20.6	35.1/23.5	40.4/24.6	38.6/26.3	43.5/28.5	47.8/30.3
Field percent						
Physical science (including mathematics)	5.4/13.9	3.6/13.5	2.5/12.7	3.8/13.0	5.0/12.8	4.6/13.1
Engineering	1.9/6.7	1.1/6.2	1.1/5.8	1.0/5.6	0.9/4.9	1.6/5.0
Life science	8.2/14.0	5.6/15.0	5.8/14.8	5.0/15.0	6.5/15.8	5.0/16.5
Social science	12.6/19.9	16.1/20.1	15.9/21.2	17.9/21.5	18.6/21.7	19.6/21.5
Humanities	8.9/17.3	8.9/16.7	8.4/16.1	8.6/15.7	7.8/15.4	11.2/14.4
Education	59.2/23.7	61.2/24.0	61.4/24.8	60.0/24.9	56.7/24.6	53.0/24.8
Professional fields/ other	3.8/4.5	3.5/4.5	4.9/4.6	3.7/4.3	4.5/4.8	5.0/4.7

*U.S. citizens only.

Source: National Research Council, Survey of Earned Doctorates (derived from annual Summary Reports, 1974–79).

all blacks enrolled in those fields (9,697 women compared to 7,020 men). Black women represented 25 percent of all black students enrolled in engineering in 1975-76. Yet black women, within their racial group, are more likely to be engineers than are white women who represent only 12 percent of the total enrollment of nonblacks in engineering.

TABLE 3

Fall 1978 Enrollment of Fulltime Black Students
by Field and Level

	Biological Sciences	Engineering	Physical Sciences
Undergraduate			
Number	16,717	17,848	5,077
Percentage of all			
black students	7.6	4.9	4.9
Total (all students)	218,793	365,129	104,161
Graduate			
Number	557	338	364
Percentage of all			
black students	2.1	1.1	1.5
Total (all students)	26,644	30,419	24,721

Source: National Center for Education Statistics (NCES), Fall Enrollment in Higher Education, 1978, Table 29 (Washington, D.C.: NCES, 1979), p. 194.

Table 4 gives preference ratings of first-time freshmen who enroll in science or engineering by field. The preferences of black students reflect patterns similar to those for all students who enter these disciplines. Since the percentage of black students in educational institutions is roughly comparable to their percentage in the population as a whole, it is clear that a differential proportion of black students are not reaching their professed goals. There are probably several reasons for this attrition. Blacks are more likely than whites to attend colleges and universities which do not have a history of producing scientists or engineers (National Advisory Committee on Black Higher Education and Black Colleges and

TABLE 4

Freshman Preference for Science and Engineering at Black and All Institutions,
Fall 1973–Fall 1977

Field	1973[a] Black	1973[a] All[b]	1974 Black	1974 All	1975 Black	1975 All	1976 Black	1976 All	1977 Black	1977 All
Biological sciences	5.1	7.0	5.0	6.7	3.7	6.3	5.7	6.2	3.9	4.7
Engineering	3.9	6.6	5.1	6.6	4.6	7.9	5.8	8.5	5.8	9.3
Mathematics/statistics	1.7	1.7	1.3	1.4	0.5	1.1	0.6	1.0	0.9	0.8
Physical sciences	1.6	2.7	2.1	2.6	1.6	2.7	1.8	2.7	1.1	2.3
Chemistry	1.4[c]	1.7[c]							0.6	0.9
Physics									0.3	0.4
Computer science									0.9	1.0

[a]Black—First-time, full-time freshmen at historically black institutions.
[b]All—All first-time, full-time freshmen at all institutions.
[c]Chemistry and physics combined.
Source: Alexander Astin et al., The American Freshman (Los Angeles: University of California, Cooperative Institutional Research Program).

Universities [NACBHEBCU] 1979, p. 18). This is due to both financial considerations and to poor academic preparation. The former condition reflects the overall financial standing of the black community; the latter is the result of inferior elementary and secondary schools which do not offer sufficient core courses in the sciences and mathematics. There is also an element of racism involved since the white undergraduate institutions blacks attend may not have the support structures necessary for their survival and degree attainment (NACBHEBCU 1979, p. 13). Other fall 1978 enrollment statistics indicate that blacks are more likely, by approximately six percentage points, to be part-time graduate students (National Center for Educational Statistics 1979, p. 194). This probably reflects financial need as well as an older student population.

The effectiveness of black colleges in educating blacks who attain graduate and professional degrees has been well documented (National Research Council, Commission on Human Resources 1977, pp. 107-19; Jay 1971; Jay 1977). That becomes even more meaningful when one recognizes that black colleges today enroll only about 20 percent of black students. The Higher Education General Information Survey (HEGIS) indicated that in the 1975-76 academic year black colleges awarded 42 percent of the bachelor degrees black students received in science. The distribution across fields is even more impressive. The HEGIS survey of all institutions reported in Mingle (1978) indicates that the percentage of bachelor's degrees from black institutions in the biological, engineering, mathematical, and physical sciences were 45, 35, 46, and 45 percent, respectively, of all blacks who received degrees in those fields. These numbers are even more impressive when one notes that not every black college offers majors in these fields. For example, in 1978-79, only 25 percent of the black schools offered an undergraduate degree in engineering, 76 percent of these institutions offered majors in chemistry, and 52 percent in physics.

STRATEGIES FOR CHANGE

This information can be used to develop a strategy for increasing black science and engineering manpower in this country. Any strategy that will be effective in dealing with this problem cannot use a single approach since many factors affect the supply of black scientists and engineers. These include poor elementary and secondary education, slightly lower representation of blacks at all degree levels, fewer role models since the percentage of successes in science and engineering is much lower than in most other fields, and a decrease in the percentage of black representation at each degree level.

The most dramatic change to alleviate the underrepresentation of blacks might be made at the doctoral level since this is
where the most glaring differences occur. Blacks now represent
less than 2 percent of the PhDs awarded every year, and recent
data and reports confirm that the number of black doctoral students
is falling (Fiske 1981). As shown earlier in Table 2, the number of
black students who received PhDs peaked in 1977 at 1,109 but declined in 1978 to 1,029 and rose slightly to 1,050 in 1979. The
most recent data from the National Research Council on PhD recipients for 1980 show that the number of blacks who received
doctorates totaled 1,097—a sign that the numbers are leveling off
more than they are rising. The data also indicate that there is still
a great deal of unevenness in the distribution of black doctorates—
602 doctorates in education and a mere 18 and 29 in engineering and
the physical sciences (Syverson 1981). These declines are occurring
despite the fact that a higher percentage of blacks are graduating
at the bachelor levels in these fields. If the black percentage of the
total number of doctorates were the same as the black percentage
of those who obtain bachelor's degrees, the PhD production rate
would increase sharply by factors of three to five.

Increasing the Number of Black Students in Graduate Schools

Several programs should be instituted to increase the percentage of black students who attend graduate school. First, there
should be a nationwide effort to assure that black students who
graduate from college have a clear idea of the options available to
them for graduate study. They should learn that they can obtain a
quality education at black universities as well as at white institutions.
The black university may be the institution of choice for some students and not only for those who may have academic deficiencies.
As Tollett points out, the black university offers credible models
for aspiring blacks to emulate, congenial settings psychologically
and socially in which blacks can develop, and transitional enclaves,
from comparative isolation to entering the mainstream American
society, without demanding competition with, or the distraction of,
the majority white group (Tollett 1978).
    These statements were aimed primarily at the four-year his-
torically black colleges, but they apply equally well to the black
universities. The point is that some students need the kind of environment that only black universities can provide. Without such
institutions, it is likely that these black students will not complete
their graduate education and hence will increase the percentage of
students who do not get graduate degrees.

An increased role for the black universities will require a larger commitment of funds to these institutions. None of the historically black institutions has the facilities to offer first-class graduate education. The fact that these schools have successfully trained graduate students and produced research reflects more the commitment of the faculty than the presence of an outstanding physical environment. None of these schools has the mechanical, electrical, and electronic shop facilities that the major institutions take for granted. None has an adequate library where all the latest journals and publications can be obtained. This is true whether the institution is supported by state or federal funds. It is almost as if there were a conspiracy to let black universities have these programs but without the resources to carry them out properly. Then, when black institutions fail, the comment is made that black institutions cannot do first-class research. I would challenge any member of the science faculty at one of the major institutions to perform more effectively than faculty at the black institutions, given the current level of support services.

Strategy for Increasing Black Scientific and Engineering Population

The first element of the strategy for increasing the black scientific and engineering population is to identify and counsel black students at the undergraduate level to continue their education at the kind of institution that can meet their particular needs. This will not necessarily mean that the graduate programs at the black universities will have to expand to accommodate this increase. But it will be necessary to address some of the present deficiencies at these institutions if students are to get all they need and deserve. Government programs should be instituted to accomplish this goal, but an effort should also be made to enlist corporate, industrial, and foundation support, since in the past black institutions have received only small amounts of funds from these sources.

The achievement of these goals will necessarily include a major effort at the historically black colleges and at the newly predominantly black colleges. The former group of colleges have demonstrated that they can produce blacks in these fields at a higher rate than their white counterparts. Not only are they producing more graduates, as Jay (1971 and 1977) has pointed out, but they are also responsible for most of the PhDs that native-born blacks receive. Jay (1981) has identified about 1,545 native-born black PhDs in the sciences. His figures compare favorably with the 1,649 black PhDs reported by the National Science Foundation (NSF 1980).

The differences are easily explained as the result of the NSF's inclusion of naturalized or resident aliens from the African and Caribbean countries. Seventy percent of the black PhDs in Jay's files obtained their undergraduate degree from historically black colleges. Clearly, these achievements and those cited above should be the basis of any effort to expand the number of blacks in the technical fields.

Research at the Black Colleges

The full utilization of the black colleges to expand the pool of black talent requires a recognition of how they differ from the larger black universities with graduate programs in science and engineering. In general their teaching loads are higher, graduate research assistants are not available, and their overall support facilities are even poorer than those of the black universities. It is clear that they are not equipped to do major research. Yet some research is important at this level to maintain the vitality of the faculty and to insure that students are exposed to the latest developments and techniques in the sciences.

How then should research be implemented at these colleges? First, it is important to recognize that individual faculty can have a profound effect on the number and quality of the students who graduate from a college in a particular field. Up to 1976, Morehouse College had produced approximately 10 percent (33) of the total number of native-born blacks who later received PhDs in chemistry. This is largely due to the teaching and inspiration of one man, Henry C. McBay. The example he gave of teaching and doing research despite enormous obstacles deeply affected each of his students. Most of the successful black colleges can point to examples of other professors who have excelled in their particular fields. It is important to identify these individuals and give them the recognition and support they need to continue and expand their work. Some effort should also be made to attract equally dedicated young faculty to these institutions to continue these traditions.

The funding agencies should support research efforts at these colleges, but with more realistic expectations for their performance. More funds are needed for research equipment, since none of these schools has an endowment for this purpose. In many of the towns and cities where these small colleges are located, it is difficult to find trained scientists who can serve as part-time faculty, in order to release regular faculty to perform basic research. Under these circumstances, it is often necessary for the principal investigators to choose between time spent on research and time spent with their students. It is unlikely that these schools will be able to attract the good postdoctoral associates that the major institutions employ to assist their faculty on research projects. Instead, they will have to hire staff on soft grant money to aid them in performing the tasks that they have specified in their grant applications. This, in turn, requires the funding agencies to consider multiyear grants to enable the principal investigator to attract quality support people. Proper timing for receiving the grant is another important factor. Often institutions receive funds in the middle of a semester, which upsets the previously established schedule. The grant monitor should arrange for the schedule to be altered or the term of the grant to be extended so that research can begin in a more orderly fashion.

In addition to funds for equipment, supplies, and support services, student support will be needed during the academic year and in the summer. Provision should be made for funds for summer salaries so that the principal investigator can involve students in the work. This is one of the most productive times for research in these colleges and every effort should be made to encourage students and faculty to remain in the area to carry on research on campus. Federal agencies and industries often attempt to recruit faculty and students for work during these months. While such efforts appear to be altruistic, too often the actual intent of the companies is to meet their affirmative action goals. Loss of student assistants during the summer months inhibits research efforts on campus which can inspire important spinoffs for other students not directly involved in the research effort. Another rationale that agencies and industrial firms give for summer hiring is that these jobs give students an inside look at their needs and problems. However, these companies could assign members of their staff to the colleges in the summer and in that way communicate their needs to students and faculty, as some firms already do.

Improving Elementary and Secondary Education

The ultimate solution to the problem of increasing the numbers of blacks in the sciences and engineering will only come when preparation of elementary and secondary black students has improved. The historically black colleges and the newly predominantly black colleges can help. Because of their location in the community, they should have a better feel for the effectiveness of the various community schools in preparing black students in science and mathematics. They should work regularly with teachers and counselors to insure that bright black youngsters take advantage of all the academic programs available to them. They can also work with teachers and students in workshops, summer sessions, and other enrichment programs to improve the level of instruction. The Saturday Academy of the Atlanta University Resource Center has successfully introduced advanced teaching techniques to local students in this fashion. A determined push in this direction could go a long way to prepare black students before they develop deficiencies that will hamper their ability to pursue scientific and technical fields in the future.

CONCLUSION

The historically black colleges have been particularly effective in graduating black students in science and engineering, and in motivating them to continue their educations in these fields. Strategies have been developed to use these institutions as a resource for increasing the pool of available black talent in this area. These strategies include:

— Establishing an information bank to inform black under-graduates in science about the opportunities available at all graduate institutions and their particular characteristics.
— Strengthening graduate programs in the sciences at black universities by providing the necessary infrastructure for these programs.
— Identifying those faculty members who are especially effective in inspiring and motivating black students to enter the technical fields and providing them with the resources to increase their effectiveness.
— Initiating programs that would encourage young black scientists to consider teaching careers at the black colleges and universities.
— Utilizing local black colleges as resources for improving elementary and secondary instruction in their communities.
— Determining and documenting effective methods of science instruction and motivation that black colleges have developed.
— Using local black colleges as laboratories to investigate the effectiveness of new teaching methods in the sciences.

It should be clear that implementation of these strategies will be costly and not all these ideas can or should be funded through federal programs. A combination of federal, state, local, foundation, and industrial support to implement new ideas and techniques could go a long way toward bringing the black community into the mainstream of the United States and hence toward solving some of the social problems that have developed in the United States over hundreds of years.

REFERENCES

Barry, John M. "The Howard connection." Washington Post Magazine, March 22, 1981, pp. 20-22.

Cummings, Frank E. Degrees, enrollment and field preference for black students in the science and engineering fields: Recent data. Report 1. Washington, D.C.: Resource Center for Science and Engineering, 1979.

Fiske, Edward B. "After steady rise, the number of black doctoral students falls." The New York Times. July 21, 1981.

Jay, James M. Negroes in science: Natural science doctorates. 1876-1969. Detroit: Balamp Publishing Co., 1971.

_____. "Black Americans in the sciences." In Minorities in science, edited by V. L. Melnik and F. D. Hamilton. New York: Plenum Publishing Co., 1977.

_____. Private communication, 1981.

McBay, H. C. Private communication, 1981.

National Advisory Committee on Black Higher Education and Black Colleges and Universities (NACBHEBCU). Black colleges and universities; An essential component of a diverse system of higher education. Washington, D.C.: NACBHEBCU, 1979.

_____. Still a lifeline: The status of historically black colleges and universities. Washington, D.C.: U.S. Department of Education, 1980.

National Center for Education Statistics (NCES). Fall enrollment in higher education 1978. Washington, D.C.: NCES, 1979.

National Research Council (NRC). Commission on Human Resources. Women and minorities in the 1970s. Washington, D.C.: NRC, 1977.

National Science Foundation. National patterns of science and technology resources 1980. NSF 80-308. Washington, D.C.: NSF, 1980.

Syverson, Peter D. Summary report: 1980 doctoral recipients from United States universities. Washington, D.C.: National Research Council, 1981.

Tollett, K. "Black colleges have important role to play, House panel told." Equal opportunity in higher education. Washington, D.C.: Capital Publications, 1978.

Black College Involvement in International and Cross-Cultural Education

Madelon Delany Stent

The United States is blessed with a largely untapped
resource of talent in the form of racial and ethnic
minorities who, by being brought into the mainstream
of educational and employment opportunities in the
areas of foreign language and international studies,
can be expected to make rapid, new and valuable contributions to America's capacity to deal persuasively
and effectively with the world outside its borders.
(President's Commission on Foreign Languages and
International Studies, 1979).

Black colleges and universities have historically served the
United States and the world by maximizing the opportunities for
black Americans and African and Caribbean peoples in higher

The author wishes to especially thank the following individuals
for their assistance on this chapter: Mariada Borgin, International
Communications Agency (Office of Private Sector Programs); Bruce
Flemming, director, Office of Black Concerns, Department of Education; Marie Gadsden, Phelps-Stokes Fund, Washington, D.C.;
Sam Myers, executive director, National Association for Equal Opportunity in Higher Education; Ruth Stutts Njiiri, director, International Education Program, Phelps-Stokes Fund; Gertrude Robinson,
formerly with Operation Crossroads, Africa; Franklin E. Williams,
former ambassador and president, Phelps-Stokes Fund; Ida Wood,
vice-president and director of Scholarship Programs, Phelps-Stokes
Fund.

education. These institutions were founded primarily for black Americans, although their charters were, in most instances, not exclusionary. Students from the Spanish, English, and French Caribbean islands, as well as from African countries, found the historically black colleges a safe, fertile environment for their growing awareness of race and of the evils of European colonialism.

The life and career of Frederick Douglass represented one of the earliest, and most unusual, involvements of black colleges in international affairs. Douglass, who supposed himself "to have been born in February 1817" (Douglass 1882, p. 26), served as a trustee of Howard University from 1871 to 1895. Born a slave, he traveled to England to speak against slavery; it was his English friends who raised the 150 pounds for his freedom, "placing the papers of my manumission into my hands, before they would tolerate the idea of my return to my native land" (Douglass 1882, p. 289). In 1871, President Grant appointed Douglass Assistant Secretary to the Commission of Inquiry to Santo Domingo, and, eight years later, President Harrison named him Minister-Resident and Consul-General to the Republic of Haiti. Barely three months later, the President added the post of Chargé d'Affaires for Santo Domingo to Douglass' responsibilities.

The black colleges have contributed immeasurably to social progress within the United States and throughout the world. Because of their unique missions, Tuskegee, Atlanta University, Howard University, and other black colleges were involved from their beginnings with world affairs. They have often aided in the development of black leadership in the educational, cultural, and political struggles of developing countries in Africa and the Caribbean. Soon after its founding in the late 1800s, Tuskegee Institute, at the request of the German government, sent a team to Togo to teach cotton cultivation. Recognized throughout the world for its approach to vocational and agricultural education, Tuskegee became the prototype for countless industrial schools in other countries. In later years, prominent Howard alumni made significant contributions in the international field: Patricia Harris, former Secretary of HEW, was appointed Ambassador to Luxembourg by President Johnson, and Thurgood Marshall, presently a Justice of the U.S. Supreme Court, was invited to assist Kenya in writing its first constitution.

As early as 1912, Claude McKay, the poet of protest and rebellion, came as a student from Jamaica to attend Tuskegee. James Weldon Johnson, a graduate of Atlanta University in 1894, served as U.S. consul in Venezuela and Nigeria from 1906 to 1913. Johnson was indisputably one of the most brilliant men on the world scene. Legal scholar, linguist, diplomat, and writer, his graduate training was rooted in the black college experience.

Mordecai W. Johnson, late president of Howard University (1926-60), was a graduate of Atlanta Baptist University, later Morehouse College. He represented Howard at the meeting of the International Association of Universities in Istanbul, at the inauguration of President Tubman of Liberia in 1956, and at the celebration of Ghana's independence in 1957. James M. Nabrit, also a graduate of Morehouse College, succeeded Johnson as president of Howard. He attended several International Labor Congresses and later was appointed by President Lyndon Johnson as U.S. Deputy Representative to the United Nations.

Out of these institutions have come outstanding leaders who have protested oppression in the United States and abroad (Woodson 1922). Martin Luther King, a Morehouse graduate and Nobel Prize winner, proclaimed to the world the need for brotherhood and global peace. Another Nobel Prize winner, Ralph J. Bunche, was a professor of political science at Howard and had a distinguished career in international affairs. His contribution in 1949 to the cease-fire in the Arab-Israeli War was widely praised and led to his award of the Nobel Prize in 1950. The U.S. Peace Corps, one of this nation's major thrusts in cross-cultural relations and the expansion of communication among peoples, was conceived by a Lincoln University valedictorian, the Reverend James H. Robinson. Speaking of Operation Crossroads Africa, established by Dr. Robinson three years before the founding of the Peace Corps, President Kennedy said:

> This group and this effort really were the progenitors
> of the Peace Corps and what this organization has been
> doing for a number of years led to the establishment of
> what I consider to be the most encouraging indication of
> the desire for service, not only in this country, but all
> around the world, that we have seen in recent years.
> (Robinson 1969).

James Robinson was a pioneer in the field of international education exchanges. He believed that such programs contributed to cultural understanding, foreign language competence, and international scholarship. He effectively integrated his own wide travel experience and contacts with the State Department, with the United Presbyterian Church, and as founder of the National Scholarship Service and Fund for Negro Students (NSSFNS). He was, therefore, able to establish linkages between African countries and institutions of higher education in the United States.

Significant international exchanges in the arts and literature have occurred at Howard and Fisk Universities. The Fisk Jubilee Singers have traveled abroad as has the Howard University Choir.

In 1949, the Howard University Players performed in Norway,
Sweden, Denmark, and Germany. James A. Porter, head of the
Department of Art at Howard, has studied African contributions to
Brazilian colonial and modern art. Mercer Cook, former Ambassa-
dor to Niger and later to Senegal and Gambia, was professor of
English at Howard for many years and later head of the Department
of Romance Languages.

Over the years, the historically black colleges have also educated the future leaders of the developing countries, forging strong
links between them and the United States. Eric Williams, the recently deceased prime minister of Trinidad, was a graduate of
Howard University; Nnamdi Azikiwe, the first president of Nigeria,
the late Kwame Nkrumah, once president of Ghana, and C. Cecil
Dennis, former foreign minister of Liberia, were all graduates of
Lincoln University. Azikiwe was so impressed with Leo Hansberry,
one of his professors at Howard University, that he offered him a
post in Nigeria's government. "You initiated me into the sanctuaries
. . . of African history," Azikiwe wrote (Barry, March 22, 1981).

FUTURE RELATIONSHIPS WITH
DEVELOPING COUNTRIES

The historically black colleges and universities, as well as
those that have become predominantly black only within the last
decade, are diverse institutions. They are public and private, religious and sectarian, large and small, relatively wealthy and poor,
and offer a variety of approaches to education. Of the 34 institutions
that are public, almost half are land-grant colleges—colleges that
have been provided funds since 1890 primarily to emphasize programs in the agricultural and mechanical arts.

The future of the United States' relationships with African nations can be determined by the strength of black political power.
The late John A. Davis and other political scientists believed that
there would be a political and racial link between the drive for black
economic and racial equality in the United States and black freedom
in Southern Africa (Davis 1969).

The small number of black Americans in the U.S. Foreign
Service and the lack of significant involvement by black U.S. political scientists in international affairs will continue to affect the kinds
of social, economic, and political relationships black colleges will
be able to establish with developing nations. These factors have had
a strong negative effect on the development of international cross-
cultural studies at the historically black colleges but not so in the
predominantly white colleges, as is clearly seen in the history and

development of international programs on their campuses. Black college graduates have played a vital part in black citizens' continuing struggle for survival. White graduates have always had opportunities to sell their talent on a broad labor market, a market which included foreign affairs, but blacks have been almost totally excluded. Smythe and Skinner wrote:

> The ability of any group to influence a country's foreign policy is directly related to its ability to influence that nation's domestic affairs. Because blacks have persistently been excluded from the national elite structure, they have had special difficulty in relating to United States foreign affairs, even over issues of vital concern to them. Consequently, past articulation of the foreign policy concerns of blacks has gone unheeded, a condition which will continue until blacks gain sufficient economic and political strength to have an effective voice in the field of American foreign relations. (Smythe and Skinner 1976).

I believe, however, that the following factors will significantly affect the role of the historically black colleges in international cross-cultural education: the international technology movement, the growth of the independent African states and the status of other developing countries, the world energy crisis and its consequent economic impact, the Adams Case, and the Report of the President's Commission on Foreign Languages and International Studies.

The International Technology Movement

Cooperation in higher education has resulted in important international ties. In an address before the American Council on Education in 1978, Dr. Jibril Aminu, the former executive secretary of the Universities Commission in Nigeria, said:

> An interesting recent development has been the renewed stress placed upon the importance of creating international linkages or establishing varying types of relationships in higher education. An international linkage in higher education is a formal cooperative agreement between two or more universities or colleges for the promotion of certain considered objectives in higher education. In other words, it is a general facilitative framework for carrying out a variety of activities aimed

> towards meeting specific objectives. One objective
> that should be achieved is the transfer of a distilled
> form of knowledge between the two systems. A phrase
> used to describe the same thing is "transfer of tech-
> nology." (Aminu 1978).

Measures to promote economic and social growth, self-reliant national development, and industrial/agricultural progress in developing countries have been targeted primarily for this exchange of
technology.

Business and industry have co-opted the term, "transfer of
technology," but such transfers are actually more likely to result
from the transfer of knowledge through higher educational channels
than from a business or contractual agreement between the government of a developing country and a foreign multinational corporation.
Technology is one area of common interest among all nations. Its
application, followed by transfer with appropriate adaptation to developing countries, can make major contributions to a new strategy
of international development to solve global problems of hunger and
peace. "Care must be taken to assure that such transfers are appropriate to the differing and particular needs of developing countries" (United Nations 1979).

The extent to which social and economic goals can be achieved
through the choice of different modes of technology is not yet known.
In the mid-1970s and early 1980s, many international scholars and
institutions of higher education were involved in projects to assess
the potential for the control of technology and its direction toward
the attainment of social goals. Black U.S. academics were hardly
ever involved in these international conferences. The September
1979 United Nations Vienna Conference, "Science and Technology
for Development," the largest conference ever held by an international body, was reported as "another donnybrook between the Third
World and the West" (Saunders 1979). White U.S. academics in
the United States delegation were unable to communicate with their
colleagues without antagonism and misunderstanding. This writer
believes that the inclusion of black U.S. academics would have
eased those tensions.

The April 1979 Nigeria-United States Workshop on Technological Development did not suffer from such a breakdown in inter-
personal communication. Black colleges and black academics were
purposely recruited in planning this conference. During analysis of
the Nigerian papers, they played a noteworthy role in interpreting
to U.S. scientists Nigerian demands for the application of scientific
knowledge to societal needs. Black academics were particularly
sensitive to the emphasis on relating technology to cultural needs

within a developing country such as Nigeria. The following recommendations for technology transfer between the United States and Nigeria can provide guidelines for program development in international education in black colleges and universities.

• Both governments should increase support for universities and related institutions concerned with development of relevant technology. Cooperation between such institutions in the two countries should be encouraged. The delivery of technologies is an area of special interest to the farmer and the small entrepreneur. In particular, the experience of U.S. land-grant colleges and their extension services should be made available on a broad basis to interested Nigerian institutions.
• The United States should support interinstitutional links between universities in the two countries. Disciplines and activities of high priority in the development of Nigerian universities (and other African universities) should receive particular attention.
• A task force of U.S. and Nigerian specialists should search for relevant technology and promote programs for its transfer.
• Nigeria should, on its own, identify priority programs to meet its developmental needs that may require the utilization of foreign technologies. The United States should then assist in identifying alternative technological options and their sources in the United States, and should facilitate direct discussions between Nigerian specialists and the United States.

The Growth and Independence of
Developing Countries

Most black U.S. students in U.S. colleges have a strong racial and ideological affinity with the independent countries of Africa and the oppressed blacks of South Africa. "Blacks in this country have always had an interest in Africa, and a few have looked beyond to black and other nonwhite peoples in Asia, Europe, Latin America, the Pacific, and elsewhere" (Smythe and Skinner 1976). It is therefore natural to assume that in the interest of international cooperation in economic and social development through higher education black colleges would tend to be most involved with the countries of Africa. Black Americans feel a kinship to Africa; the lives of young black Americans have been permeated with its music, arts, and dress. A keen interest in all aspects of their African heritage has stimulated many students to travel and study in Africa. Historically, independent black American missions like those of the African Methodist Church, have been closely aligned with black colleges, as well as major opponents of white supremacy in Africa (Arkhurst 1975). In other words, the bonds between blacks in the United States and those in African countries have been growing stronger and this relationship provides a firm basis for strong programs of international and cultural cooperation at the black colleges. Conversely, the United States' alignment with the exploitation and colonial imperialism of Europe in South Africa has established strong bonds between Americans and the English and Afrikaners of South Africa (Arkhurst 1975).

The Energy Crisis

The world energy crisis and its impact on economic growth and inflation has underscored the imbalances between oil demand and supply. These trends have affected world economic systems and are forcing changes in industrialized countries such as the United States. The historically conflicting political interests of the United States and the African states, which have been the basis for mutually antagonistic policies, will continue to cause stress in economic and social relationships. However, the ability of the United States to remain a free democratic society will largely depend upon the support of the countries of the Third World.

The 122 less-developed countries which are members of the United Nations are as diverse as their economies, "the biggest single barrier is between those who have oil and those that don't" (Saunders 1979). The increasing importance of Algeria, Angola, Egypt, Gabon, Libya, Nigeria, and Tunisia as exporters of crude petroleum requires a new examination of trade policies. Nevertheless, the 122 countries have shown remarkable solidarity and collective commitment to decolonization, reform in South Africa, human rights, economic aid and development, and disarmament (Kay 1970, pp. 45-50).

In recent years black Americans have begun to take a more active role and a heightened interest in international affairs, due in large part to the relationships established with Third World countries by former United Nations Ambassadors Andrew Young and Donald McHenry during the Carter administration. There are opportunities in the 1980s for black colleges and black Americans to cooperate with foreign countries, particularly those in Africa, as both groups become more knowledgeable about the political, economic, and social conditions of those nations.

<u>Adams</u> vs. <u>Califano</u>

Although many of the state plans to desegregate public systems of higher education have been accepted by the Department of Education's Office for Civil Rights, the <u>Adams</u> vs. <u>Califano</u> case requires that traditionally black colleges be both enhanced and desegregated. Specifically the criteria require the states to provide traditionally black institutions with nonracial missions and the resources necessary to fulfill these missions, accord them priority consideration for new programs, and eliminate unnecessary educational program duplication between them and traditionally white institutions with similar or overlapping service areas (see Chapters 3 and 11 for more on these issues). Both the criteria issued and the negotiations undertaken by the government in response to the <u>Adams</u> order emphasize that historically black colleges and universities must continue to play a significant and vital role in the education of black Americans. At the same time, state systems of higher education are being required to commit themselves to plans which promise to give black institutions a realistic chance to compete equally with historically white colleges in providing equal educational opportunity to all students.

Technology transfer projects with developing countries would, in my view, reinforce the requirement for the enhancement and desegregation of traditionally black colleges. Such international studies, activities, and programs are new and have the potential to expand the necessary redefinition of the missions of black colleges to goals of international or cross-cultural education. Many developing countries also want to increase the number of students eligible for higher education. By departing from selective admission policies and adopting new selection criteria, universities in developing countries, such as Nigeria and Zaire, encounter problems in determining whether their students are adequately prepared for college work. The predominantly black two- and four-year colleges have had the most experience in this area of student preparation (see Chapter 9).

President's Commission on Foreign
Language and International Studies

After more than a year of inquiry and deliberation, the Commission on Foreign Languages and International Studies reported unequivocably that most institutions of higher education and training for foreign language and international understanding

. . . are currently inadequate and actually falling further behind. Americans' incompetence in foreign languages is nothing short of scandalous, and is becoming worse. . . . Most broadly, the intent must be to make all undergraduates more knowledgeable about foreign societies and cultures and about major international issues in order to increase their undergraduate appreciation and competence. College graduates are the group in our population most likely to benefit from international competence. (President's Commission on Foreign Languages and International Studies 1979, pp. 5, 74)

The Commission called for the establishment of a nationally competitive program of federal grants for improving International Studies Programs at all U.S. colleges. The report specifically included colleges with high minority enrollments and community colleges and recommended programs at all degree levels with local or transnational focus.

One of the recommendations most pertinent to black colleges suggested the establishment of 60 to 70 regional centers that would focus on major world areas or, alternatively, on graduate and undergraduate training programs in transnational affairs, often at the master's degree level. The National Urban League has already called attention to the lack of "an available mechanism" through which black Americans might have a voice in the formulation of U.S. foreign policy. In The State of Black America 1980, Vernon Jordan suggests "the establishment of a Black Foreign Policy Institute at one of the major black colleges for the express purpose of undertaking research and study into foreign policy from a black perspective" (National Urban League 1980). Graduates of black professional schools of law, business, journalism, agriculture, engineering, and public health will increasingly enter careers that involve foreign relationships. Presently these schools devote little systematic attention to preparing students for work in the international field.

INTERNATIONAL PROGRAMS AT
HISTORICALLY BLACK COLLEGES

As a means of obtaining information on international involvement at black colleges and foreign students on their campuses, a questionnaire was developed and sent to the presidents of all four-year historically black colleges and universities. Included with the questionnaire and covering letter was a postcard to be mailed back immediately acknowledging receipt of the questionnaire, and checking those parts which were applicable to that institution. Telephone calls were made to all institutions that did not respond, but their informal remarks were not tabulated.

The purpose of the survey was to ascertain the extent to which black colleges participate in international studies. The underdeveloped status of international cross-cultural education in all U.S. institutions of higher education is well-documented. Despite this, U.S. colleges are recruiting foreign students in record numbers. Foreign students represent nearly 7 percent of all students in U.S. graduate schools and almost 2 percent of those in college, according to a 1979 report of the National Center for Education Statistics. The large number of students from Third World countries has contributed significantly to this increase.

Approximately 300,000 foreign students are enrolled in institutions of higher education in this country, with the number climbing 12 to 16 percent a year. . . . Students from nations in the Organization of Petroleum Exporting Countries now account for one-third of foreign students in this country, as against 12 percent in 1971-72. (New York Times, February 24, 1980).

Of all these countries, Nigeria ranks second to Iran in the number of students enrolled in U.S. colleges and universities. Black private, public, and community colleges are serving large numbers of students from both these countries. These colleges attempt to offer studies appropriate to the needs of their foreign students, but data on what these programs are and the countries of origin of foreign students have been sketchy or nonexistent.

Procedure and Results

As part of the survey, questionnaires were sent to 93 of the historically black institutions. Forty-four institutions (48 percent) responded. Eight of the 44 responded that they had no international studies programs (Lemoyne-Owens, Delaware State, Miles, Jarvis Christian, Edward Waters, Lane, Savannah State, and Virginia Union).

The questionnaire was broken down into five topical areas: (1) the number of foreign students on campus; (2) the extent to which foreign visitors came to the campus; (3) the extent to which faculty were invited abroad; (4) the number and kinds of courses in compara-

tive studies; and (5) the degree to which faculty were involved in research of an international or cross-cultural nature. The results
that follow cover each of these areas in addition to background information on the foreign students (their countries of origin, how
their education is financed, their most common academic majors)
and also provides a brief picture of the accomplishments of foreign
graduates and the existence of alumni organizations abroad.

Foreign Students on Campus

While a few institutions reported more than 500 foreign students, the average in this sample was between 40 and 60. Nigeria
was clearly the country sending most students to black colleges,
followed by Iran, the West Indies, Ethiopia, and Ghana. African
countries were mentioned four times as often as any other geographic area.

Table 1 summarizes the number of students from foreign
countries at black institutions during the periods 1970-75, 1975-78,
and as projected for 1980-81. The range is large, from institutions
with fewer than 25 students to Texas Southern with more than 2,000;
the median is at the 25 to 48 student level. Howard and Tennessee
State are the only other schools to report more than 500 students in
any of the time periods.

TABLE 1

Estimated Number of Foreign Students Enrolled
in 28 Historically Black Colleges

Number of Students	Number of Institutions		
	1970-75	1975-78	1980-81*
2,000 or more	—	1	1
1,000 to 1,999	1	3	1
500 to 999	1	—	1
250 to 499	4	2	3
100 to 249	7	6	6
50 to 99	1	8	2
25 to 49	6	5	7
1 to 24	6	2	4
None	2	1	1

*These data were projections since the survey was conducted
prior to the 1980-81 academic year.

Table 2 shows the number of different countries represented at these schools. Here, too, the range is wide, with schools having less than 10 countries represented to Texas Southern with 66, but again the median is at the low end of the scale, in the 10-14 range.

TABLE 2

Countries Represented at 29 Historically Black Colleges

Number of Countries Reported	Number of Institutions Reporting
51-66	1
26-50	2
20-25	1
15-19	2
10-14	11
5-9	8
1-4	4

Table 3 lists the most frequently cited countries of origin of foreign students at 29 historically black colleges and summarizes them by major geographic area. Nigeria, Iran, and Ethiopia were the countries which were reported most often to have had students on campus. The West Indies also had a significant representation. As indicated in Note a at the bottom of Table 3, students came most often from African countries, followed by the Middle East, the West Indies, South America, and Asia.

Source of Support

Table 4 details the sources of student support and the extent of support from each source. Foreign students' own or family funds were their major source of support at all but eight institutions; the student's government, the college or a foundation provided the remainder of their support. The U.S. government provided infrequent support and then only in small amounts. In only five institutions did the college report providing half or more of the support: Quinn (85 percent), Wiley (80 percent), Stillman (70 percent), Rust (50 percent), and Cheyney (50 percent). But Quinn, Wiley, and Stillman had few (5, 40, and 7) foreign students. In the rest of the cases, support came from the student's own government and in only three instances was this as high as 50 percent. In five instances, some support came from the U.S. government; in ten, from foundations (usually Phelps-Stokes); in one, from an unspecified church group; and, in another, from the state of North Carolina.

TABLE 3

Countries of Origin of Foreign Students
at 29 Historically Black Colleges[a]

Countries	Number of Times Cited[b]
Nigeria	25
Iran	12
West Indies	7
Ethiopia	6
Ghana	4
Kenya	3
India	3
Guyana	3
Venezuela	2
Liberia	2
Others[c]	

[a]When countries were summarized by geographical regions, the following areas received the most citations: Africa (48); Middle East (13); West Indies (7); South America (7); and Asia (5).
[b]Respondents were asked to rank order (1-3) of countries from which their students most often came. Thus, "number of times cited" includes the total of first, second, and third rankings for each country.
[c]The following countries were cited once: Brazil, Panama, Rhodesia, Saudi Arabia, Senegal, South Africa, Taiwan, and Zaire.

TABLE 4

Sources of Support for Foreign Students
in 20 Historically Black Colleges

Types of Support by Institutions	Amount of Support (in percentages)				
	75–100	50–74	25–49	10–24	Less than 10
Self, family	11	8	2	5	1
Students' government	1	2	6	8	4
College funds	2	3	1	3	5
U.S. government	—	—	—	1	4
Foundation	—	1	1	4	4
Other*	—	—	—	1	1

*This category includes funds from state and church sources.

Academic Interests of Students

Business and business administration were the subjects in which foreign students most often enrolled. There was also widespread interest in the social and physical sciences and technical and applied subjects but relatively little in health or the humanities. Table 5 indicates the dominant interest in business and business administration, since 22 of the 29 institutions responding listed these as the areas in which foreign students were most frequently interested. Biology and engineering were the only other subjects listed by more than four respondents; sociology, economics, and political science were each listed once. These are covered under the heading of social sciences.

Leadership by Graduates in Home Country

Asked the extent to which their foreign students are or were considered leaders in their country, 3 of the 22 responding institutions reported that 75 percent were; and 4, that 50 percent were. The seven institutions were St. Augustine's, which responded that almost all of its foreign students were leaders; Wiley and Benedict responded that 75 percent were; and Texas Southern, Atlanta, Hampton, and Dillard responded that 50 percent were. Of these seven, three had between 25 and 50 foreign students at the time the survey was conducted, while Texas Southern had more than 2,000. Five institutions considered that about one in four students was a leader and the other ten that few or none were.

TABLE 5

Academic Interests of Foreign Students
at 29 Historically Black Colleges

Academic Areas	Number of Times Cited[a]
Business and business administration	22
Physical sciences	17
Social sciences	18
Engineering and technology[b]	14
Humanities and education	5

[a]Figures equal totals of first, second, and third rankings.
[b]Fields cited in this category included engineering, agriculture, technology, architecture, and planning.

Only four institutions specified by name the alumni they considered prominent. Lincoln listed Nnamdi Asikiwe, former president of Nigeria; the late Kwame Nkrumah, former president of Ghana; C. Cecil Dennis, former foreign minister of Liberia; and Edward Blyden III, assistant to the president of Sierra Leone. Tuskegee listed Ptolemy Reid, deputy prime minister of Guyana; Wesley Nelson, head of Jamaica's School of Education; Michael Tomas, Region Health Officer of Ghana; and Aselfa Woldequiorgis, director of Ethiopia's Veterinary Services. Benedict noted S. Njoku, head of the Nigerian Department of Education; H. Olewunnu, a bank vice-president in Nigeria; and members of the Planning Commissions of Guyana and Nassau. Fort Valley State listed M. P. Ansah, head of the advanced teacher training college in Ghana; and Silvester Akpan, a state legislator in Nigeria. Atlanta University referred to alumni holding leadership roles in Nigeria, Ghana, Kenya, and India but gave no names.

Alumni Organizations

There was little evidence of alumni organizations abroad except in Nigeria. Only six institutions reported international alumni associations: Howard in Bermuda and Jamaica; Texas Southern in Nigeria, Iran, Sierra Leone, and Liberia; Rust in Nigeria; North Carolina in Liberia, Nigeria, and Ghana; Huston-Tillotson in Iran and Saudi Arabia; and Tennessee State in Nigeria. Obviously the Nigerian graduates, because their numbers are large, are the ones most likely to organize as alumni.

Foreign Visitors to Campus

Seventeen institutions reported short- or long-term programs which brought foreign visitors to campus for some educational purpose. Typically these programs involved fewer than 15 visitors, with only the World Cultural Center program at Cheyney State attracting more than 25. Participants most often came from Africa, with Nigeria first (7 of the 17); and Guyana (2), Ghana (2), and the Caribbean (3) noted more than once. Reference was also made to participants from Asia and, for the first time in these data, from Eastern and Western European countries, with Austria the only country mentioned by name. Looking back over past programs, respondents noted academic areas which covered the range noted earlier, but without any clear preferences. Business and public affairs were mentioned most often (4). By area, these programs involved humanities most often (15), followed by social sciences (10), business and public affairs (4), engineering and agriculture (6), education (4), and the sciences including health (4).

Faculty and Staff Abroad

Nineteen institutions reported sending faculty or staff abroad for some period of time, with only one of the 19 not specifying the frequency of such trips. One school, Quinn, noted one faculty trip abroad; 12 noted two to ten trips; and the other five reported more than ten trips. The five with extensive faculty work abroad were Texas Southern, Tennessee State, Lincoln, Tuskegee, and Huston-Tillotson.

There were 30 reported trips to Africa involving 17 different countries. Only Nigeria (6), Sierra Leone (2), Kenya (3), and Ghana (2) were mentioned more than once. Eight trips to Asia were noted, including Taiwan (3), India (2), Pakistan, China, and Thailand. The West Indies received five citations, Latin America four, the Middle East three, and England and the U.S.S.R. one each.

The academic areas most often associated with these trips were the humanities (11), foreign languages, and English; science (7), biology, chemistry, physics, and entomology; social science (8), political science primarily; education and higher education (7). Business and management (4), agriculture (2), and technology (1) were mentioned least often as academic areas associated with trips.

Courses in Comparative Studies

Fifteen institutions provided information on courses offered in comparative studies and the academic department where courses are taught. Eleven of the 15 offer between one and five courses; Howard and Lincoln more than ten. They were housed in a wide variety of departments, with social science mentioned most often, followed by the humanities and education. Howard University also offers a Master of Arts in comparative jurisprudence.

Faculty Research and Advanced Study

Asked to indicate the extent of faculty activity in research and advanced study, nine institutions listed faculty publications related to international education. Six reported research activities, but provided no details. The number of such publications is growing. They cover a wide range of subjects including South Africa's political economy, science (especially medicine), education, the politics of a divided India and Pakistan, Russia's outlook on Sino-American relations, Zimbabwe, and the personal aspirations of East Indian high school students who plan to come to the United States for higher education.

MODELS OF INTERNATIONAL PROGRAMS

The following outlines of two courses represent different approaches to international studies at black colleges. One is for students from foreign universities, the other for U.S. students interested in international trade and management.

Howard University offers a unique Master's of Arts in Comparative Jurisprudence program. Students must hold a law degree from a non-American university or its equivalent in legal, administrative, or judiciary experience, or service on a law faculty in a country other than the United States, the United Kingdom, Canada, or Australia. Through this program, lawyers develop an informed awareness of Anglo-American legal institutions, thinking, and practice. The theoretical segment of the program entails classwork at the law school, while clinical exposure is provided through various U.S. and local government agencies and the United Nations.

In 1980, Morgan State University initiated a program offering a new instructional concentration in international management in its School of Business and Management. In addition to demonstrating competence in international business, students will be expected to show mastery of various allied subjects, such as finance, marketing, economics, accounting, and management.

The university's rationale for the program is the increasing influence of multinational companies in shaping the lives of all U.S. citizens, especially those living in urban centers such as Baltimore where Morgan State is located. This program was planned to enhance the students' understanding of international management with particular emphases on international trade, analysis of international business transactions, and of effective international marketing strategy. The program consists of 57 credit hours of course work in three major areas.

Baltimore's excellent port facilities, served by a complex network of air, rail, and roadway transportation systems, has made it a recognized center for international trade and commerce. Career opportunities in international business administration should increase rapidly over the next 10 to 15 years as the projected expansion and modernization of the port progresses.

Legislation and Grants

The U.S. Department of Education's Division of International Education (DIE) administers a number of programs under a variety of legislation. Most of DIE's programs have been authorized by Title VI (Foreign Studies and Language Development) of the National Defense Education Act. The Undergraduate International Studies Program is designed for institutions or consortia of institutions of higher learning wishing to add an international component to existing curricula and to develop new methods of teaching international studies to undergraduates. In 1979, grants of $875,000 were made to 25 institutions. Typically, grantees use program funds for a one- to two-year period (consortia for one to three years) to revise and update curricula, to develop or increase faculty expertise, or to improve existing resources. A Department of Education official has said that because historically black colleges are frequently located in rural areas, and have many programs tied to the land-grant college concept, they should be successful in developing new or revised programs which emphasize agricultural development and production, programs needed in developing countries.

The Phelps-Stokes Fund has been the recipient of numerous federal grants which have been used to assist the historically black colleges. Its Caribbean-American Linkage Program (CALP) was initiated in an effort to fill a communications need in the Caribbean, to promote understanding, mutually beneficial research, and, ultimately, institutional links and cooperation.

In the past, black colleges and developing countries have maintained an uneven and undefined partnership. The developing nations, particularly those in Africa, have reaped significant economic and social benefits from the thousands of graduates trained in historically black institutions, and the latter have profited from the cross-cultural enrichment gained from contacts with foreign students. If a strategy of cooperation and collaboration could be implemented, greater equality in benefits would be possible. Ruth Stutts Njiiri of the Phelps-Stokes Fund has stated:

> Because there exists a compatibility of aspirations and needs, black colleges and educational institutions in developing nations could unite in the pursuit of economic advancement through carefully-designed institutional linkages. The sharing of human and material resources could assist in removing some of the deficiencies in educational programs caused by economic constraints. Not only does this concept of sharing of resources augur well for potential economic growth, but it supplies prospects for social development as well. (Njiiri 1980).

RECOMMENDATIONS

There has been international cross-cultural activity in black colleges and universities, but there is little available data to indicate any coordination of efforts among these institutions. Conversations with black college administrators, faculty, and students indicate that many of the colleges do not have sufficient resources or faculty to implement cross-cultural programs. Many spoke of the need to plan for informal as well as formal networks for sharing library resources and faculty. Students need increased access to international news as well as opportunities for discussion and debate on international issues. With that in mind, I recommend that the following initiatives be undertaken by black colleges and universities:

Establishment of an international or cross-cultural information clearinghouse that would serve a variety of people in the United States, the developing countries, and other parts of the world.

Exploration and reevaluation of present programs and career opportunities in agri-industrial fields, transportation, public health, marketing, banking, as well as studies on the problems of food storage and processing, energy, and water conservation should be expanded with an international focus. Tuskegee, Howard, and the University of the District of Columbia, the latter being a predominantly black college, already have well-established programs in some of these subjects. For other colleges, these fields can be studied within the related disciplines of biology, natural resource development, breeding, chemistry, engineering, medicine, and business.

The introduction of international cross-cultural components as a first step in the development of a long-range plan of incorporating international cross-cultural education into existing curriculum offerings.

In-service faculty workshops or retreats designed to increase awareness of international cross-cultural imperatives.

Evaluation and adoption by each college or university department of some of the following programs:
1. Interdisciplinary offerings on world issues, such as illiteracy, peace, health, population, pollution, and financial resources
2. Summer or semester-abroad programs
3. Student exchanges
4. Faculty exchanges
5. Language and area studies
6. Use of the often untapped resources of foreign students on campuses, and building increased understanding between them and black American students

Development of formal links for the transferral of technology to colleges and universities in developing countries through black college alumni in those countries, the United Nations University Project and its many international coordinating agencies, as well as through the World Council for Curriculum and Instruction. This council was set up to assist in professional teacher preparation on an international scale and works with Indiana University and universities in Nigeria and Malaysia. They are cooperatively developing curricular materials for world studies.

The expansion of international programs and opportunities in black colleges and universities is timely and can contribute to the necessary redefinition of their missions. Black colleges have exhibited flexibility and resiliency in responding to the complex, ever-changing relationships between the states, courts, federal government, and their own students. They must now support the new demands for international interdependence. Black college leadership needs to be acutely aware of the critical world issues and changing forces that will affect the lives of their students. This is essential if they are to coordinate and plan for international cross-cultural education.

REFERENCES

Aminu, Jibril. "International linkages in higher education: A Nigerian view." Paper delivered at the Sixty-first Annual Meeting of the American Council on Education, October 1978.

Arkhurst, Fred S., ed. U.S. policy toward Africa. New York: Praeger, 1975.

Barry, John M. "The Howard connection." Washington Post Magazine, March 22, 1981.

Davis, John A. "Black Americans and United States policy toward Africa." Journal of International Affairs 23, 2 (1969):236-49.

_____. "The revolution of color." In U.S. policy toward Africa, edited by F. S. Arkhurst. New York: Praeger, 1975. And in J. N. Rosenau, ed. Linkage politics. New York: The Free Press, 1969.

Franklin, John Hope. "A brief history." In The black American reference book, edited by M. M. Smythe. Englewood Cliffs, NJ: Prentice-Hall, 1976.

Hubbard, Louise J. "The minority student in the foreign language field." In Background papers and studies. Washington, D.C.: November 1979.

Kay, David. The new nations in the United Nations. New York: Columbia University Press, 1970.

National Urban League. The state of black America. Washington, D.C.: National Urban League, 1980.

New York Times. February 24, 1980; March 22, 1981.

Njiiri, Ruth Stutts, International education program director, Phelps-Stokes Fund. Statement to the author, 1980.

Ogbu, John U. Minority education and caste: The American system in cross-cultural perspective. New York: Academic Press, 1978.

President's Commission on Foreign Languages and International Studies. Strength through wisdom: A critique of U.S. capability. A report to the President's Commission on Foreign Languages and International Studies, November 1979.

Robinson, James H. Tomorrow is today. New York: Farrar, Straus, 1969.

Saunders, Sol. "The west vs. the L.D.C.'s: A quagmire thickens." Business Week, October 15, 1979.

Smythe, Hugh H., and Elliot P. Skinner. "Black participation in U.S. foreign relations." In The black American reference book, edited by M. M. Smythe. Englewood Cliffs, NJ: Prentice-Hall, 1976.

United Nations. International development strategy. Pamphlet published by the United Nations after Conferences on United Nations of the Next Decades, Porvoo, Finland, 1979.

Woodson, Carter G. The Negro in our history. Washington, D.C.: Associated Publishers, 1922.

PART IV

RESEARCH DIRECTIONS
OF BLACK COLLEGES

Most black colleges are undergraduate institutions and because of that fact their primary mission has been to teach. Over the last several years, research has, for many reasons, assumed a fundamental role in the functions of higher education. Research has become the yardstick on which faculty members' productivity is measured; it serves as a major criterion on which tenure decisions are determined; the receipt of research grants and contracts from the federal government and private foundations increases the prestige of institutions and departments; and, research grants and contracts bring along with them indirect costs that help in the administrative operation of the institution. Research, therefore, is a role that many black institutions may want to pursue and the following chapters by Herman Branson, Daniel Thompson, and John Monro explore variations on this theme.

Branson, Thompson, and Monroe all agree that black colleges should become more involved in research, despite the perennial problems of insufficient time, heavy teaching loads, overly competitive grant competitions, professional isolation from colleagues, and inadequate facilities and financial resources. Branson is particularly concerned with more research in the sciences; Thompson believes that there are a multitude of social and economic research issues to be studied due to changes in U.S. society; and Monro proposes the establishment of an academic research and information board to conduct black-controlled research on educational problems affecting black students. The extensive discussions promote the theses that "research fortifies teaching" and that black colleges have unique potentialities in research and scholarship by virtue of their history, locations, and involvement in massive social changes in U.S. society.

Research in
the Historically
Black Colleges

Herman Branson

Historically, teaching, not research, was considered the primary role of the vast majority of colleges and universities, including the slightly more than 100 predominantly black colleges and universities. If these institutions are to fulfill their missions, their unique responsibility as sources of black scholarship, havens for black scholars, trainers of black leaders, and protectors and articulators of black interests, requires that research be a fundamental commitment in all their educational and economic planning.

This chapter examines the feasibility of such a proposal and describes the magnitude of the research and development (R&D) enterprise in the United States. There is also an examination of the relationship between grant-getting and productivity variables, in an attempt to characterize some of the distinguishing features in the grant-giving process. There are a few hopeful signs for small colleges and universities including the black institutions. Among these are: research does not have to be done on a large scale and increasingly institutions are cooperating on such studies. As John Monro points out in Chapter 9, teachers, themselves, must be encouraged to carry on research on their work.

The term "research" came into use around 1577, but only within the last 100 years has it achieved its real vitality. In U.S. colleges and universities, the activity called research has been accorded acceptance and interest only since the early years of the twentieth century. The United States' greatest academic scientist during the last years of the nineteenth century, Professor H. A. Rowland of Johns Hopkins University, made a moving plea in 1883 for what we would now equate with research, but did not use the word in his effective summary:

The duty of a professor is to advance his science, and
to set an example of pure and true devotion to it which
shall demonstrate to his students and the world that
there is something high and noble worth living for.
(Science, February 15, 1980, p. 751).

Rowland's point of view triumphed in academic United States
to the extent that the three accepted functions of the college or university came to be teaching, research, and public service (Williams
1966). Although expressed as a triad, the three components were
not of equal strength. The research image, especially in the last
50 years, has emerged as the predominant basis for generating high
prestige for the faculty, and national and international reputations
for the institution.

FEDERAL R&D SUPPORT

A brief look at the national picture, based on available data
from the National Science Board (NSB 1979), provides an overview
of academic research and, particularly, of the research potential
of black institutions.

At present, our country's expenditures for research and development exceed those of all nations except the Soviet Union (NSB
1979). This activity represents slightly more than 2 percent of the
gross national product, down from a high of 3 percent in 1964. One
result of these generous expenditures in the United States is that
U.S. authors account for about 40 percent of the world's influential
scientific and technical journal literature. Since World War II, the
federal government has contributed more R&D funds than any other
source, although its share declined in the late 1960s and the 1970s
with the termination of the manned space program and reductions in
defense R&D spending. Development expenditures are generally
much greater than those for research, and, therefore, account for
about two-thirds of the total R&D expenditures. In the late 1970s,
defense obligations represented about one-half of the federal R&D
costs; the amount spent on space exploration fluctuated; and civilian
R&D accounted for nearly 40 percent of the total spent, with the
largest amounts expended in the areas of health and energy. Expenditures for defense R&D are likely to increase as defense budgets
grow.

Within the broad scope of R&D, basic research occupies a
special position as a long-term investment in knowledge and productivity; universities and colleges now perform the major part of this
work. In 1960, these institutions spent only 36 percent of the money

122 / Herman Branson

invested in basic research but, as colleges and universities grew in size and number and industry increasingly turned to applied work, the academic sector expanded its role until in 1975 it performed 52 percent of basic research. The major source of support for this work is the federal government. Its contributions grew in the early 1960s, gradually declined from 1969 to 1975, and expanded again in the latter half of the 1970s. The greatest share of this support has gone to the life sciences and the physical sciences, which jointly received about two-thirds of the federal contribution. In recent years, the fields of environmental sciences and engineering have grown, while psychology and the social sciences have displayed little change.

Since the mid-1960s, virtually all the basic research conducted by the academic sector (98 percent) has been carried out at institutions that grant the PhD. The figures for all federally funded research and development reveal a similar picture: approximately 100 universities receive almost all of this support and the pattern of distribution has not changed much in recent years (see Table 1).

TABLE 1

Percent of Federal R&D Funds Awarded to the
Top 100 Academic Institutions*

| | Institutions | | | |
	Top 10	Top 20	Top 50	Top 100
FY 1975	23	38	64	83
FY 1979	26	41	65	84

*The data from which these percentages are derived are based on amounts representing total federal obligations to institutions for research and development in fiscal 1975 and 1979. Total R&D obligations for 1975 and 1979 were 2,238,744,000 and 3,846,321,000, respectively; actual amounts awarded to the top 100 institutions in 1975 and 1979 were 1,870,283,000 and 3,245,139,000, respectively.

Source: National Science Foundation. Federal support to universities, colleges, and selected nonprofit institutions. (Washington, D.C.: NSF), No. 77-303 (1977) and No. 81-308 (1981).

This concentration of R&D support initially presents a somewhat discouraging prospect for the predominantly black institutions. Nonetheless, there are several more hopeful aspects which will be discussed in the following pages: not all faculty members at top universities are active in research; research need not always be conducted on a large scale with major expenditures; and new areas continually open up, as the recent growth of environmental research shows, offering room for modest beginnings. Finally, current scientific literature shows an increase in cooperative work by scientists and engineers representing different institutions (NSB 1979).

Foreign Graduate Students in U.S. Universities

American universities and colleges are recognized as having made a significant contribution to the building of world scientific and technical capabilities. These institutions have not only performed the work, but they have also educated the students. Large proportions of foreign students in the United States are majoring in scientific and technical fields. According to a 1980 study by the Analytic Sciences Corporation (Feldbaum and Potashkin 1980) using data from the Institute for International Education, in 1978-79 the largest percentage of foreign students was majoring in engineering (28.8 percent) and another 15 percent were studying math, computer, and natural and life sciences. The report goes on to show that of all the foreign students majoring in engineering, 61 percent were in baccalaureate programs, and 24.2 percent and 15 percent were in master's and doctoral programs, respectively. The latter statistics are especially important, since they indicate that foreign students account for 39.6 percent of all students pursuing a master's degree and 47.4 percent of those seeking a doctoral degree in engineering.

Foreign students also account for a substantial percentage of terminal degrees in selected disciplines. Data on 1979 PhDs reported in Syverson's summary report of earned doctorates show that foreign citizens received one-fifth of the PhDs awarded in all the sciences. Closer examination of these data for particular fields indicates that foreign students received approximately 46 percent of the PhDs awarded in engineering, 37 percent in the agricultural sciences, 32 percent in economics, and 25 percent in physics and astronomy (Syverson 1980). These figures represent a significant proportion of the individuals that U.S. universities educate in the sciences.

Who Receives Research Grants?

We emphasize the fact that a relatively small number of major institutions receive practically all federal R&D funds (as shown in

124 / Herman Branson

Table 1) in order to dispel some widespread and misleading misconceptions. One is that research funds are in such great supply that a
competent researcher in one of the top universities swims in a sea of
surplus monies. Another is that the need for research is truly recognized throughout all colleges and universities and that only lethargy
or misinformation keeps the teachers in some schools from participating. Using data from a study conducted by Roland Liebert (1977)
we will explore the accuracy of these two ideas.

GRANT-GETTING AND PUBLICATION PRODUCTIVITY

Liebert has attempted to show that there are positive and significant relationships between the process of obtaining research
grants and the productivity of scholars by using the number of published professional articles as a measure of productivity. Liebert's
sample for this study consisted of slightly more than 5,300 faculty
from roughly 300 four-year colleges and universities in the United
States (see Bayer 1973 for further details on the study design).
Subjects were administered a survey questionnaire on which they
were asked to indicate on a checklist of grant-giving agencies (17
federal and 5 nonfederal) each source from which they had received
support to conduct "scholarly work and research" as a principal investigator during the 1972-73 academic year. Table 2 gives the results, indicating the percent of scholars in this sample on grants by
type of granting agency.

The data are further refined in that they show the distribution
of these grant recipients for all institutions in the sample: four-
year colleges, universities, and PhD departments in universities.
The data show that slightly more than one-third (34.5 percent) of the
faculty in universities and four-year colleges combined had received
grants during 1972-73. Note, especially, that 21.5 percent of the
faculty in four-year colleges received grants despite the absence of
graduate programs to train students in research. Thus, it is easy
to conclude that faculty at four-year colleges do not confine themselves solely to the teaching function. Liebert cautions, however,
the reader must remember that some individuals receive more
grants than others and that the percentages provide no indication of
the size of each grant. These numbers also reveal that even in PhD
departments of universities, only about half the faculty have grants
from any agency including their own institutional or departmental
funds.

The fundamental premise of Liebert's survey is that the pattern of grant-getting by faculty is a function of the competitive advantage accrued by publication productivity, the priority accorded

TABLE 2

Percent of Scholars on Grants by Type of Granting Agency

Granting Agency[a]	All Institutions	Four-Year Colleges	Universities	PhD Departments in Universities[b]
NSF	5.2	2.6	7.2	12.3
HEW	5.3	1.7	8.3	6.9
DEFENSE	3.0	1.6	4.1	5.9
OTHFED	5.3	2.0	8.1	6.5
FNDTN	4.8	3.1	5.3	6.4
INDUSOTH	7.6	6.3	9.5	8.4
STATELOC	5.8	3.0	8.2	6.3
INTRAMUR	14.7	9.5	18.9	21.4
All agencies	23.5	21.5	44.4	50.5
Number[c]	(5,299)	(2,394)	(2,905)	(1,293)

[a] Agencies are defined as follows, with the numbers in parentheses enumerating the original 22 agency categories itemized on the ACE survey questionnaire: NSF—(1) National Science Foundation; HEW—U.S. Department of Health, Education, and Welfare, including (2) FDA, (3) OE, (4) NIMH, (5) NIH, and (6) "Other HEW"; DEFENSE—(7) U.S. Defense Department, (8) Atomic Energy Commission, (9) National Aeronautics and Space Administration; OTHFED—U.S. Department of (10) Agriculture, (11) Commerce, (12) Interior, (13) Labor, and (14) Transportation, (15) National Endowment for the Arts and Humanities, (16) Office of Economic Opportunity, and (17) "Other Federal Agency"; FNDTN—(18) Private Foundations; INDUSOTH—(19) Private Industry and (20) all other not elsewhere itemized; STATELOC—(21) State or local government; INTRAMUR—(22) Institutional or departmental funds (i.e., intramural).

[b] University PhD granting departments are those which are quality rated in the 1969-70 ACE ratings (18).

[c] About 2 percent of the cases with missing data on grants are excluded from this figure.

Source: Liebert 1977, p. 170.

125

different disciplinary fields, and the advantages resulting from particular institutional assets and specific personal characteristics of
scholars. In other words, the more one publishes, or the more significant the research one publishes, the better one's chances of obtaining a grant. Also, scholars in certain disciplinary fields receive more funds and resources for basic and advanced research
simply because of the nature of the field of study, for example, agriculture, chemistry, or any of the life sciences. Liebert's final
point is that the more prestigious the institution of the faculty member applying for a grant or the more noteworthy that member's social, academic, or professional background, the better are his or
her chances of obtaining a grant.

CAREER PRODUCTIVITY AND GRANT-GETTING

Table 3 shows the strength of association between career productivity (number of articles over the career span) and grant-getting
and also indicates the percentages of each agency's grant recipients
who were highly productive. Thus, there is a reciprocal relationship between grant-getting and publications: the person who publishes more has a better chance of winning a grant and in turn the
person who receives a grant is more likely to publish more articles.
Awards from the top five granting agencies, which include federal
departments and private foundations (called "major-league" agencies
by Liebert), appear to be those for which there is most competition.
State and local agencies, industry, and intramural research fund
providers are classified as "minor league" by Liebert and apparently
the strength of association between productivity and grant-getting is
not as strong for them as it is for the major-league agencies.

One way of explaining this differential is that major-league
funding agencies may have more well-defined criteria than the minor-
league investors; therefore, the competition may be a great deal
more stringent and rest more heavily on the prior track record of
the applicant. On the other hand, and in defense of the minor leagues,
since this study does not give any financial information on the average size of grants, the situation may be that minor leagues have more
money and resources to distribute and may not be as concerned about
fiscal stringency as the major leagues are.

Source of Grants

Table 4 shows that less than 20 percent of Liebert's sample
received grants from major-league agencies, and about 25 percent

TABLE 3

Publication Productivity and Grant-Getting

Granting Agency	Percent of Grant Receivers Having		Gamma between Grant-Getting and	
	Eleven or More Career Articles	Five or More Recent Publications	Career Articles[a]	Recent Publications[b]
NSF	73.3	49.2	.712	.713
HEW	70.4	46.7	.679	.713
DEFENSE	64.7	45.7	.730	.697
OTHFED	51.6	30.7	.449	.561
FNDTN	57.6	42.8	.523	.622
INDUSOTH	45.6	26.9	.383	.440
STATELOC	44.1	26.9	.410	.466
INTRAMUR	41.5	26.6	.395	.498
Major league	60.8	38.0	.655	.712
Minor league	41.1	24.3	.427	.518
All agencies	46.4	27.3	.580	.672
Number[c]	(5, 230)	(5, 186)	(5, 230)	(5, 186)

[a] Gammas were computed for seven-point ordinal scaled career articles with dichotomous grant-getting variables. All are significant at less than .001.

[b] Gammas were computed for five-point ordinal recent publications variable with dichotomous grant-getting variables. All were significant at less than .001.

[c] About 5 percent of the cases were deleted for lack of data on grant-getting or publications.

Source: Liebert 1977, p. 173.

received at least one grant from the minor leagues. However, over two-thirds (65 percent) of the sample received no grants at all. This finding makes it even clearer that many of the same faculty are receiving multiple grants within and across the two categories.

TABLE 4

Number and Percent Distribution of Faculty
by Grants Received

Number of Grants Received	All Grants Number	%	Major League Number	%	Minor League Number	%
None	3,470	65.5	4,308	81.3	4,017	75.8
One	1,165	22.0	742	14.0	960	18.1
Two	425	8.0	198	3.7	278	5.2
Three	170	3.2	41	0.8	43	0.8
Four	53	1.0	7	0.1	1	0.0
Five	12	0.2	3	0.1		
Six or seven	4	0.1				
Number	5,299	100.0	5,299	100.0	5,299	99.9

Source: Liebert 1977, p. 175.

Grant Distribution by Academic Field

Another way of trying to get a handle on the data is by examining the distribution of grants by academic fields as summarized in Table 5. Observe that scholars in agriculture have on an average received many more grants than those in mathematics (1.636 vs. 0.304). Scholars do more research in some fields than in others and some have more available resources. More grants for particular disciplines may also be a function of smaller grant awards to scholars in those fields. Nevertheless, there seems to be little apparent parity of the disciplines with respect to research grants.

Liebert's basic findings are that productivity variables and field differences most strongly determine whether individuals obtain or do not obtain research grants. Other data from the study (not cited here), however, show few or no positive relationships between grant-getting and institutional characteristics (for example, university status, percent of faculty with doctorates, number of periodicals in the library, and so forth) and between grant-getting and an

TABLE 5

Average Number of Grants Received
per Scholar

Field*	All Grants	Major League	Minor League
Agriculture	1.636	.608	1.041
Chemistry	1.289	.772	.473
Medicine	1.117	.714	.374
Physiology/Anatomy	1.102	.586	.517
Earch science/Astronomy	1.053	.553	.500
Biology	1.051	.547	.513
Engineering	1.041	.550	.497
Physics	.794	.557	.251
Anthropology	.700	.309	.382
Economics	.677	.269	.417
Sociology	.663	.363	.304
Political science	.578	.225	.372
Psychology	.573	.272	.319
Law	.505	.228	.277
History	.406	.141	.273
Geography	.340	.187	.152
Business	.309	.097	.210
Mathematics	.304	.184	.117
Fine arts	.296	.059	.246
Education	.268	.102	.172
Philosophy/Religion	.212	.076	.146
English language/Lit.	.211	.067	.140
Home economics	.196	.067	.111
Social work	.161	.055	.109
Foreign languages/Lit.	.155	.054	.115
Physical education	.133	.059	.079
Nursing	.120	.096	.026

*Ranked by score on all grants.
Source: Liebert 1977, p. 176.

institution's being historically black or privately supported. Liebert finds the same lack of significance if an applicant is black, female, or holds a doctorate (Liebert 1977, pp. 184-85). These results are very interesting even though the sample and the data are limited. The truth is that personal factors and institutional characteristics probably do make a difference in who receives grants, but there is a need for more conclusive research to show how these variables are interrelated. But, for the purposes of this chapter, the data from the tables and especially Table 2 demonstrate that four-year college faculty can perform research and do receive grants. This fact should be most instructive for individuals who teach at traditionally black colleges and universities.

CHARACTERISTICS OF THE GROUP

Our concern here is with about 100 black colleges and universities in the United States. Concentrated in the southeastern states, they enroll approximately 250,000 students and employ roughly 14,000 faculty members. Their combined annual budgets approach a billion dollars. Although they enroll only 15 to 20 percent of all black students in higher education, the group graduates more than 50 percent of the blacks receiving bachelor's degrees, because so many blacks are either in two-year colleges or in predominantly white colleges, where the dropout rates are higher and the graduation rates lower.

In 1978, black colleges received about 5 percent of the overall total of $7 billion federal dollars that went to all colleges and universities, but they received only 0.3 percent of the R&D funds. As one might guess, most of the federal money the group received (53 percent) was for student support (Federal Interagency Committee on Education 1979). The majority of students who enroll in these institutions are from families with low incomes, which qualifies them for most student financial aid grant and loan programs.

Research in Historically Black
Colleges and Universities

In any scheme of ranking U.S. colleges and universities by research productivity, black institutions are certainly far from the top. Thus our task is to infuse realism into our position that the predominantly black college should and must participate more effectively in research, either basic or targeted, supported by federal funds. In doing this, these institutions will move into the "mainstream" and will be less dependent on the institutional funding now directed to them in Title III of the Higher Education Act of 1965. Inasmuch as genuine research and development funds carry a reasonable overhead, black colleges could gain fiscal strength through these programs just as major universities do.

Intensive analysis is required to determine how realistic this aspiration is for the average school in this group. One of the recommendations of this article will be support of efforts in this area. But now our attention should best be directed to exploring in some detail why research should be aided in these schools, irrespective of their differing conditions or of targeted agency requirements or commitments.

Importance of Research to the Black Colleges

My basic thesis is that each of these colleges should achieve a better integration of research in its educational and economic planning. Let me make some bold statements.

First, in the predominantly black college the greatest enemy is isolation and the inevitable loss of contact with one's discipline. This is a phenomenon of all colleges, but the situation is especially serious in black colleges. The official recognition of the necessity for intellectual growth and stimulation should be programmatic. Medawar, in his delightful little book Advice to a Young Scientist (1979), emphasizes that research is "work so absorbing and deeply pleasurable." He also refers to it as "exploratory activity," a good term to emphasize its personal, individual significance.

Teaching can only be honest and effective if it is properly supported by accurate, germane knowledge. On this point Ziman (1968) observes:

> . . . contact with young fresh minds keeps the research scholar alert and undogmatic; we might equally hold that the practice of research, with all its uncertainties and difficulties, keeps the teacher humble and undogmatic and gives the student some inkling of the way in which true science is in fact conducted.

Second, administrators at predominantly black colleges must not utter pious homilies, but must insure that their faculties grow intellectually. Recognizing that only a small proportion of all academics do research, with two-thirds publishing nothing, the colleges must not pattern themselves on the "publish or perish" model. They must face reality. Even though the research results may never make

the Journal of the American Chemical Society, the teacher can still
engage in "exploratory activities" and may find a publishing outlet
in a lesser journal. Thus, the colleges should find ways to encourage, stimulate, and aid teachers in all disciplines to do the following:

— Become more active members of their professional societies;
— Subscribe to at least one journal, in addition to those sup-
plied by their professional associations;
— Attend at least one professional conference or meeting each
year;
— Attend short courses, workshops, seminars, or institutes
to keep their knowledge accurate and current;
— Prepare at least one paper annually, either for local presentation or for a wider group, and plan to eventually publish it; and
— Take leaves of absence with pay.

Third, the predominantly black colleges must actively pursue
federal, state, and industrial support for research that is within the
competency and interests of their faculties. According to the Roose
and Andersen ratings (1970), the universities that were rated "strong"
or "distinguished" did not indicate that the individual research pursued by faculty took an inordinate amount of their time: "91 percent
of the faculty members were spending 20 percent or more of their
time in research." That is not too demanding for most faculty. In
fact, a famous quip attributed to the United States' early great academic researcher, Henry Augustus Rowland, was that for research
"You don't need time; you don't need money; all you need is the will."
Fourth, the predominantly black colleges must assist their
faculties more aggressively to maintain contact with faculty at other
black colleges and especially to maintain contact with the research
leaders in their fields. A quotation from the New York Times Magazine expresses the poignancy of this need:

In science, as in other human endeavors, brilliance and
ambition and determination are not enough. Ultimate
success depends on the tenuous personal bond that may
develop between a young scientist and someone older
who can inspire him and open doors (February 17, 1980,
p. 14).

We desperately need people like these who can "inspire and open
doors," and the resulting support networks and mentoring relationships are essential.

The Larger Social Scene

The National Academy of Sciences in 1979 published a report, Research Excellence Through the Year 2000, which assesses the nature and magnitude of the "young investigator" problem in the United States. One means suggested to nurture the development of superior intellectual ability is a series of Research Excellence Awards that would comprise five-year, nonrenewable grants to tenured or nontenured faculty members nominated by a department. Black colleges and other institutions that may account for 20 to 40 percent of the black college population by the year 2000 should be seriously considered as recipients of a proportion of these research excellence awards, as well as other programs that will help to support the research of young investigators.

WHAT CAN BE DONE?

Research has been advocated as an activity through which certain essential tasks in the intellectual life of the nation are performed as a means of insuring high-quality undergraduate teaching and of fostering faculty development. Hence an agency concerned with increasing research in black colleges and universities might look at each of these categories, determine what is being done, what might be done, and how to do it.

Basic Research

Basic research is now fostered and supported primarily in the top universities, a few prestigious colleges, and only rarely in other colleges. Some of this research is carried on in the few predominantly black colleges and universities, but not enough. Of the total of $4 billion of R&D funds going to all colleges and universities, the 0.3 percent cited earlier represents only $12 million which is awarded to the black colleges and universities.

There are faculty with training at the PhD level in all these schools, so a concerted effort to increase production in research would be feasible. The approach may require certain targeted funds in research areas in which the agencies have interest. Keep in mind the reality of the competition outlined ahead: hungry, ambitious researchers of proven worth are eagerly competing for every research dollar. Unless funds are directed to these black institutions, they may get little in open competition. The agencies have an unassailable argument: We base our decisions on merit and the desire to use our funds as productively as possible.

Unfortunately some persons urging an increase in research in black colleges and universities may view it as a means of augmenting basic support through a generous overhead allowance. This may be a chimera except in our few PhD-granting institutions. If the $12 million black institutions now receive were doubled, and distributed among 100 schools with 50 percent overhead, the average budget would be increased less than 1 percent.

The motivation for supporting this type of research in black schools must stem, then, from the quality of the product, the need to establish research expertise and to train a cadre of students who can move into R&D in government laboratories and PhD-granting universities.

Research as a Means of Insuring
High-Quality Undergraduate Teaching

With black young people receiving increasingly poor education in the public schools, the federal government should be strongly supportive of the black colleges and their dedication to quality education. The one hope is that the colleges can effect such a change in these young people that they will become understanding, participating, contributing citizens of the demanding technological world of the twenty-first century. Many agencies, therefore, intent on hiring more members of minority groups should explore collaborative and consortial relationships with groups of these colleges so that faculty could be supported on agency-related research that would involve students.

If you wish minorities in a sea-grant program, for example, why not develop a five-year program with a predominantly black college's biology department in which two competent professors and five to ten of their students might work on some problem arising from the laboratory of a distinguished scientist at Woods Hole? The students and faculty would be able to spend some time at Woods Hole; the stimulation would be outstanding in comparison with the cost.

The National Science Foundation (NSF) and the National Institutes of Health (NIH) have already made impressive, effective efforts in this area: the Minority Biomedical Science Research Program and the Minority Access to Research Careers Program. More support is needed for these and similar programs, such as intensive developmental institutes with a heavy research component. Another program worthy of note is one launched by the Department of Energy in 1981 which awarded ten institutions with primarily minority students grants of $70,000 each to study current energy needs of minorities and low-income groups.

In retrospect, some federal agency might organize a series of intensive developmental institutes on research problems for the single or small-team research worker. My choice of topics would be microprocessors and molecular biology. But there are stimulating possibilities, too, in energy—both the physical and social problems associated with it. Another area that is ripe for our colleges is a more profound use of the computer in research. So many colleges have computers which are too frequently used merely to automate manual procedures.

OUTLOOK

The need for minorities to participate in and contribute to research is an expression not only of our national belief that cultural diversity is desirable, but is also an index of the success of the U.S. philosophy. Pick up a copy of The Economist or The New Scientist and you will usually find the Universities of Dar es Salaam or Zambia or Kenya advertising for a research-trained academic. With all the college-trained U.S. blacks available, few would even think of applying, because our education has somehow diverted us from the physical and social sciences. Not enough of our young people are participating in these technical fields and a great many more are needed to achieve a critical mass of minority scientists. (See Chapter 5 for data on minority participation rates in the sciences and engineering.) With the forces of anti-intellectualism riding high, and the inflationary spiral continuing, and with the increasingly difficult economic condition of the black colleges, all government agencies should feel a special urgency to enhance the effectiveness of these institutions in conducting research.

REFERENCES

Bayer, Alan E. Teaching faculty in academe: 1972-1973 (ACE Research Report 8:2). Washington, D.C.: American Council on Education, 1973.

Federal Interagency Committee on Education. Federal agencies and black colleges: Fiscal year 1978. Washington, D.C.: Department of Health, Education and Welfare, 1979.

Feldbaum, E. G., and L. A. Potashkin. Preliminary investigation of foreign graduate technical student education in the United States: Final report. Arlington, VA.: The Analytic Sciences Corporation, June 1980.

Liebert, Roland J. "Research-grant getting and productivity among scholars." Journal of Higher Education 48 (2) (March/April 1977): 164-92.

Medawar, P. B. Advice to a young scientist. New York: Harper & Row, 1979.

National Academy of Sciences. Research excellence through the year 2000. Washington, D.C.: National Research Council, 1979.

National Science Board. Science Indicators - 1978. Washington, D.C.: U.S. Government Printing Office, NSB-79-1, 1979.

National Science Foundation. Federal support to universities, colleges, and selected nonprofit institutions. Washington, D.C.: NSF, No. 77-303 (1977) and No. 81-308 (1981).

Roose, Kenneth D., and Charles J. Andersen. A rating of graduate programs. Washington, D.C.: American Council on Education, 1970.

Science. Excerpt from Vol. 20, O series, July-December 1883. Proceeding of Section B, Physics, August 1883. Reprinted in Science, February 15, 1980.

Smith, Bruce L., and Joseph J. Karlesky. The state of academic science. New York: Change Magazine Press, 1979.

Syverson, Peter D. Summary report: 1979 doctorate recipients from United States universities. Washington, D.C.: National Research Council, 1980.

Williams, Robert L. The administration of academic affairs in higher education. Ann Arbor, MI: The University of Michigan Press, 1966.

Ziman, John. Public knowledge. Cambridge, England: Cambridge University Press, 1968.

---8---

Research Areas
for Black Colleges

Daniel C. Thompson

Black colleges, as a distinct group in U.S. higher education, are generally acknowledged to be an important, perhaps an indispensable, national resource, but as far as research and scholarship are concerned, they constitute an untapped national resource, according to Stephen Wright (Wright 1979). Much more productive use should be made of their unique research and scholarship potentials.

Black colleges are particularly qualified to meet the critical need for increased social research on the black experience in U.S. society. The proposed research would take into account four distinct levels of experiences:

— The extent to which the black presence has influenced the ideology, structure, and function of specific social organizations, movements, and, ultimately, the overall nature of the U.S. social system.
— The conditions imposed upon blacks by the direct and indirect actions of white (or nonblack) individuals, groups, institutions, and special social power arrangements.
— The nature and consequences of responses blacks have made, and continue to make, to their unique situation in U.S. society.
— The contributions blacks have made, and continue to make, to their own survival and progress, and to the enrichment of the culture of the wider society of which they are a part.

Before examining black colleges as an untapped source of significant research and creative scholarship, let us look briefly at the place of research and scholarship in U.S. higher education in general.

RESEARCH VERSUS TEACHING

Both research and teaching are regarded as essential academic activities in U.S. colleges and universities, but attempting to arrive at a proper or optimum balance between these two basic functions often creates a problem (Trow 1975, pp. 39-83). Some major universities emphasize research to such an extent that classroom teaching is often regarded as a secondary activity.

> The typical graduate school offers no formal training in the art of teaching. Its professors make no effort to develop or codify a body of knowledge about what works in the classroom and what does not. . . . A graduate student . . . usually gets his Ph.D. without doing any teaching whatever. (Jencks and Riesman 1968, p. 240)

From time to time the charge is made that research frequently interferes with teaching and that, as a result, undergraduates are shortchanged in their education. On a number of occasions, students have become infuriated with what they judged to be too much emphasis on research at the expense of classroom preparation and teaching. In protesting this alleged neglect, some students have petitioned their universities to establish a dependable formal system whereby teaching excellence would be recognized and rewarded on a parity with research and publication. Since, however, there are no generally recognized criteria of teaching excellence, able and ambitious young academics tend to follow in the footsteps of their tenured colleagues and opt for research and publication as the most certain avenues to professional advancement and recognition (Keast and Macy 1973; Wilson 1972, pp. 102-03).

One of the most provocative discussions of the place of research in U.S. higher education is presented by J. E. Hexter (1971). He writes in "defense" of the "publish or perish" policy, which he claims is the "hard line" taken by "twenty to forty great universities" in this country. These universities, he states, are the "pacesetters" for higher education at large, for "where they lead, the rest of academia follows." Hexter concludes:

> In higher education in America the classroom teacher, however excellent, who refuses to present the appropriate offerings before the brazen idol of publication set up by the great universities, finds fewer and fewer places to hide, and those places more and more dingy and repellent. (Hexter 1971, p. 25)

Finally Martin Trow's exhaustive analysis of data gathered for the Carnegie Commission on Higher Education in 1969 indicates that the search for an optimum balance between teaching and research continues, and that "any notion that teaching generally takes second place to research is certainly not borne out," at least as far as four-year institutions are concerned. Instead there is a diversity of teaching-research patterns designed to blend these two academic functions since they are regarded as essential to academic excellence in higher education (Trow 1975, pp. 39-53).

Research and teaching at any institution, therefore, should not be pitted against each other, for the two activities are complementary. Research fortifies teaching and teaching invigorates research. Both should be encouraged by institutional officials and faculty should understand their parallel importance and value.

THE NEED FOR MORE BLACK RESEARCHERS

The paucity of productive black social researchers and scholars compared with the relatively large number of whites who interpret the black experience from a white perspective has been a perennially frustrating problem for black educators, scholars, and leaders. The research findings and interpretations of white social scientists and educators are frequently used as bases for the formulation of broad social policies and practices directly and indirectly affecting blacks (Clark 1965, pp. 74-80).

The negative consequences of biased research and scholarship on social policies and practices affecting blacks was the central theme of a conference of black sociologists convened by the Center for Policy Study and the Department of Sociology at the University of Chicago in 1972. After long and careful discussion, conference participants generally concurred that

> Sociologists, especially white sociologists, are too apt to accept traditional "middle-class" values and established moral norms as a basis for their analyses, insights, and interpretations of the black experience (Thompson 1974, p. 22).

Charles V. Willie calls attention to the extent to which the biased research of white scholars, such as Daniel Moynihan and Christopher Jencks, may victimize blacks and stymie their efforts to move into mainstream U.S. life (Willie and Edmonds 1978). Willie is particularly concerned that, because of their great prestige as scholars in top flight universities, these scholars tend to

have more credibility than black intellectuals. Their research findings quickly become bestsellers and have "a major impact upon race
relations programs in our national life, with ripple effects in other
institutions" (Willie and Edmonds 1978, pp. 5-11).

Therefore more top level research and scholarship are needed
to form sound bases for the improvement of educational policies and
practices affecting blacks. The same level of research and interpretation is also needed to understand and influence the wide range
of social policies and practices which affect various aspects of black
life as blacks strive to become a more significant part of mainstream
U.S. life. (For fuller treatment of this topic, see Chapter 9.)

For instance, Martin Trow enunciates the position generally
held by scholars and educators:

> Research . . . is one of the core functions of American
> higher education. Despite the fact that it is not carried
> on by all American academics, not even encouraged in
> all institutions, its influence is felt in every academic
> function, both through its effects on the growth of knowl-
> edge (and thus on the contents of higher education every-
> where) and through its role in providing the basis of in-
> stitutional prestige (Trow 1975, pp. 5-38).

According to Fulton and Trow's (1975) analysis of faculty research activity based on the 1969 Carnegie Commission Survey,
about 79 percent of the faculty in "high-quality" universities had engaged in some publishable research in the last two years before the
study; 54 percent of those in "high-quality" colleges; even 29 percent in "low-level" colleges, and 14 percent in junior colleges.
Overall, almost half (48 percent) of all faculty in U.S. institutions
of higher education were, or had been recently, engaged in publishable research.

From 1968 to 1973, I conducted a comprehensive study of private black colleges. Members of my research staff conducted formal interviews with about 400 representative teachers in 51 black
colleges and with over 300 other knowledgeable persons directly or
indirectly related to black colleges. Comments and opinions expressed in this chapter on black colleges are drawn primarily from
that study. We found:

> Only 5 or 6 percent of the teachers in the sample had
> ever published a book; just 12 percent had ever con-
> tributed to any published work, and a mere 4 percent
> had ever published in a scholarly journal. . . . only
> 7 percent were at that time engaged in scholarly re-
> search (Thompson 1973, p. ix).

Therefore, while research is generally regarded as the intellectual heart of the university, and the most prestigious avenue for professional recognition and advancement in "top-quality" colleges, it tends to be deemphasized and regarded as a more or less secondary or peripheral academic activity in black colleges. The research level in black colleges is far below that which is characteristic of U.S. institutions at large, including junior colleges.

Research and Publication Are Not Usually Expected

When teachers in the sample colleges were asked what academic activities are expected of them as faculty members, none cited research or publication. When asked to state their colleges' position on research, they generally agreed that they were not expected to do research. Sixty-four percent of the faculty, however, did feel that research activity and publication would bring them greater recognition and professional prestige.

> None of the deans and only one of the department heads interviewed suggested that creative scholarship might be a reason for an increase in salary or promotion in academic rank. . . . Only 10 teachers (2.5 percent) in the sample felt that research or publication was important to their professional welfare in their colleges (Thompson 1973, pp. 155-62).

Even in institutions where research and publication are normally expected, a significant proportion of faculty persons manage to survive and advance without engaging in publishable research. Thus Logan Wilson points out that "the 'publish-or-perish' dictum . . . is in actuality more fiction than fact in the average institution." He reported that a tabulation of the writing of approximately 1,000 faculty in a university system revealed that 32 percent had not published any articles and 71 percent had not published a book (Wilson 1972, p. 103). Consequently, if research is often neglected in institutions where pressure to do it is strong, little or no research is likely to be found in institutions where there is no obvious pressure for it.

Lack of Time to Do Research

Black college administrators usually insist that their colleges are essentially "teaching institutions." By this some apparently mean that teaching and related institutional routines should occupy the total professional time of the faculty, and that research activity should be confined to the teachers' spare time. Actually none of the administrators interviewed expressed any concern at all with the issue of "balance" between teaching and research.

As a rule, both teachers and administrators in the sample colleges expressed the conviction that since a large majority of their students come from low-quality, often culturally isolated, segregated high schools, teaching must be a broadly defined, demanding, full-time activity if students' great academic deficiencies are to be effectively met (Kannerstein 1978). Teaching is emphasized a great deal more in black colleges than in U.S. colleges in general primarily because such a large proportion of their students require excellent classroom instruction plus personal counseling and extensive informal instruction and guidance if they are to overcome centuries of accumulated academic neglect. The truth is, if the graduates of these colleges are to be prepared to go on to graduate and professional schools to enter promising careers, their teachers must devote a great deal of time to out-of-class, face-to-face instruction.

In addition to the fact that teaching in black colleges is many-faceted and time-consuming, the faculty teaching loads are usually comparatively heavy. The Carnegie study (1969) found teaching loads varying from a norm of as few as three courses per year in high-quality universities to five or six courses per term in junior colleges (Trow 1975, p. 47). Black colleges are very similar to junior colleges with respect to teaching loads. Faculty in black colleges who carry less than four or five courses per term are very likely to be engaged in some other institutional activity, such as administration or development. In many instances they are left with less spare time for research and writing than are some other teachers with "full" teaching loads.

When the issue of optimum balance between teaching and research in black colleges is raised, two basic facts stand out: first, teaching must be the overriding concern in these colleges because the unique educational challenges presented by their students demand it; and second, the financial stringencies characteristic of just about all black colleges usually result in heavy teaching loads for their faculty members. Consequently, if there is to be any significant increase in research activity, there must be an infusion of funds earmarked for released time so that a much larger number of competent, ambitious faculty can engage in research.

Professional Isolation

For one reason or another the great majority (68 percent) of the faculty in the black colleges studied were almost completely isolated from their colleagues in other institutions (Thompson 1973, pp. 156-57). Only 6 percent had attended a meeting of their professional associations during the two years before the study was conducted, and only five of the 400 faculty in the sample had ever held an office in one of these professional associations. Only three of those in the sample indicated that they had ever participated in joint research with a faculty member in another institution. It was rare indeed to find any faculty member in the black colleges who was or had been engaged in any meaningful intellectual interaction with colleagues in top-quality institutions of higher education.

The professional isolation of most teachers in black colleges prevents them from having the intellectual stimulation needed for meaningful research and writing. They simply do not operate in the competitive, creative intellectual environment characteristic of the campuses of top-quality institutions.

If black colleges could find ways to break down the intellectual isolation of their faculty, they would be taking an important step toward cultivating their untapped scholarly resources. Providing a significant number of their most competent, ambitious faculty with ample funds to develop and engage in important research projects in which they could employ highly qualified staffs and expert consultants would be a good beginning. Some members of the faculty should be able to develop and sponsor research among institutions, sometimes involving predominantly white institutions. Certain interracial research projects might be much more sound and unbiased than those conducted by black or white institutions independently. Several black colleges already have well-established and effective cooperative programs in engineering with top-quality universities (Kirschner 1980).

Insufficient Funds

Throughout their histories, black colleges have had to survive on uncommonly scarce funds; seldom have funds been allocated specifically for research. Generally, funding agencies have tended to overlook or discount the scholarly potentials of black colleges. They have apparently adhered to the unstated principle that the bulk of their research grants should be made to a relatively few of the most productive, well-established professors in major research universities. Thus Herman R. Branson, in Chapter 7, points out that in

1975 a small number of major universities (100) received 98 percent of all research funds granted to institutions of higher education, and these grants were primarily to well-known, productive scholars. Consequently, black colleges which are not major research institutions and seldom have a significant number of nationally recognized research scholars, are either left out of the research-granting activity altogether or are given relatively small, token grants. For instance, Earl J. McGrath reported that in 1960 black colleges received barely one-tenth of 1 percent of the funds appropriated for "organized research" in institutions of higher education in this country (McGrath 1965, p. 180). The same situation apparently continues today.

Exclusion from the Inner Circles of
Academic Power in the United States

While there seem to be little hard data to support it, evidence suggests that much of the research done in the United States is a result of long, sustained relationships between established research scholars in a relatively few affluent research universities and funding agencies. All too often unsolicited applications for research funds from unknown teachers in black colleges must compete with applications for similar research from nationally respected scholars in elite institutions. The result always seems to be the same: the well-known professors in the elite institutions are chosen over the unknown teachers in black colleges, who are clearly the greater investment risk from the point of view of past performance and institutional support.

Black institutions of higher education must have an equal opportunity to establish themselves as strong, productive research centers, or at least subcenters, if they are to tap, expand, and develop their scholarly resources. This means that certain carefully selected faculty members in these institutions must receive grants to engage in meaningful research and writing.

The research activities of several black institutions could be coordinated through an advocacy committee composed of productive scholars who possess the academic skills needed to conduct sound social and scientific research. The various skills and activities of these scholars could be coordinated through a central research center. The research department of the United Negro College Fund would be an ideal structure to function as the coordinator of such a research consortium. (See John Monro's proposal for the establishment of an academic research and information board in Chapter 9.)

This proposed research consortium would have several functions: (1) to seek out and screen potential researchers in black institutions; (2) to overcome professional isolation by conducting regularly scheduled research seminars in which selected scholars in
black colleges and universities would have sustained interaction with
well-established, productive scholars in predominantly black or predominantly white institutions; (3) to stimulate and encourage joint
research among scholars in black colleges, and between black and
nonblack institutions; and (4) to assist little-known, but promising
black scholars in their efforts to secure proper financing for meaningful projects (LeMelle and LeMelle 1969; McGrath 1980).

BLACK COLLEGES AS CENTERS FOR
THE STUDY OF SOCIAL CHANGE

Most black colleges are located in geographic regions and
communities where far-reaching, basic social changes have been
occurring for approximately 25 years. The major changes have
centered around the desegregation of schools at all levels and the
political process, but they are apparent in almost every aspect of
the social order (Blackwell 1975; Conyers and Wallace 1976; Fellman 1974; Joint Center for Political Studies 1979; Jordan 1979,
1980, 1981; Marden and Meyer 1978; Paris 1978; Pettigrew 1971;
Tobin 1979). The forces which united to bring about the election of
black mayors in key cities, especially in the South, also have been
responsible for a number of less spectacular but still significant
changes in other institutions, agencies, and in public opinion in general. For instance, almost all formal racial barriers, which a generation ago symbolized a completely segregated society in the South,
have now disappeared.

The many obvious and basic changes that have been taking
place in the South have national and even international reverberations,
but they have received only passing, superficial research attention.
Most of what is known about these changes has come from the mass
media, which are too often biased or narrow in their accounts, and
from occasional special reports developed by social agencies that,
for the most part, are soon forgotten. Little effort has been made
to systematically study the often conflicting forces that bring about
these changes or the forces opposing them, and the consequences
they have for the social system at large, and for the black experience in particular.

For one reason or another, prestigious white universities and
researchers have almost completely ignored these changes in black-
white relations, which have caused strains in almost every institution

in the South. Consequently there is a great need for objective research on the changing social system of the South where both black and white "perspectives" would be systematically studied. Studies of social changes in the South would be important for three reasons: they would test fundamental theories of social change by submitting them to empirical validation; they would gather valuable data which could be used in the formulation of social policy; and they would hasten the discovery and development of black scholars as a part of this country's national resources.

The best approach to study social change is through consortial arrangements. Certain carefully selected black colleges could enter into a consortium or "Center for the Study of Social Change" coordinated perhaps by the United Negro College Fund, whereby specific, independent research on the subject might be encouraged and adequately funded.

It might be especially productive for promising scholars in a number of strategically located black colleges to engage in joint studies of changes in a limited number of key social systems (such as education, government, employment, health, criminal justice, sports, and organized religion) common to the various communities where the colleges are located. The studies would employ the same methodology and test the same general hypotheses, so that the resulting data would be comparable and could form a basis for conclusions to aid in the formulation of social policy, as well as in the clarification of basic social theory.

In the October 1979 special issue of Change Magazine, Stephen J. Wright raised a basic, challenging question: "Why Don't More Blacks Study Blacks?" He called attention to the paucity of useful research on the black experience, particularly by blacks themselves. He believes that black researchers could give new dimensions and provide illuminating insights to the study of the black experience which white researchers usually overlook (Wright 1979, pp. 62-63).

I would extend Wright's proposition by suggesting that since the black experience in the United States has not always been enmeshed in the larger U.S. society, it must be understood as an integral part of the total culture, not as an independent unit apart from it. This means that all aspects of the black experience reflect sustained historical interaction with the various institutions, values, and traditions that constitute U.S. society. Consequently the "white experience" and the "black experience" both have a "black" and a "white" dimension. Therefore black researchers could enhance the authenticity and value of a variety of major social studies, not just those affecting the lives of black people. Combining with counterparts in white colleges to form effective research teams for the study of major social changes which affect their total communities is also worthy of consideration.

Education

For more than 25 years the process of desegregating educational systems throughout the United States, especially in the South, has been a major, socially disruptive issue. To enlighten social policy, much more needs to be known about this process as it has affected blacks, whites, and other minorities in the various communities in which it has been introduced. Among the issues that might be researched are:

— The nature of the desegregation process in different types of communities: What have been the nature and intensity of forces which resisted court-ordered desegregation? How were these forces dealt with or overcome in different situations?
— To what extent has school desegregation affected race relations in other aspects of community life?
— The plight of black principals in desegregating school systems.
— An evaluation of the different desegregation strategies adopted by various school systems.
— What has been the role of the news media in the school-desegregation process; the role of white power figures and groups; of black leaders and organizations?
— The achievements of black students in all-black schools compared with their achievements in predominantly white schools in various communities.
— The achievements of black students in traditionally white colleges compared with their achievements in traditionally black colleges.
— The achievements of white students in traditionally black colleges compared with those of white students in traditionally white colleges.
— The nature, function, and validity of selected standardized tests, such as the Scholastic Aptitude Test (SAT) and the National Teachers' Examination (NTE). How are the results of blacks' scores on such tests reflected in social policy?
— Academic standards of schools before and after 1960.
— The nature and consequences of academic innovations affecting black students in various school systems since 1960. The changing racial composition of school boards in different communities since 1960.
— A profile and interpretation of the black high school dropout compared with that of the academically successful high school student.

148 / Daniel C. Thompson

Public Affairs and Government

Some scholars and lay observers believe that the prevailing
political structure is the most reliable indicator of social change.
Thus in most areas of the South, blacks were virtually excluded
from meaningful political participation until the passage of the 1965
Voting Rights Act. This exclusion was reflected in their powerlessness and in the lack of esteem in which they were held in almost
every other area of community, state, and national life (Key 1949).
In this connection, the following questions raise issues which
require research:

- Exactly what impact has the Voting Rights Act of 1965 made
  in the racial composition of the electorate in various types
  of communities?
- There have been changes in blacks' involvement in local
  and state government since 1965. Have they shared in the
  political "spoils"?
- Have there been significant changes in the racial structure
  and control of local and state political organizations since
  1965?
- How are the major dilemmas of black elected officials resolved?
- A profile of black elected officials compared with their
  white counterparts in various communities and states.
- To what extent have the purposes and missions of black
  political factions changed since 1965?
- Have there been significant changes in the campaign rhetoric
  of erstwhile white supremacist candidates since 1965?
- In what ways have white politicians responded to the new
  black enfranchisement?
- To what extent have blacks become active and effective
  players in the decision-making process in public affairs
  since 1960?
- What has been the social impact of federal programs, such
  as CETA, social welfare, and compensatory education programs since 1960?
- How has the new black enfranchisement affected the welfare
  of the black community? The larger community?

THE CHANGING SOCIAL STATUS OF BLACKS

One of the issues now being debated widely in the United States
is the nature and extent of black advancement since the 1960s. On
the one hand, some informed observers would agree that

When education, occupation, and income are used as criteria of middle-class status, we find that there has been
a significant increase in the size and composition of the
Black middle class in the United States since 1955. . . .
The upward social mobility of Blacks has been especially pronounced since 1960 (Thompson 1974, p. 217).

On the other hand, some knowledgeable observers express
serious doubts about the nature and significance of black advancement during the last 20 years. Some agree with the interpretation
of Vernon E. Jordan, Jr., former president of the National Urban
League, who wrote:

For black Americans the decade of the 1970s was a time
in which many of their hopes, raised by the civil rights
victories of the 1960s withered away; a time in which
they saw the loss of much of the momentum that seemed
to be propelling the nation along the road to true equality for all its citizens. . . . The 70s, however, brought
forth in Black America a mood of disappointment, frustration and bitterness at promises made and promises
unkept (Jordan 1980, p. 1).

We need extensive, definitive data on the social gains and
losses of blacks in representative communities since the comprehensive Civil Rights Movement of the 1960s. Among the questions
that should be studied are the following:

— How did the Civil Rights Movement of the 1960s affect race
  relations in particular communities? What were the key
  demands of local versus national black leadership?
— What is the plight of the black underclass today compared
  with 1960?
— What are the status and life styles of the black middle
  class today compared with 1960?
— What has been the social role of black intellectuals in different types of communities?
— To what extent have black entrepreneurs benefited from the
  Civil Rights Movement in different communities?
— How has the crime rate in the black community changed
  since 1960?
— To what extent have black employment opportunities in-
  creased since 1960?
— Has the delivery of medical care for blacks improved in
  specific communities since 1960?

— Does an analysis of the 1980 Census data show key changes
in the status of blacks?

Finally, researchers gathering and interpreting data on the
topics and questions listed above could examine and, when deemed
necessary, reformulate key, traditional theories pertaining to the
nature, processes, and consequences of social change. Such data
should also go a long way toward unmasking deeply rooted black
stereotypes and misconceptions which have haunted, embarrassed,
and frustrated blacks, hampering their long struggle for survival
and advancement in U.S. society. Such a comprehensive study of
social change might produce reliable information which would be
essential in the formulation of sound, effective social policies at
all levels of public life in this nation.

Perhaps the most fundamental and lasting effect of the broad,
in-depth study advocated here would be to provide concrete opportunities for black colleges to discover, nurture, and utilize the great,
largely untapped, intellectual resources of their faculty and students.
Such concerted research efforts would certainly enhance the image
and influence of black colleges in the world of higher education and
also in U.S. society.

REFERENCES

Blackwell, James E. The black community. New York: Dodd,
Mead, 1975.

_____. Black colleges as a national resource beyond 1975. Atlanta,
GA: Southern Educational Foundation, 1976.

Carnegie Commission on Higher Education. 1969 Carnegie Commission survey of faculty and student opinion. Berkeley, CA: Carnegie Commission on Higher Education, 1969.

Clark, Kenneth B. Dark ghetto. New York: Harper & Row, 1965.

Conyers, James E., and Walter L. Wallace. Black elected officials.
New York: Russell Sage Foundation, 1976.

Dobbins, Charles G., and Calvin B. T. Lee. Whose goals for
American higher education? Washington, D.C.: American
Council on Education, 1968.

Fellman, David. Black city politics. Madison, WI: Dodd, Mead,
1974.

Fulton, Oliver, and Martin Trow. "Research activity in American higher education." In Teachers and students, edited by Martin Trow. New York: McGraw-Hill, 1975.

Hexter, J. E. "Publish or perish: A defense." In The professors, edited by Charles H. Anderson and John D. Murray. Cambridge, MA: Schenkman, 1971.

Jencks, Christopher, and David Riesman. The academic revolution. New York: Doubleday, 1968.

Joint Center for Political Studies. National roster of black elected officials. Washington, D.C.: Joint Center for Political Studies, 1979.

Jordan, Vernon. The state of black America. Washington, D.C.: National Urban League, 1979, 1980, 1981.

Kannerstein, Gregory. "Black colleges: Self-concept." In Black colleges in America, edited by Charles V. Willie and Ronald R. Edmonds. New York: Columbia University, Teachers College Press, 1978.

Keast, William R., and John W. Macy, Jr. Faculty tenure. San Francisco, CA: Jossey-Bass, 1973.

Key, V. O., Jr. Southern politics. New York: Vintage Books, 1949.

Kirschner, Alan H. UNCF statistical report of the member colleges. New York: United Negro College Fund, 1980.

LeMelle, Tilden J., and Wilbert J. LeMelle. The black college: A strategy for achieving social relevancy. New York: Praeger, 1969.

Lipsett, Seymour Martin. Rebellion in the university. Boston, MA: Little, Brown, 1971.

Marden, Charles F., and Gladys Meyer. Minorities in American society. New York: D. Van Nostrand, 1978.

McGrath, Earl J. The predominantly Negro colleges and universities in transition. New York: Columbia University, Teachers College Press, 1965.

_____. A letter to the editor. Change Magazine 12 (January 1980).

Paris, Peter J. Black leaders in conflict. Philadelphia, PA:
Pilgrim Press, 1978.

Pettigrew, Thomas F. Racially separate or together. New York:
McGraw-Hill, 1971.

Thompson, Daniel C. Private black colleges at the crossroads.
Westport, CT: Greenwood Press, 1973.

_____. Sociology of the black experience. Westport, CT: Green-
wood Press, 1977.

_____. "Black college faculty and students: The nature of their
interactions." In Black colleges in America, edited by Charles
V. Willie and Ronald R. Edmonds. New York: Columbia University, Teachers College Press, 1978.

_____. "Black colleges: Continuing challenges." Phylon 40 (2)
June 1979.

Tobin, Gary A. The changing structure of the city. Beverly Hills,
CA: Sage Publications, 1979.

Trow, Martin, ed. Teachers and students. New York: McGraw-
Hill, 1975.

Volpe, Peter E. "Teaching, research and service: Union or co-
existence?" In Whose goals for American higher education?,
edited by Charles G. Dobbins and Calvin B. T. Lee. Washington, D.C.: American Council on Education, 1968.

Willie, Charles V., and Ronald R. Edmonds, eds. Black colleges
in America. New York: Columbia University, Teachers College
Press, 1978.

Wilson, Logan. Shaping American higher education. Washington,
D.C.: American Council on Education, 1972.

Wright, Stephen J. "Why don't more blacks study blacks?" Change
Magazine 11 (October 1979).

_____. The black educational policy researcher: An untapped na-
tional resource. Washington, D.C.: National Advisory Committee
on Black Higher Education and Black Colleges and Universities,
1979.

The Need
for Black-Controlled Research
on Black Educational Problems
(A View from the Classroom)

John U. Monro

The central purpose of this chapter is to assert the need, as seen from the author's classroom perspective, for a major effort, controlled by the U.S. black community, to conduct an intensive, ongoing program of research and publication. Such a program would improve the educational experience and opportunities of black youth in the United States.

It would involve the establishment of an academic research and information board, with headquarters on one of the major black university campuses, and a board of trustees which would assure attention to the wide spectrum of black educational concerns. These include:

— Improving elementary and secondary education as well as college and graduate school education
— Testing
— In-depth examination of black students' learning styles, motivations, and special problems
— Development of constructive relationships with white colleges and universities
— Establishment and encouragement of research on black educational problems on a number of traditional black campuses
— Training a strong new cadre of young black professionals in educational research

As Stephen Wright made clear in his investigation of this problem in 1979, up to now "the education of blacks in America has been determined largely by white perceptions of their educability and of their role in society" (Wright 1979). Write states that at every level of education from first grade through graduate school, there is little black input into research or policies affecting the education of black youth. In white graduate schools, senior professors discourage black graduate students from doing research on black educational problems. Black college faculties are preoccupied with teaching, and have little time and are given little support for research. Funding agencies seem not to be very interested either.

There are important institutionalized research efforts already in operation on behalf of black colleges and black youth. One thinks of the energetic and productive Howard University Institute for the Study of Educational Policy, the Clark College Southern Center for Studies in Public Policy, and the more recent effort of Tennessee State University in Nashville to pull together information and expertise in remedial basic studies education. The Institute for Services to Education (ISE) in Washington, D.C. has served the black colleges well by sharing information and making a concerted effort, among a number of colleges, to design and operate a modern, effective basic studies program.

THE EDUCATIONAL PROBLEMS OF BLACK YOUTH

Despite these efforts, the evidence is accumulating that the education of blacks in the United States at all levels fails to bring about equal opportunity. At the elementary and secondary school level, it fails to prepare young people for a productive role in society, or to go on to further schooling; and at the college and university level, it fails to prepare the black scholars and professionals our society must have. It may well be that two of the most tragic and dangerous social problems our country will face in the years ahead are the mistraining of our youth and the high school dropout rates, which are partially responsible for the high levels of unemployment and unemployability of black youth in our center cities. Increasing mechanization, lack of social planning, race prejudice, and the policies of multinational corporations constantly seeking a cheap labor force, also have contributed to the unemployment and unemployability of black youth. The time is right to mobilize the intelligence and experience of the U.S. black community in a serious, institutionalized, broadly supported effort to study the educational failures and successes of black youth.

At least at the college and university level, the country has made encouraging progress over the past ten years. As a consequence of desegregation and the civil rights struggle, the United States has moved from an enrollment of some 200,000 black students in college in 1960 to just over one million enrolled today (National

Advisory Committee on Black Higher Education and Black Colleges
and Universities [NACBHEBCU] 1980). Yet on closer inspection,
the data on black college and graduate school enrollments are grounds
for concern and renewed struggle:

• Fifty-five percent of black students entering college now enroll
in two-year community and junior colleges, compared to 35 percent
of white students, and the large majority of blacks do not transfer to
four-year colleges. Twenty-seven percent of white students between
the ages of 16 and 34 were enrolled in colleges, while 21 percent of
black students in the same age group were enrolled (National Association for Equal Opportunity in Higher Education 1980).

• In fall 1978 total black enrollment in higher education was
divided as follows (NACBHEBCU 1980):

	Number	Percent
Two-year institutions	442,617	42.0
Majority universities and colleges	420,263	39.8
Historically black universities and colleges	166,284	15.7
Predominantly black colleges	26,800	1.6
Total black enrollment in higher education	1,055,964	99.1

Though black colleges enrolled less than 20 percent of all black
students in recent years, they awarded 37 percent of the baccalaureate
degress in 1975-76 and 1976-77.

• From 1970 to 1980, the historically black colleges graduated
300,000 students, over half the black college graduates in that period
(NACBHEBCU 1978, p. 22). There are 105 historically black colleges compared to 3,000 white colleges in the United States.

• Black students constitute 10 percent of the total undergraduate
enrollment in all of the nation's colleges but in 1976 received only 6
percent of the baccalaureate degrees (NACBHEBCU 1978, p. 22).

• Black students in 1976 represented only 6 percent of the enrollment in graduate schools and 4.5 percent in professional schools
(NACBHEBCU 1979, p. 17).

• In 1980 the average first year enrollment of blacks in each of
152 medical schools was 7 students; in each of 58 dental schools,
3 students; in each of 160 law schools, 11 students; and in each of
798 graduate schools, 47 students. To achieve anywhere near the
number of graduate professionals necessary to meet the nation's
needs in the future, the number of black students entering each medical school should be 37, each dental school 24, each law school 29,
and each graduate school 78 (NACBHEBCU 1980).

● A December 1980 report prepared for President Reagan's
staff by the National Association for Equal Opportunity in Higher
Education (NAFEO) states:

> Black higher education seems to be deteriorating and
> needs to see some current trends reversed. There is
> an increasing gap between the percentage of blacks ver-
> sus whites in the 25 to 34 age group completing four or
> more years of college. Black graduates have increased
> in numbers but not at a rate to keep pace with the num-
> bers of whites. Only about 50,000 out of close to a mil-
> lion baccalaureates each year go to Black Americans.
> . . . Black enrollments in graduate and professional
> schools peaked in about 1974 in absolute number and
> percentage. Since 1976, there has been a decline in
> the numbers of blacks enrolling in Law Schools, Medi-
> cal Schools, and Ph.D. programs. All students, black
> and white, who enter college in two-year colleges have
> only about $1\frac{1}{2}$ chances in 10 of earning a B.A., compared
> to about 6 to 7 chances in 10 for those entering four-
> year colleges. . . . Blacks tend to be enrolled in two-
> year colleges. . . . Simply put, Black progress in
> higher education is at a standstill at the undergraduate
> level and has regressed at the graduate and profes-
> sional levels (NAFEO 1980, p. 3).

● In its report, Target Date, 2000 A.D.: Goals for Achieving
Higher Education Equity for Black Americans, the NACBHEBCU
(1980) stated:

> Between 1960 and 1975, an annual average of 300,000
> would-be black college enrollees were not accommo-
> dated due to inequities in higher education opportunities
> for black and white Americans. Had parity existed in
> 1960, over the fifteen years 1960-1975, an additional
> 4.75 million blacks would have enrolled in college.
> . . . The effort to attain true equity is staggering
> (p. 9).

At every level of our national educational program, from
grade school through graduate and professional training, we are
failing by a wide margin to provide equal opportunity for black
youth, and failing to prepare the trained black leaders and professional people our society needs. To put it bluntly, when the complete tally is in, nearly half our black youth today are being shut out

of the system. In our great urban centers, discouraging percentages of black students simply drop out of school. And though more than a million black men and women are now attending college, itself an important gain, we must note that the deck is still stacked against their having an equal chance to enroll in the prestigious and best-endowed undergraduate and graduate institutions. So, despite the apparent gains, millions of young blacks continue to be badly educated, underprepared, locked out of the system. If we are to succeed as a society, this trend must be turned around.

CHANGES IN EDUCATIONAL NEEDS

The 1980s and 1990s are sure to be periods of rapid and difficult change for all American education, especially for colleges, and most critically for black colleges. All colleges face a shrinking population of young people and thus growing competition for students. The best current projection is that the number of high school graduates, 2,833,000 in 1978, will diminish each year to a low of approximately 2,150,000 in 1993, a reduction of about 683,000 in 15 years. The black colleges face a period of continuing grave economic crises and retrenchment.

At the same time, public discontent with the quality of education in all our schools is steadily mounting, expressing itself in demands for excellence, firmly established levels of student competency, and in increasing requirements that teachers and administrators at each level be held accountable for sound educational results. Francis Keppel (1980) recently observed that the federal and state governments may be impelled to establish their own educational quality standards, over and above the standards of the present accrediting agencies, as a basis for justifying grants in support of individual colleges and universities. Past experience suggests that such government evaluation may well take the form of standardized achievement tests administered to a college's graduating students to ensure minimum competence.

Another major change on the horizon for black colleges is the interest that a number of major white universities and colleges have shown in the problems of educating underprepared freshmen. Given the generous federal financial aid programs and the impending shortage of students, almost all educational institutions are now of necessity admitting and retaining students they previously would not admit. To tackle this job effectively requires considerable educational know-how, knowledge of student backgrounds and motivation, of placement and diagnostic testing, and of student learning styles. The new admissions efforts will require new programs of testing, teaching, curriculum planning, and evaluation of results.

It would be easy for black colleges to see white colleges and universities as antagonists. But in the long run we will make more progress if the two types of colleges see themselves as involved in the same national effort, and share research and information. Black and white institutions have much to learn and much to gain from working together. The black colleges, considered as an institutional power center for the black community, must be concerned with the quality of education offered to black students, 80 percent of whom attend white colleges. It is essential that in any such joint effort the black community, working through the black college leadership, have a voice in a major, continuing, unified research effort on issues affecting black youth. In the end, not only black youth, but all U.S. schools and colleges and untold millions of nonblack, minority, and impoverished young people, will benefit from such a major research and information effort by the black colleges.

Finally, for its own protection, and especially the protection of its youth, the U.S. black community must have a strong, broad, concerned, continuing program of research on all aspects of black education, initiated and directed from within. With such a major research and information effort on its side, the black community will be able to:

— Affect educational programming for black youth in center city schools
— Counter racist research seeking to demonstrate "genetic inferiority"
— Challenge standardized admission tests that cut off thousands of black youth from major colleges and universities every year
— Cope with the impending possibility of standardized, government-sponsored competency tests which could well threaten the accreditation and support of black colleges
— Disseminate programs of instruction which work well with black students

If we fail to take the initiative in developing such a research effort, we can expect that black youth and their educational prospects will continue to be at the mercy of white-directed research operations, with the same tragic results that have confronted the black community for over a century.

NEEDED RESEARCH AREAS

The rest of this chapter will delineate areas where a continuing educational research effort and the sharing of information and results are essential to black colleges and to the general education of black youth. This discussion is illustrative rather than comprehensive. It grows out of the day-to-day experiences and observations of one college teacher, normally involved with the problems of teaching basic language skills to freshmen. Public school teachers and administrators and other college teachers will surely have research agendas of their own. But this list will serve, at least, to indicate areas of considerable need.

Let us consider these research needs under three headings: testing, instruction, and administration.

Testing

Admissions Testing

Nowhere are the vulnerability and unfair treatment of black students more obvious than in the area of admissions testing. And nowhere is there a greater need for a strong, respected institutional representation of the black case, coupled with the development of testing instruments or other admissions criteria which will more objectively estimate a student's academic potential. The present critical reevaluation of the College Board's Scholastic Aptitude Test (SAT) is dramatic and important, but the fact is that such evidence about the test has been accumulating for 30 years.

In the 1950s, in a well-publicized effort, the Ford Foundation supported an effort by the National Scholarship Service and Fund for Negro Students (NSSFNS) and the College Board itself to help able southern black students to go North to white colleges. The project involved a major recruiting effort by counselors from Howard University, and in the end several hundred black students entered selective northern colleges. Most of the students scored significantly below the usual SAT average of the colleges in which they enrolled, but almost all succeeded in college.

In 1969, Alexander Astin reported on a study of the college records of some 36,000 men and women, and reached the following conclusions:

> The low representation of blacks among entering college freshmen and the de facto segregation that exists in many colleges is attributable in part to the use, in the admissions process, in particular, of scores of tests of academic ability. As predictors of the individual's chances of success in college, test scores and school grades are subject to considerable error. Thus, other criteria could probably be employed in

the admissions process with only minor unfavorable
effects on the level of academic performance and on
the dropout rate (Astin 1970).

In another study, "The Myth of Equal Access in Public Higher
Education," published in 1975, Astin showed that one consequence
of traditional selective admissions programs based on standardized
tests was that "low income and minority students tend to be disproportionately concentrated in institutions at the bottom of the hier-
archy." By "institutions at the bottom" Astin referred to two-year
and certain four-year colleges having poorer educational resources
and lower faculty salaries than would be found in the major selective
colleges and universities. Astin noted that the United States prides
itself on "equal access to higher education," but that in terms of the
quality of institutions open to most poor and minority youth, equal
access is "more of a myth than a reality."

The SAT score and the ACT composite score are key factors
in Astin's identification of more or less selective colleges. High-
selective, four-year colleges use a cut-off score of 1000 in the SAT,
and a composite score above 22 on the ACT; medium-selective colleges cut off on SAT scores from 900 to 1000, or 18 to 22 on the
ACT. In the university group, high selectivity means an SAT score
above 1149, or an ACT composite score above 25. Medium selectivity calls for an SAT of 1000 to 1149, or an ACT score between 23
and 25. Astin concludes:

> If one accepts the idea that colleges exist to educate,
> then the model of selective admissions based on test
> scores and prior grades makes little sense. If an in-
> stitution exists to educate students, then its mission is
> to produce certain desirable changes in students, or,
> more simply, to make a difference in the student's life.
> This kind of "value added" approach to the goals of high-
> er education suggests that admission procedures should
> be designed to select students who are likely to be in-
> fluenced by the educational process, regardless of the
> student's entering level of performance. Instead, ad-
> missions officers in selective institutions function
> more like race track handicappers: they try merely to
> pick winners (Astin 1975).

Anyone involved in even the most exacting college admissions
knows that, outside the narrow band of students who score high on
aptitude tests, there is a very large population of students who score
low on the tests. Many of these applicants are admitted anyway,

come to college, graduate on time, and   well after graduation.
They often include the "special" admissions known to all colleges:
gifted athletes, sons and daughters of alumni, faculty sons and
daughters, and sons and daughters of the rich and influential. If
there is a strong special reason, the college blinks at the SAT score
and admits. If there is not a strong special reason, the low SAT
score becomes a reason for rejection.

Across the South, and indeed across the nation, one major
state flagship university after another has a black student enrollment of 15 percent or under. A great many of these institutions
now govern admissions by a cutoff score on one or another set of
admission tests. Whatever the announced purpose of the cutoff
scores, the effect is to send most aspiring black students in the
South to black state colleges, and elsewhere to the two-year community colleges.

As presently used, the tests become a way of denying black
youth a fair chance at a first-rate college education. In the black
colleges, students by the hundreds, with caring, professional instruction become first-rate college students and go on to graduate
school, in spite of low scores on the tests.

A respected, continuing educational research and information
program is needed that could stand up to the College Board, the
Educational Testing Service (ETS), the ACT, the selective universities, the social scientists, and the power of the media. It should
provide valid research on test results, alternative modes of testing
and evaluation, and data about the record of students who do well in
college despite low entrance test scores.

Placement and Diagnostic Testing

All but the most selective colleges need a reliable, informa-
tive battery of placement and diagnostic tests for incoming freshmen. The purpose of this testing is to discover at what level of instruction students should be placed, and what their individual learning skills and communication problems may be. This presents quite
different problems than those related to admissions tests. Too often,
colleges have been overly impressed by the virtues of well-known,
shrewdly marketed, standardized, quick and easily scored tests.
Once these tests are used at matriculation for placement or diagnosis, they tend to be used again at the end of the semester or college year to give a "before and after" measure of the student's progress or competency.

From my own experience, I can comment on certain difficulties in the use of the Nelson-Denny Reading Test, the McGraw-Hill
English Test, the ETS Cooperative English Test, and the Missouri

College English Test. These are all well-known, widely used, standardized tests, but each has limitations.

The Nelson-Denny Reading Test in practice gives only a gross indication of placement (quite good reader, mediocre reader, poor reader), which helps some but not nearly enough in placement; and it gives little or no useful diagnostic information. Although the Nelson-Denny Test is often used as a posttest, it gives no real indication of students' ability to write accurately, in their own words, notes or summaries of material they have read. Thus the test is not specific to a main element in a college reading program.

The three main English tests (McGraw-Hill, ETS Cooperative, and Missouri College) have time-tested virtues, but they all depend heavily on the ability of the student to proofread (detect other people's errors) and to edit. They also are overly concerned with finicky details of spelling, diction, and grammar. Thus, as pretests they tell us next to nothing about the students' ability to write well, i.e., to generate ideas about a topic, to organize the ideas into an outline, and to construct good sentences and paragraphs of their own. Once any one of these three English tests is used as a posttest by which students and their teachers will be judged—the result is a distortion, or frustration of the central effort to interest students in writing, and to teach them how to write well.

None of the reasons for adopting such standard placement tests seem very good to me, but they are convincing to many. All the tests have been on the market a long time, and have an established reputation. The English tests provide a rough classification of students according to the intensity and success of previous standard grammar instruction in school. All have a built-in statistical apparatus for measuring the local group of students against the national average, which is to say against the records of other students who have taken the test some time in the past. The tests are inexpensive and easy to score. And, perhaps above all else, the students' scores come out reduced to concrete numbers (e.g., grade level 7.6; or 42 correct/51 questions). The numbers reassure many educators that the tests are actually measuring something important. If you get one set of numbers in August and another followup set in May, you can measure the progress for any student or for all students, and the effectiveness of the teacher.

The final and most important reason for using these tests seems to be that their results, by appearing to show in "concrete" and "objective" terms student progress and competence, become a basis for impressing a foundation or government agency and securing a grant. For such financial purposes, homemade or teacher-made tests, no matter how well they may reflect classroom results, are not so concrete and objective and so are suspect in the arcane world of grant-seeking. All this makes the selection of pretests and post-tests difficult. Too often, the commonly used tests do not measure any skill or information that anyone can positively identify, or that serious teachers would normally set as a high priority for their classes.

There are concrete examples everywhere. I visited one major community college (not a traditional black college) where the students are kept in the first basic English course until they can "pass" the ETS Cooperative English Test. It is a heavy burden to everyone concerned, except ETS and the people who set the requirement. Another major four-year college recently adopted a handsome, expensive, and not particularly relevant freshmen English textbook, partly because it brought with it a standardized, easily scored, but not especially relevant placement exam.

What we need for placement and diagnosis on the one end and for evaluation on the other end, are sound achievement tests related to curriculum which will accurately indicate students' particular skills, that we want them to have, and that we are prepared to teach them. This can mean teacher-made or staff-made tests; or, better still, tests on which a group of teachers from several colleges can agree. It should be one of the main responsibilities of the proposed new Academic Research and Information Board to oversee the discussion and development of such diagnostic achievement tests in all the basic areas—writing, reading, mathematics, speech, social sciences, and natural sciences.

After some 35 years of working with many kinds of placement and competency tests, I am satisfied that the first requirement should be, not that a test be easy, quick, and inexpensive to score, but that it give students a chance to show what they know and what they can do, and what skills and information they have been taught. By and large the best test of students' writing skills is their ability to sit down under exam conditions and write short essays (300 words or so) on a reasonable topic. Without greatly distorting a sensitive evaluation, it is possible for two or three readers to agree fairly quickly upon a simple set of numbers to appraise the significant elements of an essay (quality of ideas, organizational ability, control of sentences, strength and accuracy of vocabulary). Having done all this in August, it is possible and reasonable to repeat the exercise in May, and get a measurable record of a student's progress. Most important, such a test will give students and teacher a meaningful instructional objective to work on for an academic semester or for a whole year.

Similarly, for reading, I am impressed by the effectiveness of teacher-made tests which require students to summarize in their own words the meaning of a given sentence, paragraph, or brief essay. Surely that is the task students will be asked to perform countless times in their college work and in professional or business activities after college. I have been relatively unimpressed by reading tests that place the major emphasis on speed or that use multiple choice questions to ascertain whether a student has understood the central point of a paragraph.

In short, we need a thoughtful exploration of all our existing methods of pretesting for placement and diagnosis, an exploration conducted by teachers of first-year college students and testing experts working together. We should develop a new, authoritative, effective set of placement and diagnostic tests which relate to our students and their instructional needs that we in the colleges will respect and use.

Posttesting (Competency, Evaluation, Monitoring)

What has been said above about pretesting applies with added force to tests used at the end of a course or program. Emphasis is added because the posttest becomes the "objective" yardstick against which everything in the program is monitored and evaluated—student skills, information, and progress; teacher effectiveness; and (not least in consideration of grants) program effectiveness. Whatever the posttest may be, it reflects heavily on the whole teaching program. Students need to do well to pass a critical competency exam; teachers need to do well to keep their jobs; the management needs good scores to satisfy the donor.

As with pretesting, my main point here is not that posttesting per se is bad. On the contrary, a good, broad, demanding posttest can be a central ingredient in establishing a strong academic program. Such a test gives students and teachers alike clear, well-defined, and explicit objectives, and, when these objectives are met, a fair measure of accomplishment. The trouble with most standardized posttests in writing or reading is that they relate only tangentially, if at all, to the fundamental learning students must accomplish if they are to become competent readers and writers. It is often difficult, even after close study, for a teacher to figure out exactly what is being examined.

For a reasonable model, I am tempted to return to the old-style, pre-1930 College Entrance Examination Board exams. These were essay-type exams, given at the end of each high-school year, consisting of an old-fashioned array of "spot questions" (key questions of substance sprinkled throughout the exam, the answers to which immediately tell whether the student knows the subject matter being tested) and essay questions all related to an explicit syllabus of instruction devised by committees of teachers representing the colleges and schools and published by the schools. If students wanted to go to college, their goal was to learn a stipulated body of information and skills in every course every year they were in high school, and to be able to report in their own words all that they had learned during the annual board exams. I am not foolish enough to think that our high schools or their faculties would ever consent to return to such a rigorous, stipulated system of evaluation of work actually accomplished. I am convinced, though, that the model may be helpful for teachers of first- and second-year college students, who must somehow salvage the education of the hundreds of thousands of able students graduating from high schools who are unable to read or write or do basic arithmetic.

In faculty discussions about testing, a surprising percentage of college teachers display a deep, almost passionate conviction that to work explicitly to help students pass a plainly delineated final competency exam is somehow unprofessional, maybe even dishonest. The idea seems to be that teachers should have no advance knowledge of what the exam will cover; that teachers who do have any advance knowledge about the exam, even in the most general terms, will try to teach their students how to pass it, which, heaven forbid!

Finally, in designing a meaningful posttest, it is important that the exam be broad and demanding enough to assure that the students learn all they should in a course, and not settle for a few insignificant elements, making a relatively narrow exam. For example, a brief essay written under exam conditions is an excellent test of students' ability to generate, organize, and write down their thoughts. But if that is the whole of a final competency exam, it will allow students and their teachers to settle for simple, manageable forms in paragraphing, sentence structure, and vocabulary; and to practice mainly these forms, to the exclusion of a great deal else that should and could be accomplished in first-year English studies.

Clearly, in posttesting, just as in other testing areas, remedial educators need the expert study, consultation, publication, and back-up support that can come best from a coherent, ongoing research and information effort spearheaded by the black colleges.

Curriculum and Instruction

Everyone involved in education has his or her own perspective on what matters most. Mine is that of a classroom teacher, more narrowly of a classroom teacher persuaded that what probably matters most in college work is how it all begins, that is, what happens in first-year courses. Students' experiences with first-year teachers give them their most vivid, enduring ideas of what college is all about. And, for the large majority of students entering American colleges today, full of hope but ill-prepared in basic skills and information, what happens in the first year, or perhaps in the first few weeks, makes a critical difference in whether they fail or succeed.

A major problem in the whole U.S. educational system is that first-year studies are still held in low esteem by many senior faculty although basic skills teaching is critically important. Typically, college teachers think of themselves as specialists in an important subject—anthropology, ancient classical languages, mathematics, or others—prepared to do research in and to teach that subject. In a word, college teachers aim not to teach students but to teach their subjects. Most first-year teachers are different. They are like elementary and secondary school teachers in that they are concerned with the less prestigious business of teaching individual students. The belief is that college teachers add luster to their colleges, and strength to their folders, by publishing obscure and narrowly focused research articles in limited circulation professional journals. Thus, scholarly publication is the "proper" road, the high road, to academic recognition and tenure. Teachers who spend their time teaching individual students how to read, write, figure, and think are on the low and bumpy road to oblivion.

Working with first-year students who have developed bad study habits over 12 years of schooling is an intricate, demanding, professional job. It involves an intense and accurate awareness of students' experiences at home and in school, their strengths and ambitions, how they learn, and how to hold their attention. It means discovering how to lead them on into the new world of books and ideas, to use their good minds energetically and with discipline toward a major professional objective, to make them aware of their growing obligations to others, to society—obligations which grow along with their own improved opportunities. Beyond all this, the successful first-year teacher must care deeply about each student as an individual, care enough to spend unmeasured amounts of time when it is needed. The good teacher will be at once professional, dealing with the materials at hand, and personal, letting students know that someone on the campus knows them, respects them, likes them as individuals, and is ready to encourage or goad, support, correct, or hold up objectives, as the situation requires.

First-year teachers tend to expend most of their energies in day-to-day work with individual students. And, if they do have the time and energy to conduct research on basic studies, they usually encounter certain obstacles. First, research these days is apt to be directed toward obtaining or retaining a foundation or government grant, and thus will be operational and optimistic rather than fundamental and realistic; second, research on problems of teaching first-year students and how they learn usually cuts little ice with college bigwigs establishing policy and awarding tenure.

A power struggle is often triggered by the development of a unified Basic Studies Program. Too often traditional academic departments tend to view the development of a separate, coordinated program as a major loss in their budget, faculty positions, and academic power. So it is usually an uphill task, politically, to establish a separate program, and equally hard to keep it going (see Chapter 13 for more on this issue). One of the important developments of the past 15 years is the recognition by the major foundations and the Department of Education that experimental first-year study programs should be encouraged. Thus, an opportunity has been presented and now is being realized on many campuses. But the opportunity may prove to have been only temporary when current grants disappear.

My own strong and obvious prejudice is for a separate, coordinated first-year program of instruction. Such a program could bring together the efforts of all first-year teachers, giving them an academic home base where good work is encouraged. Most important of all, teachers can be held strictly accountable for what skills and information have been learned at the end of the first year. The immediate casualty of returning this responsibility to the traditional departments is apt to be the loss of any focused and effective accountability for educational results.

One major purpose in establishing an academic research and information board for black colleges would be to give systematic attention to all the threshold problems of teaching and learning that first-year students and their teachers are trying to address. The contemplated board could direct professional research on major educational efforts, pull together active teachers from all corners of the black school and college world for serious discussions of the problems and of the research findings, and publish the results.

Another focus of the new board should be support of the efforts now underway in some colleges to extend remedial programs into the upper-class years. Experience suggests that each four-year college will have to develop a sequential program of its own, depending on the local general education requirements. The joint research and information effort could help validate the importance of remedial work at the upper levels, and help develop curriculum ideas and models. For example, the reader might give some attention to the works of Piaget (1972), Shaughnessy (1977), Garrison (1974), and Whimbey (1975) which all have relevance for classroom studies where students need professional attention.

Study of Title III and AIDP Programs

An objective evaluation and descriptive report of the most successful first-year programs undertaken in recent years, supported by the AIDP and other Title III funds, should be conducted. Examining the Title III and AIDP records would be a good way for the Research and Information Board to begin to identify the most effective programs currently in black colleges. As noted earlier, teachers rarely have the time or the research skills to keep detailed records on class work and to assess how well they have succeeded. But the Title III and AIDP grants required fairly strict behavioral objectives, accountability, and careful record keeping. These records are piling up, and deserve a close look.

Thirteen Colleges Program

I would urge the new board to assemble from the Institute for Services to Education (ISE) in Washington all available records of its remarkable Thirteen Colleges Program curriculum effort of the late 1960s, and evaluate their work for the use of all colleges. The program was too rich and important to be forgotten.

Vocabulary

Finally, I hope that some authoritative educational research group will look into the essential question of how we can effectively expand our students' vocabularies. College teachers have found that most students come to college with weak vocabularies, too weak for reading academic material or for comprehending classroom discussions. One favored approach to building vocabularies involves a study of Latin and Greek word roots, prefixes, and suffixes. This method is perhaps of some use if the student is thoroughly schooled in ancient Latin and Greek, but not much help otherwise. Another approach is having students jot down in a notebook the words they encounter that they do not know. This seems to work fairly well for conscientious students, but overall strikes me as a fairly haphazard method.

About ten years ago, I decided to tackle the problem by examining the frequency of word use. It occurred to me that there might be some relationship between the words my students knew and the frequency with which certain words are used. I gave a simple little test—based on the frequency of word use—and the results were interesting (see Thorndike and Lorge 1944 for early studies on this topic). My students had quite good command of the 3,000 to 4,000 most frequently used words. But beyond that basic everyday level, their understanding and control quickly diminished. This finding suggested developing and teaching a list of important words drawn from the next level, in the frequency range of 4,000 to 6,000. It took a year of working with word books and dictionaries and field testing to develop a list of some 900 words to be taught at the rate of 30 a week during the 30-week academic year. That total translated into a regular class activity of six new words a day, every day, for five classes a week. The program worked well in my classes. Clearly the students needed to know these words, and they appreciated the specific assignments. We scheduled a brief, ten-minute class warm-up each day, going over the current word list, and reviewing for the biweekly tests.

But the idea never caught on in other classes and never appealed to any other teachers. Perhaps it is just too old-fashioned. So the problem of how to systematically expand students' vocabularies remains.

Administration

College administrators have at least three major areas of responsibility that would be served by the work of the academic research and information board: monitoring and evaluation; development of new program directions; and initiating effective relationships with other colleges

Monitoring and Evaluation

Modern data processing equipment makes it possible and relatively inexpensive for any college to keep track of its students and faculty, to record and study how well they are performing from year to year, and to discover the strengths and weaknesses of their day-to-day operations.

Monitoring and evaluation programs of this kind require coordination of the curricula and development of evaluation tests, and the proposed Research and Information Board could be helpful in such efforts. For example, should a student's ability to perform on an essay exam be considered an important skill to develop and thus should it be tested each year through four years of college? In what courses in the second, third, and fourth years should there be responsibility for strengthening writing skills, and how should these efforts be coordinated and tested? Should the college administer an essay competency exam at the end of the second year, as is now done in Georgia, as a condition for moving on to the third year and a major field? Should a college examine the student's developing knowledge in various subjects at the end of the second, third, or fourth year? If so, what information or skills should be tested? What attention should be paid to departmental course syllabi and

final examinations? Is there now available a useful set of achievement tests for measuring students' intellectual growth as they move
through college? If there is not such a set of tests, could one be
devised? What would be tested? Could a college faculty at the request of the administration devise such a set of progress exams?
We need expert research help on these issues, and others.

Consortial Arrangements

Finally, the new board could help black colleges share ideas
and develop a strong institutional outreach program to learn about
promising developments at major white colleges and universities.
The white colleges have much to learn from the black colleges, and
vice versa. And now is a good time to set up the necessary structure for serious sharing.

In the past few years, at least three outstanding efforts at
interinstitutional sharing have been developed: the Education Improvement Program (EIP) sponsored by the Southern Association of
Colleges and Schools on behalf of the Title III program Developing
Institutions in the South; "Alternatives to the Revolving Door" initiated and supported by the U.S. Fund for the Improvement of Postsecondary Education (FIPSE); and the already mentioned Thirteen
Colleges Program of the Institute for Services to Education.

The Education Improvement Program, presided over by Joseph
Thompson of the Southern Association of Colleges and Schools in
Atlanta has brought the Title III first-year faculties together for at
least three or four meetings a year, to share new and useful ideas
in many fields of study. In past major meetings, the group discussed
the work of Piaget and Whimbey. In addition, EIP publishes a regular newsletter reporting on recent meetings and presenting new ideas.
EIP has had good results helping teachers on the firing line keep in
touch with each other to share ideas, and keep track of major new
developments in their areas of work.

FIPSE initiated the "Alternatives to the Revolving Door" project in 1974 to bring together a national group of 12 open-door two-
year and four-year colleges which have had outstanding results in
basic skills programming. Not one traditional black college qualified for institutional membership in this important national seminar.
The Bronx Community College in New York led the seminar. There
were two years of meetings of representatives from the successful
programs who discussed their efforts and produced a valuable set of
reports. When "Revolving Door" ended, FIPSE funded a continuation
of the publication effort under the title "Networks."

ISE's Thirteen Colleges Program coordinated the efforts of black colleges to develop and operate new first-year curricula in basic studies and in natural sciences and social sciences, and brought the teachers and counselors together for regular workshops and sharing sessions.

These three projects have made an especially important contribution in recognizing successful threshold programs scattered through the country. The projects are important models of what black colleges could accomplish if they established a similar research and information program on their own.

CONCLUSION

There is obvious need for the black community to establish, under black control, a strong, broadly based program of research and information concerned with improving the educational experience and opportunities of black students in the United States.

Even though considerable progress has been made in opening up educational opportunities for blacks over the past 20 years, there are still obstacles and shortcomings in the system. Among these are the high dropout and unemployment rates of black youth in the center cities; the severe limitation of access to major universities; the shunting of almost half of black college-age students into two-year colleges; and the still discouragingly low representation of black students in graduate and professional schools.

The suggested programmatic research and information effort focusing on educational problems should be controlled and directed by individuals and institutions representing the black community, and should be concerned with all manner of educational problems from kindergarten through graduate school. The most likely headquarters for such an effort would be one of the black universities, especially one with graduate and research capabilities.

One of the major objectives of the research and information effort would be the development of educational research programs on a number of black college campuses, and the preparation of a new generation of black scholars to undertake such basic research as their major professional responsibility.

How might black educators set about establishing such a center for educational research and information? Three tactical models come to mind. One is the College Entrance Examination Board, which grew out of the efforts of 12 forward-looking college presidents and school leaders who decided in 1900 that it would be extremely beneficial if the colleges could agree on acceptable entrance

172 / John U. Monro

exams that could be conducted anywhere in the country. Today the
board numbers 451 colleges and 1,777 schools.

The United Negro College Fund could also serve as a model.
It was initiated in 1943 when 14 black college presidents met at
Tuskegee Institute under the leadership of then president Frederick
D. Patterson, to consider whether the black colleges could work to-
gether in an annual, nationwide fundraising drive.

A third possible model is the College Scholarship Service (CSS),
founded in 1953 when six college presidents in the Northeast decided
that their colleges' financial aid programs were wasting far too much
money in their attempts to attract honor students through large
scholarship awards. The presidents concluded that it would be possible to agree on a common system of financial need evaluation, to
share information about scholarship candidates, and to bring the
expensive competition under control. In the long run, the CSS helped
pave the way for federal financial-aid programs based on individual
need. College Scholarship Service has grown from a membership
of 18 colleges in 1954 to 1,021 colleges and schools today.

Black colleges and universities, like all higher education institutions, will be immediately faced with shrinking enrollments.
Their survival will depend to a large extent on their continued success in educating students who lack the necessary preparation for
college. The academic research and information board recommended
here would be an invaluable resource for these colleges. Not only
could it serve as a clearinghouse for new programs, but could also
begin to assist high schools in developing new educational strategies.
The potential for success is great, but the initiative must be taken
now.

REFERENCES

Astin, Alexander W. "Racial considerations in admissions." In
The campus and the racial crisis. Proceedings of the 1969 annual
meeting of the American Council on Education. Washington, D.C.:
American Council on Education, 1970.

_____. "The myth of equal access to public higher education."
Paper delivered at conference of the Southern Education Founda-
tion (SEF), Equality of Access to Postsecondary Education. Atlanta,
GA: SEF, July 1975.

Garrison, Roger H. "One-to-one: Tutorial instruction in freshman
composition." In Implementing innovative instruction: New
directions for community colleges (II, 1). San Francisco:
Jossey-Bass, 1974.

Institute for the Study of Educational Policy (ISEP). The black college primer. Washington, D.C.: Howard University Press,
1980.

Keppel, Francis. "Education in the eighties." Harvard Educational
Review (May 1980).

Lawson, Anton E., and John W. Reaver. "Piagetian theory and
biology teaching." The American Biology Teacher (September
1975).

National Advisory Committee on Black Higher Education and Black
Colleges and Universities (NACBHEBCU). Higher education
equity: The crisis of appearance versus reality. Washington,
D.C.: NACBHEBCU, 1978.

_____. Black colleges and universities: An essential component of
a diverse system of higher education. Washington, D.C.:
NACBHEBCU, 1979.

_____. Target date, 2000 A.D.: Goals for achieving higher edu-
cation equity for black Americans. Washington, D. C.:
NACBHEBCU, 1980.

_____. Black higher education fact sheet. Washington, D.C.:
NACBHEBCU, 1980.

National Association for Equal Opportunity in Higher Education
(NAFEO). "America's historically black colleges and the Reagan
administration." Paper prepared for President Reagan's staff,
December 1980.

Piaget, Jean. "Intellectual evolution from adolescence to adulthood."
Human Development 15 (1972).

_____. "Cognitive development in children: Development and
learning." Journal of Research in Science Teaching (1964).

Shaughnessy, Mina. Errors and expectations: A guide for the teaching of basic writing. New York: Oxford University Press, 1977.

Thorndike, E. L., and I. R. Lorge. The teacher's word book of
30,000 words. New York: Columbia University, Teachers
College Press, 1944.

Whimbey, Arthur. Intelligence can be taught. New York: E. P. Dutton, 1975.

Whimbey, Arthur, and Jack Lockhead. Problem solving and comprehension (A short course in analytical reasoning). Philadelphia, PA: Franklin Institute Press, 1980.

Wright, Stephen. The black educational policy researcher: An untapped national resource. Washington, D.C.: NACBHEBCU, 1979.

PART V

EXTERNAL FACTORS AFFECTING FUTURE DIRECTIONS AND MISSIONS OF BLACK COLLEGES

Regardless of which traditional missions black colleges decide to continue or which new roles they wish to pursue, all institutions will have to contend with a variety of external forces over which, customarily, they have had little control. Public policies established by the federal government and states and enrollments are two principal concerns. The first two papers in this section by John Williams and Mary Carter-Williams carefully discuss those issues and recommend strategies to give black colleges some leverage over public policies and their enrollments. The final chapter by John Matlock deals with a specific public policy of concern to many public black colleges, namely, desegregation and its effects on the role and functioning of black institutions. Declining enrollments, shifting federal and state public policies toward higher education, and the inevitable possibility of more mergers among colleges and universities portend a bleak future for U.S. postsecondary education. However, Williams, Carter-Williams, and Matlock delineate several researchable topics that should help institutions to better prepare for these adverse situations.

Public Policy and
Black College Development:
An Agenda for Research

John B. Williams

Research on the relationship between government and black
colleges and universities emerged over the past two decades during
what seemed to be a period of unlimited growth throughout postsecondary education. Most colleges and universities were expanding
their enrollments, and predominantly white colleges and universities
began for the first time to admit substantial numbers of blacks from
the increasing pool of eligible students. In light of this new trend,
special efforts were required for black colleges to participate in the
increasingly competitive marketplace of potential college enrollees
(Bowles and DeCosta 1971; Carnegie Commission 1971; LeMelle and
LeMelle 1969; McGrath 1965).

One of the purposes of this research was to suggest ways for
the federal and state governments to promote the development of
traditionally black colleges and universities. Recommendations ran
the gamut of then existing public policy options: from providing un-
encumbered direct grants to institutions, to increasing student financial aid across the board in higher education, to mounting technical
assistance and demonstration projects in institutional management
and classroom instruction. The initiation of federal action, such as
Title III of the Higher Education Act of 1965, aimed at strengthening
"developing" institutions, may have been the outcome of public concern and of some of this work.

AMBIVALENCE TOWARD BLACK INSTITUTIONS

At least two important aspects of the 1960s and 1970s research deserve attention. First, researchers concerned with the

development of black colleges and universities have taken responsibility for articulating a rationale for public support of these institutions. Ever since the late nineteenth century, when most of the
black colleges were founded, government leaders and public policymakers have been ambivalent about the prospect of their continued
growth and expansion. This uncertainty about the future of black
institutions manifested itself in many ways (e.g., Browning and
Williams 1978). Today such uncertainty centers upon how government should value the institutional diversity exemplified by black colleges and universities. Is it ethically and politically correct for the
U.S. government to promote the existence and growth of ethnically
identifiable black institutions on the one hand, and at the same
time to pressure for desegregation or full and equal participation
for blacks in all other U.S. public institutions? Furthermore, do
institutions maintained primarily for the advancement of black U.S.
residents constitute an unwarranted contradiction of U.S. law,
public policy, and politics which evolved out of recent attempts to
integrate public school systems? This is the point of view expressed in the famous Brown decision (347 U.S. 483 Supreme Court
1954), that racially separate institutions are by definition unequal
regardless of which ones, black or white, are rated superior. Or
do black colleges offer public benefits nowhere else available and
therefore transcend incremental attempts to achieve equity?

Some state politicians have suggested that black colleges
should close their doors, reasoning that desegregation in education
has become the policy of the nation, and that black students should
therefore attend the more affluent white state institutions. Others
concerned with the problem press for expansion of the black colleges.

Needless to say, substantial disagreement of this type makes
the job of establishing a consistent and viable public policy of equality in higher education difficult. For some officials, comparable
quality between similar black and white institutions within a single
system is called for, but for others achieving equality is an integration problem, requiring a desirable racial and ethnic mix of
students, faculty, and administrators at every institution. For
others, attempting an incremental approach, equity criteria are
only applied to predominantly white institutions.

The absence of a broad consensus in higher education on
race equity standards makes desired and reasonable distributions
of public funds difficult to achieve. The U.S. Department of Education's 1980 Report on the President's Black College Initiative
provides a recent account of inequality of federal support. The
report concludes that "obligations to black institutions increased in
FY 1979, but declined as a percentage of the federal government's

obligation to all colleges and universities.* The Federal Interagency Committee on Education reports little change, with year-to-year declines in the percentage of federal funds awarded to black colleges and universities over the period 1972-80 (FICE, 1973-81).

Clearly, ambivalence about the importance of black colleges, underlying government's failure to establish clear signals about what should be considered equity criteria, is only one reason for timid and unequal public support of black institutions. It is an important one, however, which can be addressed through useful policy research and analysis.

BLACK COLLEGES AND FEDERAL FUNDING

A second important aspect of this period is that widespread efforts to obtain increased federal funds for all postsecondary education were also taking place. At a time when educational costs were increasing rapidly and college student protest had reached a new peak of intensity, controversy over the federal role in higher education focused in 1970-71, when the 1965 Higher Education Act was reauthorized (Gladieux and Wolanin 1976). Debate over this issue spawned numerous policy research studies assessing the poor financial state of higher education and recommending alternative federal policy options (e.g., Carnegie Commission 1970; Cheit 1971; Committee for Economic Development 1973; National Commission on the Financing of Postsecondary Education 1973).

These studies took the position that inflation and costs were rising at a rate the colleges could not accommodate alone without compromising the integrity and breadth of their important educational service to the nation. Cheit (1971), for example, recommended substantial federal direct institutional aid for the nation's higher education systems. A later report, prepared by a Department of Health, Education and Welfare task force named after its chairperson, Frank Newman, former president of the University of Rhode Island, took another approach, arguing that higher education was in need of reform rather than major infusions of direct institu-

---

*This unpublished report, prepared by Meldon Hollis, then Director of the Black College Initiative Project, was not "accepted" by officials of the Department of Education and, to this writer's knowledge, was never transmitted to President Carter. It is not known, therefore, whether any of the report's contents were issued publicly.

tional aid from federal funds to continue to operate the same programs. Colleges and universities, by operating more efficiently
and adopting more responsive instructional offerings, could better
serve traditional student clienteles, while expanding enrollment by
attracting new clients from age groups which, until then, had not
participated in higher education in large numbers. Education would
become a lifelong endeavor with students attending institutions that
more specifically served their needs at appropriate stages in their
lives.

The Cheit recommendation and that of the Newman report
raised a clear choice for Congress. Federal policymakers had to
choose between aid directly to institutions and financial aid to students. Arguably, an overall policy of direct grants to institutions
tended to reward colleges at a time when student protests and other
controversies made major changes in higher education seem necessary to the public. Also, unrestricted federal aid seemed to allow
colleges and universities to remain inefficient and unresponsive to
demands for change, and to offer little incentive for them to admit
and educate poor, minority students successfully. On the other hand,
a financial, aid-to-students approach established an "academic marketplace," which fostered efficiency, provided incentives for change,
encouraged colleges to recruit and admit new students, and improved educational opportunity. Such a policy also seemed to bring
colleges into line with public needs and to make them more accountable to the public. In 1971, policymakers chose this route: the
Education Amendments of 1972 clearly emphasized student aid as a
vehicle for federal supports (Lynn 1980).

A solution to the problem of the decline of black colleges was
being sought as this new federal policy debate occurred. Achieving
both goals—survival of black colleges and of U.S. postsecondary
education in general—seemed antithetical. In short order, Title III
became the largest of only a few remaining direct-aid-to-institutions
programs. The new federal aid-to-students policy increased competition between white and black institutions for Title III funds.
Title III constitutes a necessary and substantial source of federal
aid to black colleges, even though the program's guidelines have
never clearly corroborated the fact that it was established in 1965
for this purpose (Cobb 1977).

Moreover, the federal financial-aid-to-student policy was formulated and continues to be administered in a way that even today
does not favor the participation of black colleges and universities.
Such a policy, by establishing a higher education marketplace, may
be desirable for improving efficiency and effectiveness; on the other
hand, it probably does not promote equality between black and white
institutions. Free-market conditions in industry do not always

result in desired parity among businesses, and it is not reasonable
to expect that free-market conditions in higher education will result
in equity for black colleges and universities which are in a disadvantaged financial and political position. The absence of growth and
expansion in student enrollment heightens their disadvantage.

AN AGENDA FOR PUBLIC POLICY RESEARCH

An agenda for public policy research on the development of
black colleges should aim at establishing equality between black and
white institutions, especially those within the same state system.
Toward this end, contradictions in existing public policy that prohibit equity may be partially resolved. Such analyses should
capitalize on advancements in knowledge, theory, and methodology
in the recently expanded field of higher education research and
development.

At least three types of research will contribute to resolving
policy contradictions and fostering equality for traditionally black
institutions. These types, corresponding to trends in the much
larger volume of research on higher education, are:

— Assessments of the implementation and impact of specific
programs;
— Applications of analytical models of innovation and development to suggest possible improvements in the organization
and governance processes of higher education which can
then be targeted for public policy intervention;
— Historical studies describing responses of an institution
or network of institutions to a variety of important social,
economic, or political situations and from which new
frameworks for knowledge about black college development
can be obtained.

ASSESSING CURRENT PUBLIC POLICY PROGRAMS
AND BLACK COLLEGE DEVELOPMENT

Initially, policy researchers need to determine the differential
impact upon black institutions of existing public higher-education
policies. Some studies have assessed the impact of higher-
education policy as far as access and retention of blacks in predominantly white colleges and universities are concerned (e.g.,
Astin 1982; Thomas 1981). But in the past few have dealt sufficiently
with differential impacts upon black institutions. It is important to

know that minority students have access to, and are retained, at predominantly white institutions or within the postsecondary system as a whole; but the only way to assess the benefit of public policy for black colleges is to compare the outcomes over time of federal and state funding programs at these institutions with those at white ones in the same system, adopting the individual colleges as units of analysis. There appears to be some hesitation about collecting data of this kind at a time when higher education claims to be embarking upon a new era of enlightenment in its attitudes toward full participation by minority groups.

Impact of Federal and State Financial Aid Policy

The impact of federal and state student financial aid policy deserves immediate attention. Student financial aid management problems reported at black colleges do not arise solely from technical inadequacies and personnel deficiencies at the campus level, but also from the ways financial aid policies are formulated and implemented, and from the unique aid requirements of the students. For example, although the Pell Grant Program aims at enabling low-income students to attend college and at enabling poorer institutions to compete for students, the way it is administered has the opposite effect. The Pell Program limits the amount of financial aid a student can receive to 50 percent of the cost of attending the institution:

> With a grant ceiling of $1600 (in 1978-79), this restriction affects people enrolled in schools where the cost is less than $3,200 a year. Consider a low-income student. If he or she is poor enough to qualify for the maximum grant, then for every dollar less than $3,200 that it costs to attend the college of his or her choice, the half-cost limitation will serve to reduce the grant fifty cents. Perversely, the main impact of this provision is felt by students otherwise eligible for the largest grants . . . and it is felt by them only if they select a relatively low-priced college or university (Finn 1978, pp. 70-79).

Black colleges and universities have tended to be low-cost institutions, serving low-income students. Federal student financial aid policy embodied in the Pell program does not favor such institutions.

A recent study authorized by the U.S. Commission on Civil Rights is designed to measure the impact at black and Hispanic

institutions of reductions and threats to reduce federal student aid
by the current administration. The study documents the adverse
and differential effects of such reductions. It shows, for example,
that simple failure to publish Pell grant eligibility rules on time
resulted over a two-year period in enrollment declines at some
black and Hispanic institutions (Advanced Technology 1983).

In more general ways, existing student and federal categorical
programs may offer poorer assistance to black institutions. Technical expertise and understanding of funding requirements notwith-
standing, there exists, overall, a different set of financial management problems at black institutions. These stem primarily from
the inability of the institutions to pass on increased operation costs
to students, and from past discrimination particularly by state government. These facts of life may not be reflected in existing policy
and delivery mechanisms. It is less realistic, for example, for
poorer institutions to undertake cost-reimbursement contracts,
simply because no reserve funds are available to cover immediate
costs involved in operating such a contract. Poorer institutions
encounter cash-flow problems when cost reimbursement at the
federal level is slow. Lacking substantial capital for fund raising,
poorer institutions usually cannot afford even the costs of proposal
preparation and grantsmanship.

Public Policy Research on Government Regulation

Policy analysts usually divide public policy in higher education into three categories: student financial aid, institutional support, and regulation. An analysis of the impact of the policies in
each category generally consists of measuring the extent to which
prescribed goals were achieved using delivery systems—usually
funding mechanisms—delineated in the policies themselves. Since
policy research is conducted in this manner, many policies which
fall into the regulatory category go uninvestigated and the unintended
consequences of such policies are seldom explored (Finn 1978).

This is an unfortunate shortcoming since two of the three
most significant recent federal policies in higher education—affirmative action and desegregation—involve mostly regulatory activities.
And perhaps more substantially than financial aid policies, both of
these policies clearly reflect ambivalent and inconsistent goals for
black colleges. Lack of clarity in federal desegregation and affirmative action regulations makes research on their impact important, particularly where limited evidence exists of specific unintended consequences of these policies for black college development. According to informal accounts, such undesirable outcomes

may include increased administrative costs, racial polarization, and the imposition of impersonal governance structures which disrupt the sense of community established at the college campus.

Mounting evidence also exists of the failure even to implement court-ordered desegregation in 19 state higher education systems cited for past race discrimination policies (Adams v. Richardson, 356 F. Supp. 92,94 [D.D.C. 1973]). Ambivalence of desegregation policy reflected in this decision, and among responsible policymakers, probably constitutes a reason for nonimplementation (Adams v. Bell, 430 F. Supp. 118 [D.D.C. 1983]; U.S. Commission on Civil Rights 1981; Williams 1981).

Policies and Programs at the State Level

A research program which surveys the effects on black institutions of higher education policies, policy options, and their outcomes at the state level is also needed. Options exist in various areas of state policy: in student financial aid, in the development of instructional programs, in the allocation of general revenue funds, in the maintenance and construction of campus facilities, and desegregation.

Little is known of the comparative aspects of policies at the state level, except for the work presented periodically by groups such as the Southern Regional Education Board and the Department of Education's Office of Civil Rights. But these sources have not developed an historical perspective on the evolution of state policies over the past century: how state policies have changed (where they have been in existence sufficiently long), and the consequences of those changes for the development of public black colleges and universities. William Trueheart's recent study, The Consequences of Federal and State Resource Allocation and Development Policies for Traditionally Black Land-Grant Institutions (1979), and a discussion of state policy barriers prepared by the National Association for Equal Opportunity in Higher Education provide useful beginnings for such an exploration (NAFEO 1977). But clearly debates over the proper formulation of state policy for black-college development lack this historical dimension. For example, some southern states have in the past appropriated supplementary institutional aid to public black colleges. But in some instances where such programs were established during the early 1960s, the unabashed aim of policymakers was to deflate growing criticism of racial discrimination, allowing state-college systems to remain segregated. Today these same policymakers cite such past practices as evidence of their intent to foster black-college development through state action. One way to explore the intent of such awards would be to compare the duration, levels, and kinds of funding to white and black institutions over the years using some standard of comparability. And such complicated but possible calculations of the longitudinal impact of state-funding policies would be instructive for other purposes as well.

Exploring New Approaches

The impact of innovative alternative public policies for black-college development should also be explored. One such alternative would be establishing a development bank for raising endowments at black colleges and universities, instead of awarding financial aid (or in addition to this type of assistance). Initiating a policy to assist selected states to develop at least one major black research university would be another unorthodox alternative, one which would rest firmly on the conviction that ethnic identity is an aspect of institutional diversity in U.S. higher education that should be preserved.

New approaches of this kind already exist in the literature. For example, the Carnegie Commission recommended in 1970 that:

> . . . a special subdivision of their [black colleges'] development be created within the National Foundation for Development of Higher Education proposed in Quality and Equality. This division in which Negroes should have a vital role in advisory and management capabilities would aid black colleges in developing and implementing new programs and activities that respond to the challenges confronting them as institutions in transition (Carnegie Commission 1970, pp. 57-58).

Following upon this recommendation, a White House working group appointed by President Nixon designed a package of legislative proposals, including the provision of federal foundation funds for black colleges. The package was introduced in Congress in March 1970, but it never emerged from congressional committees for want of what many believed to be a lack of involvement, but not necessarily disapproval, by the "higher education establishment" (Pelavin et al. 1981). To the extent that such recommendations have already been partially implemented—the Fund for the improvement of Post-secondary Education, for example, may correspond to what the Commission labeled a "National Foundation for Development"—

research and development studies can investigate the impact they have had on black-college development and suggest the feasibility of more complete implementation of the original recommendation.

Assessing Existing Policies

On the whole, a thorough assessment of the impact of existing public policy on the development of black colleges will set the stage for more informed judgments about the "ends" as well as the "means" of current and future federal and state action. Pluralist notions of higher education and development become politically palatable options when racially distinct institutions seem to serve the interests of all affected client groups. An example is the 1978 Tribally Controlled Community College Assistance Act designed to assist Native Americans (P. L. 95-471, Title 25, Section 1801, U.S. Codes, October 17, 1978). Title I of the Act authorizes grants for the operation and improvement of tribally controlled colleges to insure the continuation and expansion of educational opportunities for Native American students.

At this time, both whites and blacks are upset over the per-ceived inferior status of black colleges—blacks because they want their institutions to attain equal status, and whites because they be-lieve the black colleges constitute an unnecessary drain on limited financial resources. Reaching a pluralist accommodation will de-pend upon the likelihood of achieving institutional parity through public-policy intervention. The public benefits are drawn clearer in this way. How genuine this possibility is can only be tested through assessments of what has already been accomplished, of what has taken place inadvertently, of what can be corrected, and of bold new attempts aimed at attaining the pluralist ideal in U.S. higher education. Assessments of existing policy, in particular the intervention programs in states affected by the Adams decision and the nationwide student financial aid programs, may similarly sug-gest the extent to which integrationist approaches are realistic. Such assessments can point out ways of changing policy so that equal benefits accrue to black institutions and thus enhance the prospect of desegration.

The federal government has never made a forthright attempt to enhance the development of black colleges. The argument against further expenditures of public funds for black-college development unfortunately reflects the incorrect judgment that large amounts of money have already been spent for this purpose and, having failed to achieve good results, increasingly limited public money should now be given to "more advantaged" colleges. But on the contrary, a close inspection of federal programs reveals that attempts to provide added funds and to "equalize" expenditures to black institutions have failed because of the obscure fashion in which the legislation creating programs such as Title III (Aid to Developing Institutions) was written (Cobb 1977). The intended recipients were black colleges, but the legislation written by Congress was not that specific. Such programs may have established the moral basis for federal support to black institutions and may have created a more favorable public attitude toward the prospect of their optimum development. But no firm development goals for black institutions, separate from the entire network of postsecondary education, are reflected in past federal law and policy. The clear impetus and intent of Title III, for example, may have been to enhance the prospects of black colleges at a time when most colleges were prospering. The legislation, on the other hand, provides federal funds to "developing institutions," a political euphemism for black colleges and universities. There may be good reasons why Title III was started in this way, but the program did not limit eligibility to black institutions and left open the possibility for competition with relatively advantaged white colleges. Today such competition is increasing.

The fact that money may have been wasted as a consequence of the way federal programs are structured is not solely the fault of black colleges. In many instances federal legislation fosters failure (Jacobs and Tingley 1977); further data to resolve this debate may, in the final analysis, await the passage of legislation that clearly attempts to develop black or other racially identifiable institutions. If such a policy is undertaken, its results should be documented through competent research assessing the impact of demonstration policy programs aimed at strengthening representative institutions.

ANALYTICAL MODELS OF COLLEGE DEVELOPMENT, PUBLIC POLICY, AND BLACK COLLEGES

To some extent, any attempt by government to accelerate the development process at black colleges will be impeded by a lack of general knowledge about normative development and innovative processes at any college campus. Most attempts to describe ways in which colleges develop take the form of analytical models, and most were created prior to the recent depression in higher education. Consequently, they rely to a great extent upon econometric assumptions of unlimited expansion and bureaucratic governance assumptions about decisionmaking processes (St. John and Weathersby 1977). For the most part, the public policy response

to declining enrollments and financial exigencies in higher education
has been to propose and support new management practices and
systems. Much of the research on black college development deals
with improving management through the application of planning
models. In addition to the fact that the management systems may
adopt incorrect assumptions, interventions aimed at improving
management may have a profound, undesirable impact upon aspects
of other college organizations. More specifically, a "modest" system that suggests or predicts appropriate management practices
and systems at a college campus may not include variables that
describe the more intangible elements of the culture or politics of
the college setting.

Effects of Changes in Management Systems

Internal management is closely associated with the formal
structure of an institution in the theoretical literature on organizations (St. John and Weathersby 1977). But aspects of college organization other than formal structure are important, if development
and innovative processes are to be understood. As Pascarella
points out in a recent review of the impact of college on students:

> Within such organizations, student behaviors, atti-
> tudes, and educational outcomes are influenced not
> only by the institution's structural factors (e.g.,
> organizational size, living arrangements, administra-
> tive policies, academic curriculum), but also through
> interactions with the important agents of socialization
> (peers, faculty, administration).
>   Clearly, not all interactions with socializing agents
> in college will be of a formal, structured nature such as
> lectures or class discussion. Nor is it clear that such
> formal activities are regarded by those being socialized
> as an influence of any notable importance on such areas
> of development as attitudes and values (Feldman & New-
> comb 1969; Lehmann 1963). Rather, it may well be, as
> suggested by Asch (1952), Newcomb (1943), and Sherif
> (1952) on reference groups, and by Katz and Kahn (1978)
> on organizational behavior, that effective social learning
> of normative attitudes and values in college is strongly
> influenced by informal interaction with the agents of so-
> cialization (Pascarella 1980).

Consequently, public policy interventions based upon formal structure and management systems may result in undesirable changes in

the college's informal setting that could not be foreseen from the limited perspective of such models.

This may already have happened in HEW's Title III Developing Institutions program, where attempts were made to build more efficient and sophisticated management systems at "developing institutions." An unanticipated outcome may have been the overdependence of the colleges on the federal government for maintaining the new structures and other services that were inadvertently introduced by management interventions (GAO 1979). Furthermore, the possibility of provoking undesirable consequences through uninformed policy interventions has increased because integration has recently become a firm goal of public policy in higher education.

Leaders of black institutions maintain that the survival of black colleges as distinctive institutions is at issue in the Adams states. Many opponents of the decision argue that achieving structural reforms in those states may have the unfortunate consequence of changing elements of the institutions' informal structures such as faculty-student interaction which make it possible for black students' achievements. An example of such a reform is granting full membership to black colleges in state coordinating bodies to increase their state funding.

The voluminous research on higher education innovation and development is silent on the effect of structural reforms on informal behavior patterns. Instead, it is characterized by the use of a variety of analytical models that describe developmental and innovative processes of all types. In a recent review of the literature on change, purposive change, and innovation in higher education, Dill and Friedman (1979) categorize such models and discuss the theory underlying each type. The four types of models they describe are drawn from: (1) theory of complex organizations; (2) social conflict theory; (3) diffusion theory; and (4) planned change or organizational development research. As these authors point out, no model is necessarily superior except where specific research problems are considered. Since the assumptions underlying each type are different, so too are the kind and range of variables each attempts to measure.

The major shortcoming of this body of research is that few researchers have explored relationships among the numerous models, not even among models designed to describe the same developmental processes, because variables were not specified clearly enough. "Much of the research has set and generally attained the modest goal of demonstrating conformity to a general model. . . . This approach is useful but must be extended if knowledge in this important area is to be scientifically increased" (Dill and Friedman 1979, p. 412).

In other words, while it may be possible using available models and data to describe significant changes in formal structure and management that have come about through policy formulation and implementation, little is known about how to sustain and extend elements of informal campus structure supportive of black students' aspirations while improvements in administration and managements are being made. Because of the way the models are constituted, the research literature does not deal with relationships between formal and informal structures or between complex organization and social conflict variables.

The Office for Civil Rights and state higher education commissions have already formulated policies aimed at influencing the rapid development of black colleges and universities in some Adams states, such as assigning new instructional programs to black institutions. As suggested above, research should be undertaken to assess the impact of these new policies, as with all other federal policy programs. But in addition to assessing Adams policies, existing analytical models, particularly those unflawed by unlimited growth and corporate or collegiate governance assumptions, should be studied. Such an assessment should include research which would attempt to draw relationships between elements of more than one type of conceptual model and more than a single defined aspect of institutional development. It will be important to apply the models at black colleges and universities because developmental processes at these institutions may be unique. It is reasonable to expect this will be so if black colleges are the first to experience decreased enrollments. Black institutions have had a long history of adapting to diminished resources.

Changes in public policy, whether aimed at integration or pluralist goals, will be accomplished more easily and with fewer adverse effects if there is more knowledge about the appropriateness of new analytical models of college development and about ways of using them in planning, implementing, and predicting results of public-policy programs. Any viable standard of equality among institutions must take into account ways in which colleges operate. Understanding underlying structures, both formal and informal, at work in any college community and differentiating those at black institutions will improve the accuracy of predictions of desired policy outcomes. The increasing application of analytical models will constitute a way of understanding structures and processes, and thus of achieving a viable standard of equality through public policy intervention.

Historical Research, Public Policy, and
Black College Development

Salient trends in historical studies of the relationship between
public policy and black college development suggest other directions
for future research. Studies in this small category illustrate continuing ambivalence about the value of black collegiate institutions
(Bond 1976; Dyson 1971; Graham 1975; Logan 1969; Neyland & Riley
1963; Robinson 1953). Even in instances where public policy seemed
to support the maintenance of collegiate institutions established
primarily for the advancement of blacks as a class or racial group,
the development of such institutions was circumscribed by the
policies themselves or by broader elements of social, economic,
and political structure (Browning and Williams 1978; Wolters 1975).

Furthermore, studies of the recent history of black colleges
indicate a limitation of policies that aim at full assimilation of
blacks into other collegiate institutions, however unlikely the prospect. Only if full and optimum assimilation of black students occurred, would the issue of maintaining black institutions be moot. As
a nation, the United States would still not have confronted the more
basic issue of its identity: whether it is possible to simultaneously
maintain racial, ethnic, and institutional diversity while achieving
social progress. It would remain for other nations to explore the
possibility of attaining cultural pluralism.

Despite these contributions, existing histories of black colleges and universities fail to give the full picture of how their value
as educational institutions is influenced, and of the cyclical historical processes which determine this value. The failure reflects an
important problem of American social history—understanding the
impact upon educational institutions of complex social and economic
forces. In other words, how have a burgeoning economic system,
social and public policy demands for sometimes contradictory goals,
and U.S. pluralism influenced the character and progress of higher
education? Overall, in the case of black U.S. citizens, there still
remains the question of how the tension between industry's changing
manpower needs, fear of assimilation stemming from racial prejudice, and the political ideals of freedom and equality will work out.
Accounts of the development of black colleges can provide evidence
of this broad historical drama. They may also demonstrate the
need for new policies which more accurately take into account a wide
variety of environmental forces which, left unnoticed, can detract
from attempts by the government and the universities themselves to
further their development as institutions.

Adopting historical approaches which examine concurrently
the nature, articulation, and impact on black college development of

changes in the economic system, in social theory and knowledge, and in political ideology underlying government actions is consistent with advances that have taken place in other arenas of educational history (Graham 1974; Katz 1975; Tyack 1974). For the most part, the history of black colleges has focused on the growth and expansion of their individual leaders. Examining the leadership aspect of college development under current no-growth circumstances will be important, but further lessons for public policy can be derived from historical analyses of economic forces at work in the communities surrounding the colleges. These include changes in local and national attitudes toward blacks as a racial minority, changes in social knowledge among educated groups in the communities, and how that knowledge was translated through political means into public policy. Beginning such history at the local level would seem the most productive approach since substantial federal policy involvement in higher education is a fairly recent occurrence, and since the details of the impact of local political forces and social and economic trends is unknown. Such data will be the basis for broader analyses perhaps on a state-by-state basis.

Determining Goals of Black Colleges

A more useful analysis of the historical development of black colleges would also include a different perspective on the goals of the black college. Much of the historical research presents the view that black colleges attempt to achieve the same goals as all other colleges in the United States, and thus endorse the same social and cultural values. In many cases, however, black college development was overtly limited, some were not allowed to offer liberal arts curricula, and others were simply not given sufficient funding to establish instructional programs like those at white institutions. There is some evidence, therefore, that they could not and did not endorse the same values (Browning and Williams 1978).

Some studies of black colleges and universities have reflected social processes and the culture of predominantly white, "prestigious" institutions (Jencks and Riesman 1968). Comparisons are drawn between elements of the culture and history of white colleges and what seem to be similar elements at black institutions. The result has been a presentation of black institutions as simply having failed to achieve the cultural goals of predominantly white, major research universities.

Leaders of black colleges may have realized that their institutions would not be allowed to adopt the same missions as white colleges and, furthermore, that they should not attempt to do so

even when possible, not because black students were incapable of
achieving as well as whites or because racism would prevent even
the most highly educated and well-assimilated blacks from achieving appropriate rewards or acclaim. Black leaders may have rejected existing social values simply because such values were un-
worthy. They may have attempted through their institutions to
enhance other values. Some black colleges may represent what
Grant and Riesman (1978) suggest are

> attempts to reform society, to rebel against values,
> adopting goals and establishing cultural norms which
> were intended to be fundamentally different from
> those of other institutions. . . . attempts not only to
> [establish and maintain new institutions], but to set
> forth new ideal . . . reforms pointing toward a dif-
> ferent conception of the ends of [college] education.

In this view some colleges constitute "telic reforms" approaching
"the status of social movements or generic protests against contemporary American life" (Grant and Riesman 1978).

One would not expect the development of black institutions to
parallel nor necessarily mimic that of predominantly white colleges;
not because the black colleges have failed to achieve cultural parity,
but because their goal was to create a fundamentally different college culture. It is important to compare the words of black college
leaders with their actions, with what actually occurred at black
institutions, and with public responses, some of which took the
form of piecemeal development policies. Public policy has been
important to black colleges not because of what the policies attempted to accomplish, but rather because of what they enabled the
colleges to do. Ambivalence over the value of black institutions,
resulting in contradictory policies and contradictory goals, rendered
achieving equality impossible, but such confusion and indecision
did allow black college leaders to pursue the development of their
institutions, perhaps in the direction of unorthodox goals.

The uncommon development of black colleges and universities
has been influenced by a myriad of social forces which lay beyond
the institutions themselves and beyond the purview of public policy
intervention. Understanding this sets the stage for identifying important influences of this kind, for redefining policy while taking
external factors into account, and perhaps for improved interventions. Such knowledge will also contribute to the formulation of
improved models of internal college operations, and, in turn, to
improved governmental development policies.

REFERENCES

Advanced Technology Incorporated. Study of the effects on Black and Hispanic institutions of recent reductions in student aid: Draft report to the U.S. Commission on Civil Rights. Reston, VA: May 17, 1983.

Asch, S. Social psychology. New York: Prentice-Hall, 1952.

Astin, A. W. Minorities in American higher education. San Francisco, CA: Jossey-Bass, 1982.

Bond, H. M. Education for freedom. Princeton, NJ: Princeton University Press, 1976.

Bowles, F., and F. DeCosta. Between two worlds. New York: McGraw-Hill, 1971.

Browning, J. E. S., and J. B. Williams. "History and goals of black institutions of higher learning." In Black colleges in America, edited by C. V. Willie and Ronald R. Edmonds. New York: Columbia University, Teachers College Press, 1978.

Bullock, H. A. History of Negro education in the south. Cambridge, MA: Harvard University Press, 1967.

Carnegie Commission. Quality and equality. New York: McGraw-Hill, 1970.

_____. From isolation to mainstream. New York: McGraw-Hill, 1971.

Cheit, Earl. The new depression in higher education. New York: McGraw-Hill, 1971.

Cobb, H. C. Report on an examination of the Developing Institutions Program. Washington, D.C.: United States Office of Education, September 1977.

Committee for Economic Development (CED). Management and financing of colleges. New York: CED, 1973.

Dill, D. D., and C. P. Friedman. "An analysis of frameworks for research on innovation and change in higher education." Review of Educational Research 49 (1979):411-35.

Dyson, W. Howard University. Washington, D.C.: Howard University, 1971.

Federal Interagency Committee on Education (FICE). Federal agencies and black colleges, FYs 1972-1980, Vols. 3-9, Nos. 2-8. Washington, D.C.: FICE, 1973-1981.

Feldman, K., and T. Newcomb. The impact of college on students. San Francisco, CA: Jossey-Bass, 1969.

Finn, C. E., Jr. Scholars, dollars and bureaucrats. Washington, D.C.: Brookings Institution, 1978.

General Accounting Office (GAO). Report to Congress: The federal program to strengthen developing institutions of higher education lacks direction. Washington, D.C.: GAO, 1979.

Gladieux, L. E., and T. R. Wolanin. Congress and the colleges. Lexington, MA: Lexington Books, 1976.

Graham, E. K. A tender violence. Unpublished manuscript, 1975.

Graham, P. A. Community and class in American education, 1865-1915. New York: Wiley and Sons, 1974.

Grant, G., and D. Riesman. The perpetual dream. Chicago, IL: University of Chicago Press, 1978.

Jacobs, F., and T. Tingley. "The evolution of eligibility criteria for Title III of the Higher Education Act of 1965." In The development of colleges and universities. Appendix A. Cambridge, MA: Harvard Graduate School of Education, 1977.

Jencks, C., and D. Riesman. The academic revolution. Garden City, N.Y.: Doubleday, 1968.

Katz, D., and R. Kahn. The social psychology of organizations. 2nd edition. New York: Urley, 1978.

Katz, M. B. Class, bureaucracy and schools. New York: Praeger, 1975.

Lehmann, I. "Changes in critical thinking, attitudes and values from freshman to senior years." Journal of Educational Psychology 54 (1963):305-15.

LeMelle, T., and W. LeMelle. The black college: A strategy for achieving social relevancy. New York: Praeger, 1969.

Logan, R. Howard University. New York: New York University Press, 1969.

Lynn, L. Designing public policy. Santa Monica, CA: Goodyear, 1980.

McGrath, E. The predominantly Negro colleges and universities in transition. New York: Columbia University, Teachers College Press, 1965.

National Association for Equal Opportunity in Higher Education (NAFEO). State policy impediments to black colleges. Unpublished manuscript, November 15, 1977.

National Commission on the Financing of Postsecondary Education. Financing postsecondary education in the United States. Washington, D.C.: GPO, 1973.

Newcomb, T. Personality and social change: Attitude formation in a student community. New York: Dryden Press, 1943.

Newman, F. Second Newman report: National policy on higher education. Cambridge, MA: MIT Press, 1973.

Neyland, L. W., and S. W. Riley. The history of Florida Agricultural and Mechanical University. Gainesville, FL: University of Florida Press, 1963.

Pascarella, E. T. "Student-faculty informal contact and college outcomes." Review of Educational Research 50 (1980):545-95.

Pelavin, S. H., B. J. Hayward, D. C. Pelavin, and M. E. Orland. An evaluation of the Fund for the Improvement of Postsecondary Education. Durham, NC: NTS Research Corporation, 1981.

Robinson, W. H. The history of Hampton Institute, 1868-1949. Doctoral dissertation, New York University, 1953.

Sherif, M. The psychology of social norms. New York: Harper Brothers, 1952.

St. John, E. P., and G. B. Weathersby. "Institutional development in higher education: A conceptual framework for evaluation." In The development of colleges and universities, Appendix B. Cambridge, MA: Harvard Graduate School of Education, 1977.

Thomas, G. E., ed. Black students in higher education. Westport, CT: Greenwood Press, 1981.

Trueheart, W. E. The consequences of federal and state resource allocation and development policies for traditionally black land-grant institutions. Doctoral dissertation, Harvard University Graduate School of Education, 1979.

Tyack, D. B. One best system. Cambridge, MA: Harvard University Press, 1974.

U.S. Commission on Civil Rights. The Black/White Colleges. Washington, D.C.: U.S. Commission on Civil Rights, 1981.

U.S. Department of Education. Report on the President's Black College Initiative. Part I. Unpublished report. Washington, D.C.: U.S. Department of Education, July 1980.

Williams, John B. Outcomes of postsecondary desegregation. Nashville, TN: Vanderbilt Institute for Public Policy Studies, 1981.

Wolters, R. The new Negro on campus. Princeton, NJ: Princeton University Press, 1975.

The Effect
of Desegregation Policies
on Historically Black Public
Colleges and Universities

John Matlock

From the U.S. Supreme Court's landmark <u>Brown</u> v. <u>Board of Education</u> decisions in 1954 and 1955 up to the present, considerable attention has been directed to desegregation of elementary and secondary schools in the United States. Declaring "the fundamental principle that discrimination in public higher education is unconstitutional" (<u>Brown</u> 1955), the Court made no distinction between various levels of public education—elementary, secondary, and higher education. Yet, public institutions of higher education managed to escape the impact of the <u>Brown</u> mandates, and continued to exclude blacks legally, leaving them no choice but to attend historically black institutions. Prior to <u>Brown</u>, the Supreme Court had dealt narrowly with several issues associated with segregation in public higher education: <u>Gaines</u> v. <u>Canada</u> 1938; <u>Sipuel</u> v. <u>Board of Regents</u> 1948; <u>McLaurin</u> v. <u>Oklahoma</u> 1950.

OVERVIEW OF THE <u>ADAMS</u> CASE

In 1969, the Office for Civil Rights (OCR) in the Department of Health, Education and Welfare (HEW) concluded that ten states (Louisiana, Mississippi, Oklahoma, Arkansas, Pennsylvania, Georgia, Virginia, Maryland, Florida, and North Carolina) were operating racially segregated higher education systems in violation of the 1964 Civil Rights Act. OCR used enrollment data in establishing these violations. Racial enrollments at historically black and historically white institutions were basically the same as they had been when higher education institutions were legally segregated in these states. In other words, historically black schools were still nearly all black, and historically white schools were still virtually all white.

Based on OCR's conclusions, HEW requested the ten states to develop and submit plans designed to desegregate their dual higher education systems. Arkansas, Pennsylvania, Georgia, Maryland, and Virginia developed and submitted plans, but Louisiana, Mississippi, Oklahoma, North Carolina, and Florida refused. Furthermore, the five plans submitted to HEW were deemed unacceptable.

In 1970, the NAACP Legal Defense and Educational Fund, Inc. (LDF) filed a class action suit against HEW stating that the agency had been derelict in its duty to enforce the Civil Rights Act because it had not taken steps to compel states to desegregate their racially segregated systems of higher education. The suit requested that HEW take action to cut off federal funds to these states. HEW countered by asking that the suit be dismissed because it had the authority to decide what actions, if any, should be taken against the ten states.

In 1973, over three years after the suit was filed, the U.S. District Court in Washington, D.C. ruled that the states were in violation of the Civil Rights Act and that HEW had a duty to begin enforcement proceedings (Adams v. Richardson). The court ordered HEW to initiate enforcement proceedings within 60 days.

Black Colleges' Arguments

Various civil rights groups and educators were elated with the court's mandate, but other groups, particularly those representing black colleges and universities, viewed the mandate skeptically. Their concerns were that the desegregation mandate would be utilized by states to diminish the role of public black colleges and universities; the mandate potentially endangered the future existence of these institutions.

HEW appealed the ruling to a circuit court which upheld the lower court's ruling, but gave HEW additional time to obtain desegregation plans from the affected states. During the appeal, the National Association for Equal Opportunity in Higher Education (NAFEO), an organization of presidents of historically black institutions, intervened as amicus curiae. NAFEO argued that the historically black public institutions had not practiced segregation and discrimination, and stressed that these institutions had a unique role in higher education. NAFEO also stated that these colleges had provided compensatory and reparative educational services to black students, who historically suffered from segregated school systems as well as discrimination in employment.

Obviously swayed by NAFEO's argument, the court ruled that it was important that desegregation of public higher education be resolved on a state system-wide basis, rather than on an individual institutional basis. The court noted:

> The problem of integrating higher education must be dealt with on a statewide rather than a school-by-school basis. Perhaps the most serious problem in this area is the lack of statewide planning to provide more and better trained minority group doctors, lawyers and other professionals. A predicate for minority access to quality post-graduate programs is a viable, coordinated, statewide higher education policy that takes into account the special problems of minority students and of black colleges. As amicus points out, these black institutions currently fulfill a crucial need and will continue to play an important role in black higher education (Adams v. Richardson, D.C. Cir. 1973).

With the exception of Louisiana, which refused to submit a plan, and Mississippi, which had its plan rejected because it did not include community colleges, the states submitted desegregation plans to the Office of Civil Rights and they were accepted. OCR evaluated the plans and later said they were not specific in delineating how the delineated goals and programs would desegregate the states' higher education systems. The NAACP Legal Defense Fund filed a "Motion for Further Relief" on the basis that HEW, by accepting inadequate plans, had not lived up to its court-imposed obligations.

Again, NAFEO filed an amicus curiae brief in opposition to the "Motion for Further Relief" request. NAFEO contended that the roles and missions of traditionally black institutions were valid, and that they provided equal education to black students. According to NAFEO, without the historically black public institutions there would be no mechanism for providing education to blacks who had received inadequate training from public elementary and secondary schools as the result of segregation.

In early 1977, the court granted the Legal Defense Fund's request for relief noting that the plans accepted by HEW were inadequate, and that HEW had not fulfilled its obligation under the court order. The court ordered the plaintiffs and defendants to draft an order that HEW could utilize in negotiating acceptable plans from the six states, Arkansas, Georgia, Virginia, Oklahoma, North Carolina, and Florida, which, by law, had operated racially segregated public higher education systems. A federal court in Maryland enjoined HEW from initiating enforcement proceedings against Maryland, and Pennsylvania intervened as a defendant in the Adams case and agreed to a separate negotiation with the plaintiffs and HEW.

HEW and the plaintiffs could not reach an agreement and HEW requested an extension of time in late March 1977. On April 1, however, the court, while granting HEW an additional two months, issued a supplemental order requiring the agency to develop and issue specific criteria for the states to utilize in developing their desegregation plans. The result was a document entitled Amended Criteria Specifying the Ingredients of Acceptable Plans to Desegregate State Systems of Public Higher Education, which was accepted by the court.

The criteria developed by HEW were to apply to the six states listed above. Desegregation was to be accomplished on a statewide basis and the states were required to take affirmative steps to overcome the causes and effects of prior discrimination in public higher education. Specific goals and timetables were to be developed for desegregating faculty, administrators, nonacademic staffs, and governing boards of state public higher education systems. The states were cautioned to consider the characteristics of higher education systems which would make desegregating them different from public elementary and secondary schools. Finally, the states were instructed to recognize the unique role of the historically black colleges.

The Special Mission of Black Colleges

On this final criterion, the court in its Second Supplemental Order (Adams v. Califano 1977), specifically stated:

> The process of desegregation must not place a greater
> burden on black institutions or black students' oppor-
> tunity to receive a quality public higher education.
> The desegregation process should take into account the
> unequal status of the black colleges and the real danger
> that desegregation will diminish higher education oppor-
> tunities for blacks. Without suggesting the answer to
> this complex problem, it is the responsibility of HEW
> to devise criteria for higher education desegregation
> plans which will take into account the unique importance
> of black colleges and at the same time comply with the
> Congressional mandate.

Despite the court's caution concerning HEW's criteria for developing desegregation plans, supporters of black colleges and universities wondered if states that previously perpetuated segregated public-higher education systems, and for many years neglected and underfunded black institutions, could now do an about-face. Would these states provide the resources and leadership necessary to expand and enhance the historically black institutions? And are predominantly white institutions, which in the past excluded blacks, now committed to advancing educational opportunities for blacks, or are they more interested in filling the empty chairs that demographic data show will exist in the future?

It was the court's premise in <u>Adams</u> that long-range planning offered the best and most realistic promise for desegregating within a reasonable time, since instant desegregation probably could not be achieved. As the result of court mandates, governmental policies, and the desegregation planning processes of state higher-education systems, the current and future roles of historically black colleges and universities most certainly will change. This chapter focuses on the impact desegregation planning is having on these colleges and will have on their future roles in higher education.

PROGRESS OF DESEGREGATION PLANS

In late 1983, desegregation of higher education was still unresolved in a number of <u>Adams</u> states. In others, progress was being made toward a plan, but all were in different stages of development. The original court order required that the NAACP Legal Defense Fund approve the plans submitted by the Department of Education (DOE), but the LDF has not approved all plans accepted by the DOE. The DOE's Office for Civil Rights has approved plans in Alabama, Delaware, Kentucky, Louisiana, North Carolina (university system only), South Carolina, Missouri, Texas, Virginia, and West Virginia. Plans submitted by Arkansas, Florida, Georgia, North Carolina (community-college system), and Oklahoma had been rejected as of July 1983; Pennsylvania had just submitted its plans. Arkansas and Florida were told to add to their plans "measures designed to increase the recruitment of black students at traditionally white institutions and to increase the number of blacks employed in academic positions"; North Carolina and Oklahoma were told to submit supplemental information on how they planned to increase black enrollment at certain institutions; and Georgia officials were advised to provide specific steps to increase the amount of black faculty and staff members, as well as "to further enhance and desegregate the state's traditionally black public institutions" (McDonald 1983). All

revised plans were due to DOE on August 15, 1983 and, if they were
rejected, the affected states could face the loss of federal education
support.

A UNIQUE MERGER: TENNESSEE STATE UNIVERSITY AND THE UNIVERSITY OF TENNESSEE AT NASHVILLE

On July 1, 1979, after a ten-year court battle, the traditionally white University of Tennessee at Nashville (UTN) was merged
into historically black Tennessee State University (TSU) (Matlock
and Humphries 1979). The merger was the result of a court order
upheld by the U.S. Supreme Court when it declined to review the
case. While Tennessee is a non-Adams state, the desegregation
principles the court advanced are similar to those in the Adams
case. It was the first merger of two institutions—one traditionally
black and the other traditionally white—where the black institution
emerged as the surviving institution.

Historical Overview

In 1968, a class action suit was filed by Rita Sanders (now
Rita Geier) in the U.S. District Court in Nashville, Tennessee on
behalf of all blacks living in Tennessee, as well as all white residents, students, and faculty at Tennessee State A & I University
(now TSU), and students attending Tennessee public high schools.
The governor of Tennessee, the UTN's board of trustees, the
Tennessee Higher Education Commission (the coordinating agency
for Tennessee higher education), the U.S. Department of Health,
Education and Welfare (HEW), and the State Board of Education (the
governing body for TSU) were named as defendants in the suit.
The suit sought an injunction to prohibit UTN from expanding
its downtown Nashville campus by constructing a new building. The
basis of the suit was that expansion of UTN's Nashville campus
would perpetuate segregation at TSU and a dual public higher-
education system based on race in Tennessee. HEW was named
in the suit because it was providing some of the funds for the construction of the downtown building. HEW was eventually excused as
a defendant in the suit and then joined with the plaintiffs. It asserted
that the maintenance of several white institutions and one black institution in Tennessee violated the Fourteenth Amendment's Equal Protection Clause on the premise that students at TSU received inferior
education opportunities. HEW requested a court order requiring

that the state dismantle the dual system and that the defendants submit to the court a statewide plan for desegregating public higher education in Tennessee.

Tennessee's public higher-education system previously was segregated by law under the state constitution of 1870, and no blacks were permitted to attend any of the numerous white public institutions until 1960. Tennessee State, founded in 1912 as a land-grant institution for Negroes, was the only choice for black students prior to this time. In 1947, UTN was established in downtown Nashville, the state capital, as a two-year extension center, to provide evening instruction for part-time students employed by business and governmental agencies. UTN was accredited in 1971 to award external degrees.

After holding hearings, the court denied the plaintiff's injunction request that would have prevented the construction of UTN's building, but mandated that the defendants submit to the court a plan for desegregating higher education in Tennessee. The court said that UTN did not show intentions of becoming a degree-granting institution and was not in direct competition for students with TSU since the two schools served vastly different clienteles. The court concluded that expansion of UTN would not contribute to the perpetuation of a dual public higher-education system in the state.

The defendants submitted a plan that offered recommendations rather than specific plans of action. These recommendations included recruiting black high-school students to attend white colleges and universities, increasing black faculty at white campuses, recruiting white students and faculty to go to TSU, and providing joint TSU and UTN academic programs. The court was neutral on the plan and directed the defendants to report on their recommendations and to develop a more specific plan.

The defendants submitted numerous reports over a period of years. The court continued to maintain that, while progress was being made in breaking up the state's dual educational system, the recommendations aimed at resolving the problems associated with white UTN and black TSU were not satisfactory. The court finally indicated that the plan submitted by the defendants would not work and ordered that a new plan which would involve developing programs at TSU to attract white students and to desegregate its faculty. The defendants were also asked to consider the possibility of merging TSU and UTN.

A second plan was submitted which the court accepted as minimal. This plan included selecting white faculty at TSU over black applicants, special TSU scholarships for white students, constructing a business building and a library, and transferring UTN's social work program to TSU's campus but maintaining it under UTN's control.

    Several subsequent reports reflected little progress on the plan. TSU had attracted few white students. Additionally, UTN was given degree-granting status in 1971. UTN now offered undergraduate degrees in approximately 22 areas including a master's degree in business administration. Furthermore, the Tennessee Higher Education Commission (THEC) recommended that merger was the only way to eliminate the segregated public higher-education system in Tennessee.

    Finally, in 1977, while accepting the statewide desegregation plan, the court ordered the merger of TSU and UTN and stipulated that the merger be completed within three years from July 1, 1977. The court noted the failure of the various previous plans in desegregating TSU and UTN. In 1977, enrollment at TSU was 84 percent black, 15 percent nonblack, and 1 percent foreign students; 23 percent of the 284 faculty members were white. The court indicated that, while most of the white institutions had made significant progress in desegregating their institutions, TSU had had little success in attracting white students.

    At the time of the merger order, TSU was under the direction of the Tennessee State Board of Regents (SBR), which was formed in 1972 as the governing board for six regional universities and ten community colleges in Tennessee. The UTN system comprises four campuses and has a separate governing body. One of TSU's major concerns was that the SBR, not TSU, was given authority by the court to plan and implement the merger. In many cases, TSU could only make recommendations to the SBR for their consideration.

    TSU was in the position of being ordered by a court to have another institution merge with it, without retaining control of selection of personnel or organizational structure. Additionally, the chancellor of the SBR at the time of the merger had been UTN's chancellor prior to his appointment in 1975.

    The defendants appealed the decision; but, on April 13, 1979, the U.S. Sixth Circuit Court of Appeals in Cincinnati, Ohio upheld the decision. The appeals court supported the lower court's finding that, although the state's plan for desegregating public-higher education in Tennessee was acceptable, TSU "required special attention because it was the heart of the dual system," and that previous plans and the expansion of UTN "impeded the required dismantling of the dual system." The appeals court decreed that the district court did not exceed its power in ordering the merger. The defendants appealed the case to the U.S. Supreme Court, which declined to hear it.

Impact of the Merger and Desegregation Policies

As the result of the merger, TSU's enrollment rose from 5,358 students in fall 1978 to 8,438 in fall 1979. In fall 1978 the enrollment of UTN at Nashville was 5,419; 805 or 15 percent were black students. So the combined enrollment could have been close to 11,000 students, but many white students from UTN did not enroll in TSU after the merger.

TSU's enrollment declined from 83.1 percent black in 1978 to 60.5 percent black in 1979 after the merger. In 1978, 63.3 percent (219 of 346) of TSU's faculty was black. After the merger only 44.5 percent were black (216 out of 406). The percentage of black administrators dropped from 90.8 (59 of 65) in 1978 to 68.8 (64 of 93) after the merger.

The merger created an interesting mix of students, exclusive of race. Formerly UTN was a commuter school attracting part-time, older, working students compared to TSU's residential, younger, full-time student body. After the merger, TSU acquired the UTN facility on a lease arrangement. The campuses, four miles apart, remain much the way they were prior to the merger, causing some concern that there are still a predominantly white and a predominantly black campus. This will probably change in the future as TSU administrators shift programs and activities between the two campuses. To reduce the shock of the merger, full integration of the two campuses did not occur during the first year.

From 1977 to 1979 throughout the state college system, excluding TSU, desegregation efforts have resulted in only small percentage increases in black student enrollment—from 11.6 percent to 18.8 percent (15,137 to 15,495). The percentage of black undergraduates increased from 12.5 to 12.6 of total undergraduate enrollment (13,748 to 13,892). Black graduate enrollment rose from 7.2 percent (1,305) of total graduate enrollment to 8.5 percent (1,603). There were only slight increases in the percentage of black faculty (3.1 to 3.4 percent) and of black administrators (3.7 to 4.2 percent).

IMPACT OF DESEGREGATION ON
BLACK INSTITUTIONS

One major criticism of desegregation plans by officials at historically black institutions was that black administrators had little input into the planning process (Haynes 1979, 1980). In some cases, they were asked to submit data, but institutional self-studies and other plans were disregarded.

Desegregation planning has resulted in a closer scrutiny of historically black institutions in various states. Not only were these institutions underfunded in the past, but they were given far less political, technical, and management support than other institutions. In other words, as long as the institutions educated only black students, they received little assistance or attention. Now, as states attempt to desegregate these institutions, the management and fiscal abilities of the administrators are being called into question. Numerous historically black schools are undergoing management reviews that are resulting in administrative changes from presidents on down. For example, the University of North Carolina system has begun a study to assess the administrator of its five traditionally black schools; and the Tennessee Board of Regents conducted a yearlong evaluation of the president of TSU and his administration almost a year prior to the merger of UTN into TSU.

Role Changes for Black Colleges

In some cases, the states' new activities recommended for historically black institutions appear to alter the roles and missions of these institutions. For example, one state has selected its black university to become an urban institution, despite its being a land-grant institution. This could drastically alter its status and role. Furthermore, some states propose activities and programs for their historically black institutions that disregard the existing roles and missions of the institutions, instead of enhancing and expanding those roles.

Few states, in their desegregation plans, acknowledge having any prior responsibility for the problems of their public black institutions, despite years of underfunding, neglect, and the building of neighboring, competing higher-education institutions. In fact, one gets the impression from several plans that the states almost blame the black institutions for their problems.

Administrators at historically black institutions see these efforts as a ploy to discredit the black institutions. One administrator noted that most fiscal problems at black schools are the result of underfunding. He stated that all state colleges and universities are audited each year and are not permitted to have a deficit budget. He wondered why these fiscal problems and deficits were not identified by state auditors years ago, and why the states did nothing to help the traditionally black schools to resolve them.

Emphasis on Attracting White Students

As Haynes (1979, 1980) noted, some desegregation plans show little evidence of any sound rationale or logic for determining the academic requirements of the historically black institutions. Programs are proposed for these institutions without the benefit of analysis of employment needs and opportunities in the state. The concern appears to be to develop academic activities at the black institutions to attract white students, rather than to address the needs of the institutions and the state and local communities.

Black institutions generally have not been successful in attracting white students, despite the statewide implementation of desegregation plans. Yet there has been a significant increase in the number of black students attending predominantly white institutions. Enrollment at historically black institutions continues to drop as black students have greater access to other educational settings including community colleges, proprietary schools, as well as the white institutions. The desegregation plans do not adequately address this problem, nor that of the decreasing numbers of blacks who are entering colleges and universities.

Goals to increase the number of black students at historically white institutions tend to be low and are easily obtained in some of the desegregation plans. For example, a 150 percent increase of black students in a discipline that enrolls an abnormally low number of black students will still result in small numbers, although the percentage goal may have been reached.

Faculty Changes

On the other hand, white schools have not been successful in attracting black faculty and administrators, despite the desegregation and affirmative action plans. In some states, where white institutions have increased their black faculties, they have done so by "raiding" historically black colleges. The result is little overall change in the number of black faculty in a particular system. Most of the desegregation plans compare faculty salaries among institutions but do not make it possible to reach conclusions regarding their equity; important variables such as years in rank, discipline, highest degree awarded, and sex are not controlled.

How Will Desegregation Be Funded?

While the intent of the court was to eliminate public higher-education segregation through systemwide planning in the <u>Adams</u>

states, some plans show considerable evidence of individual institutional planning rather than systemwide planning. The quality and consistency of statistical data included in the desegregation plans vary considerably. It is apparent that states that lacked an adequate data base relied more on data submitted by individual institutions.

The funding mechanisms of the desegregation plans reviewed seem very unrealistic. For example, one plan suggested that it would take approximately $90 million to bring the state's traditionally black institutions up to par with their counterparts, but the plan did not indicate the source of the additional funds. Furthermore, several states suggested that funds to assist the historically black schools would come from higher education allocations, thus inviting a competitive environment among institutions that see little chance of obtaining the necessary resources to adequately operate their campuses.

A key omission in all the desegregation plans, primarily because it was not required, is a description of the legislative process relative to higher education in each state. For example, what involvement do the governor and the legislature have in the budget development and approval process?

Monitoring and Evaluation

Some plans leave the monitoring of the desegregation process to the agency that develops the plan. In one state, no provisions were made for a citizen's advisory board to monitor the progress of the desegregation process. Some plans also fail to establish an adequate process for evaluating the impact of proposed changes on various institutions. Yet, careful evaluation is a requisite of any ongoing desegregation plan.

RECOMMENDATIONS

More detailed research is needed on the potential effects that desegregation has had and will have on the historically black institutions. Without this information, it will be difficult to develop and evaluate plans for the inevitable changes that will come. Considerable analytic research has been conducted on the impacts of desegregation in elementary and secondary schools but there is a paucity of research that examines the actual impact of desegregation on public higher education, especially at the institutional level. The following recommendations for change (which are directed to black institutions, states, and students), therefore, depend on impact analysis or must incorporate research and evaluation in the planning and execution of programs.

• Before various academic programs and policies are implemented, historically black public institutions should conduct impact analyses to determine potential effects of the programs and policies on their campuses, as well as on how the programs meet the needs of the community and the state. Such analyses will help to identify needed institutional support and resources to sustain new programs and the effect these new initiatives will have on current and future enrollments.

• Research is needed on the economic and social impacts that black institutions have on their communities, and whether a new and different clientele will alter their historic roles and missions.

• Historically black public institutions will need to determine what impact their state's proposed changes and desegregation planning efforts will have on them, review and revise their missions, develop long-range plans and strategies, and collect and analyze longitudinal data. Moreover, they should take an active role in the desegregation process, primarily to assure that proposed plans concur with their self-studies.

• Black institutions, as a group, should develop and implement improved recruiting and marketing strategies, in order to effectively compete with other institutions.

• Black institutions should conduct analyses of their management and resource allocation/utilization processes, to determine how effectively and efficiently they operate, how programs and staff are evaluated, and how limited funds are distributed and utilized.

• State desegregation plans should be consistent with educational and other master plans, rather than treating them separately from other statewide long-range plans.

• The states must define clearly what factors constitute a desegregated public higher-education system, and collect data on attrition, graduation, and transfer rates of minority students. They should also expand the roles of historically black institutions in the areas of research, graduate studies, and public service activities. Too much attention has thus far been placed on processes rather than significant outcomes.

• States should analyze salary inequities between black and white institutions, develop strategies for increasing the graduation rates of black high-school students, and increase the number of black students in undergraduate and graduate programs. This will not only influence future student enrollments but will also have an impact on the future available pool of black faculty.

• Additional research is needed on the high attrition rates of black students, particularly at white institutions, and why a higher percentage of black students complete their studies at black institutions. Finally, some data to determine why there are large numbers of black students attending community colleges would be useful. Would these students attend historically black public and private four-year institutions if they had the opportunity or do they represent a unique group that would not attend any other type of institution?

This chapter revealed that some historically black public institutions have benefited from the desegregation process, while others have not. As a result of desegregation planning, changes are now being implemented that might alter and diminish their roles and missions in the future, rather than enhance and expand them. Officials at many black public institutions feel that desegregation will be used to eliminate or merge them into neighboring historically white institutions. Only the future will show whether the Adams principles will enable all citizens to attend a higher-education institution of their choice, and whether current desegregation planning will strengthen and expand the long-standing and viable roles of historically black public institutions in U.S. higher education.

REFERENCES

Adams v. Richardson. 356 F. Supp. 92 (D.D.C. 1973).

_____. 480 F 2nd 1159 (D.D.Cir. 1973).

Adams v. Califano. Civil Action No. 3095-70, United States District of Columbia, Second Supplemental Order, April 1, 1977.

Bell, Derrick. "The politics of desegregation." Change, October 1979.

"Black colleges show black percentage drops." Memphis Commercial Appeal, April 13, 1980.

Braddock, Jomills. The perpetuation of segregation across levels of education: A behavioral assessment of the contract-hypothesis. Baltimore, MD: Center for Social Organization of Schools, Johns Hopkins University, October 12, 1979.

Braddock, Jomills, and James McPartland. The perpetuation of segregation from elementary-secondary schools to higher education. Unpublished study. Baltimore, MD: Center for Social Organization of Schools, Johns Hopkins University, 1980.

Brown v. Board of Education. 347 U.S. 483 (1954).

_____. 349 U.S. 294 (1955).

Carter-Williams, Mary. Profile of enrollments in the historically black colleges. Washington, D.C.: Institute for Services to Education, 1978.

Change magazine. "Report: Faith, hope and parity." October 1979.

Coalition for the Concerns of Blacks in Postsecondary Education. Report Number 3. Columbia, SC: Coalition for the Concerns of Blacks in Postsecondary Education, March 1, 1980.

Commercial Appeal (Memphis, TN). "Iranians lament tuition measure." June 30, 1980.

_____. "Tuition hike for Iranians is temporarily prohibited." July 4, 1980.

Crain, Robert, and Rita Mahard. High school racial composition, composition, achievement and college attendance. Santa Monica, CA: Rand Corp., 1977.

Crossland, F. E. Minority access to college: A Ford foundation report. New York: Schocken Books, 1971.

Davis, J. A., C. Burkheimer, and A. Borders-Patterson. The impact of special services programs in higher education for "disadvantaged" students. Princeton, NJ: Educational Testing Service, June 1975.

Fields, Cheryl M. "U.S. accepts 5-year, $19.8 million plan to desegregate South Carolina's colleges." The Chronicle of Higher Education (July 27, 1981).

Florida State Department of Education. Florida's commitment to equal access and equal opportunity in public higher education. Tallahassee, FL: State University System of Florida, Revised Plans for Equalizing Educational Opportunity in Public Higher Education, February 1978.

214 / John Matlock

Geier v. Dunn. 337, F. Supp. 573, 1972, U.S. District Court for
the Middle District of Tennessee.

Georgia State Board of Regents. Fourth segment of a plan for the
further desegregation of the university system of Georgia. Submitted to the Office for Civil Rights, HEW. Atlanta, GA: Georgia
State Board of Regents, October 19, 1978.

Goodrick, Welch. "Minorities in two year colleges." Community
and Junior College Journal (December–January 1972-73).

Haynes, Leonard L., III. A critical analysis of the Adams case:
A sourcebook. Washington, D.C.: Institute for Services to
Education, 1978.

_____. The Adams mandate: A blueprint for realizing equal edu-
cational opportunity and attainment. Washington, D.C.: Institute
for Services to Education, 1979.

_____. An updating of desegregation planning and its effect upon
historically black public colleges and universities. Paper presented at the American Association for Higher Education, Washington, D.C., March 7, 1980.

Haynes, Leonard L., III, Henry Cobb, and Robert T. Homes. An
analysis of the Arkansas–Georgia statewide desegregation plans.
Washington, D.C.: Institute for Services to Education, 1979.

"Hearings for University of North Carolina system on ending federal
funding begin July 22nd." Minority Higher Education Reports 1
(July 4, 1980).

"Improved access found at two-year colleges, but other problems
cited in report." Minority Higher Education Reports 1 (June 20,
1980).

Institute for the Study of Educational Policy. Minorities in two-year
colleges: A report and recommendations for change. Washington, D.C.: Howard University, 1980.

Kolstad, A. Attrition from college: The class of 1972 two and one-
half years after high school graduation. Washington, D.C.: Department of Health, Education and Welfare, National Center for
Education Statistics, 1977.

Lloyd, Crystal. Adams vs. Califano: A case study in the politics of regulations. Cambridge, MA: Sloan Commission on Government and Higher Education, Revised 1978.

Maryland State Board for Higher Education. Fourth mid-year desegregation status report for public postsecondary education institutions in the state of Maryland. Annapolis, MD: Maryland State Board for Higher Education, July 1978.

_____. Summary of the fifth annual desegregation status report for public postsecondary education institutions in the state of Maryland. Annapolis, MD: Maryland State Board for Higher Education, 1979.

Matlock, John, and Frederick Humphries. The planning of the merger of two public higher education institutions: A case study of Tennessee State University and the University of Tennessee at Nashville. Paper presented at the Association for Institutional Research Nineteenth Annual Forum. San Diego, CA, May 13-17, 1979.

McDonald, Kim. "U.S. rejects college desegregation plans of 5 states, threatens to cut off funds." Chronicle of Higher Education (July 13, 1983).

McLaurin v. Oklahoma. 339, U.S. 637 (1950).

McPartland, James R. Desegregation and equity in higher education and employment: Is progress related to the desegregation of elementary and secondary schools? Baltimore, MD: Johns Hopkins University's Center for Social Organization of Schools, May 1978.

Middleton, Lorenzo. "A black university in Oklahoma is given a new urban mission." The Chronicle of Higher Education (August 7, 1978).

_____. "Desegregation in 5 states slowed by decrease in black enrollment." The Chronicle of Higher Education (January 21, 1980).

_____. "Louisiana proposes compromise on higher education desegregation." The Chronicle of Higher Education (June 23, 1980).

_____. "Desegregation Plan for N.C. colleges labeled 'sellout' by NAACP lawyer." The Chronicle of Higher Education (July 15, 1981).

Mingle, James. Black enrollment in higher education: Trends in the nation and the South. Atlanta, GA: Southern Regional Education Board, 1979.

_____. Black and Hispanic enrollment in higher education, 1978: Trends in the nation and the South. Draft document. Atlanta, GA: Southern Regional Education Board, 1980.

Missouri, ex rel. Gaines v. Canada. 305, U.S. 337 (1938).

Morris, Lorenzo. The role of testing in institutional selectivity and black access to higher education. Paper presented at the annual meeting of the American Educational Research Association. San Francisco, CA, April 1979.

National Advisory Committee on Black Higher Education and Black Colleges and Universities. Access of black Americans to higher education: How open is the door? Washington, D.C.: U.S. Government Printing Office, January 1979.

"N.C. to assess 5 black colleges." The Chronicle of Higher Education (June 16, 1980).

New Orleans Times Picayune. "The States-Item. Accord gives millions to La. black colleges." August 22, 1981.

North Carolina University Board of Governors. The revised North Carolina state plan for the future elimination of racial inequality in public higher education systems, phase II: 1978-83. Chapel Hill, NC: North Carolina University Board of Governors, May 1978.

Payne, Ethel. Black colleges: Can they survive? Challenges and changes. The Ford Fellow in Education Journalism Report. Washington, D.C.: George Washington University's Institute for Educational Leadership, January 1979.

Peterson, Marvin, R. T. Blackburn, Z. F. Gamson, C. H. Arce, R. W. Davenport, and J. R. Mingle. Black students on white campuses: The impact of increased black enrollments. Ann Arbor, MI: University of Michigan Press, 1978.

Pettigrew, Thomas. "Continuing barriers to desegregated education in the South." Sociology of Education 38 (Winter 1965).

Savannah State College Desegregation Committee. A plan for the desegregation of Savannah State College. Savannah, GA: Savannah State College Desegregation Committee, June 26, 1978.

Sipuel v. Board of Regents. 332 U.S. G31 (1948).

Southern Regional Education Board. Fact book on higher education in the South: 1975 and 1976. 1977.

_____. Racial composition of faculties in public colleges and universities in the South. 1979.

Sweatt v. Painter. 339, U.S. 628 (1950)

Tennessee Higher Education Commission, State Board of Regents, University of Tennessee Board of Trustees. 1979 desegregation progress report. Nashville, TN: Tennessee Higher Education Commission, January 17, 1980.

U.S. Commission on Civil Rights. Social indicators of equality for minorities and women. Washington, D.C.: Government Printing Office, August 1978.

United States Court of Appeals for the Sixth Circuit. Case Number 77-1621 and 77-1623; 77-1625; Geier, et al. vs. University of Tennessee, et al. Cincinnati, Ohio. Decided and filed April 13, 1979.

_____. Case Number 77-1622 and 77-1624; Richardson, et al. vs. Blanton, et al. Cincinnati, Ohio. Decided and filed on April 13, 1979.

U.S. Department of Health, Education and Welfare. Criteria specifying the ingredients of acceptable plans to desegregate state systems of public higher education. Prepared by the Department of Health, Education and Welfare pursuant to the Second Supplemental Order of the U.S. District Court of the District of Columbia entered on April 1, 1977, Washington, D.C., July 5, 1977.

_____. National Center for Education Statistics. Traditionally black institutions of higher education: Their identification and selected characteristics. Washington, D.C.: HEW, 1978.

Watson, Bernard. "Through the academic gateway." Change, October 1979.

Weinberg, Meyer, Charles Grigg, David Sly, and Louis Pol. Three myths: An exposure of popular misconceptions about school desegregation. Atlanta, GA: Southern Regional Council, 1976.

12

Student Enrollment
Trends in Black Colleges:
Past, Current,
and Future Perspectives

Mary Carter-Williams

The dramatic growth in black access to predominantly white institutions since 1968 has been accompanied by increasing speculation about the survival of the historically black colleges. Although black-college enrollment patterns have not been subjected to comprehensive empirical analysis, existing research indicates that they tend to parallel those in predominantly white institutions (Blake, Lambert, and Martin 1974).

Given the grim outlook projected for higher education through the year 2000 and the emerging sociopolitical and economic climate of the nation, the fact that black college enrollments reflect national enrollments raises serious questions about the future of these institutions. This chapter will examine past and present trends that influence black-college enrollments with emphasis on the implications for the size and composition of future enrollments, the future roles of these institutions, public policy, and future research.

Historically, the clientele of the black colleges has tended to be female and from families earning less than $6,000 per year, although in recent years a significant proportion have been from families with incomes of $10,000 or more. Few of these students are drawn from the top 10 percent of their high school graduating classes (Morris 1979) and approximately 90 percent of them would not be admitted to the more selective predominantly white institutions based on their standardized test scores (Kumi and Williams 1979). Although the black colleges presently enroll less than 20 percent of the blacks in higher education, they produced approximately 40 percent of the total number of black baccalaureates in 1976.*

---

*Caution must be employed when assessing the enrollments of the black colleges by race because available data on them are frag-

TRENDS IN HIGHER EDUCATION ENROLLMENTS

There has been a phenomenal change in the size of higher education enrollments over the past 20 years. In 1965, an estimated 5.5 million students were enrolled in institutions of higher learning; by fall 1978 the total enrollment had escalated to 11.5 million, more than double the earlier figure. Fall enrollment in 1982 exceeded 12 million. This unprecedented increase in enrollment was accompanied by sharp changes in the composition of the student population. Prior to 1965, most students in higher education were white, male, and between the ages of 18 and 21—the traditional college age. By 1976, approximately half the students were older than the traditional college age, nearly half were women, and a significant percentage were minorities. By fall 1979, more than half of all college students were women (5.9 million versus 5.7 million men).

The growth in higher education enrollments between 1966 and 1976 (Table 1) paralleled the similar but more accelerated growth in black enrollment in higher education. As Table 1 shows, black enrollment increased by 277 percent between 1965-66 and 1976-77, while total enrollment doubled during that period. Much of this increase, as Arce noted in 1976, was due to the increased admittance of blacks into predominantly white institutions between 1968 and 1974.

Despite these gains, an examination of the flow of students through the educational system brings into focus the serious gaps in equity blacks still face. Rough approximations of the number of black and white first-graders (per 100) who enter at various levels and remain in the educational system are presented in Figure 1. Figure 1 illustrates that blacks continue to lag behind whites in high school completion rates (76 blacks versus 85 whites), college-enrolling rates (36 blacks versus 41 whites), and college-completion rates (4 blacks versus 14 whites). Significant losses in black students occur between the tenth and twelfth grades, between high school graduation and entry into college, and during the first year of college.*

---

mented and inconsistent. The enrollment-related studies prepared by the Institute for Services to Education, Inc., the American Council on Education, the Southern Regional Education Board, the United States Bureau of the Census, and the Bureau of Labor Statistics, Department of Labor, were particularly useful in preparing this paper.

*In order to arrive at actual numbers of students in each stage, the reader must remember that each figure represents the proportion of students from the previous stage who continue their studies. Thus, 98 white and 97 black students complete grade 10; and 87

FIGURE 1

Typical Education Flow Pattern: Black and White Students

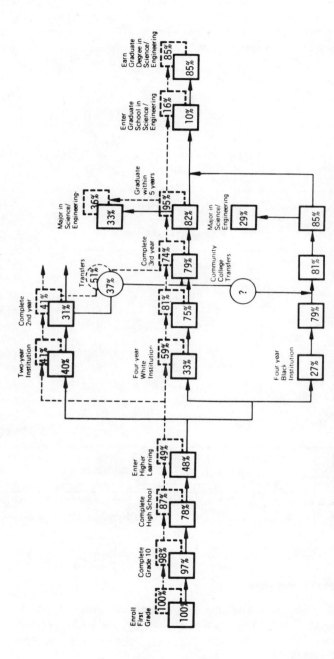

Note: Each figure represents the proportion of students from the previous stage who continue their studies.
Source: This chart is a modification of the student flow chart included in Joel B. Aronson, An analysis of supported projects to test methods for increasing the access of ethnic minority students to careers in science and technology, National Science Foundation, November 1976, p. 43.

221

In addition, Figure 1 indicates not only the disproportionate number of blacks who enroll in two-year institutions, but also the disproportionate number who drop out of these institutions. Approximately four of every 18 black students who enter two-year colleges graduate, and only one of these transfers to an upper division institution.

TABLE 1

First-time and Total Enrollments
of Black Colleges, 1966-78

Year	First-time First-year Enrollment	Total Enrollment
1966	42,615	129,444
1967	40,007	148,301
1968	40,825	154,977
1969	40,024	161,709
1970	42,674	168,328
1971	42,814	178,143
1972	41,378	181,209
1973	39,372	184,559
1974	44,265	189,001
1975	54,498	211,170
1976	50,411	211,713
1977	49,161	212,574

Sources: E. Blake, Jr., L. K. Lambert, and J. L. Martin, Degrees granted and enrollment trends in historically black institutions (Washington, D. C.: Institute for Services to Education, 1975) and unpublished reports of the Institute for Services to Education, 1978.

---

percent of 98 white students and 78 percent of 97 black students complete high school, which equal 85 and 76 students, respectively. Therefore, the numbers get progressively smaller as one moves through the various stages.

What lies ahead for both blacks and whites in higher education will be determined by a broad range of factors: tuition costs, family income, inflation, public policy, student values and choices, among others. The structural diversity of higher education, family income, and public policy will also have particular relevance in determining the number of blacks who enter and succeed in college.

FUTURE TRENDS IN BLACK COLLEGE ENROLLMENTS

Size of Future Black Enrollments

In 1971, the Carnegie Commission projected that black enrollment in higher education would reach 1.1 million by 1980 and that the enrollment in the historically black colleges would reach 300,000 by the year 2000. By 1977, the national black college enrollment had exceeded the Commission's yearly goal by 3,000 students, even though the somewhat larger increases that occurred in the previous decade and the early 1970s were no longer evident (see Table 1). In the same year, the total enrollment of the black colleges reached a high of 212,574 students—70.8 percent of the number predicted by the commission for the end of the century (see Table 1).

Hence, between 1966 and 1977, the total enrollment of the black colleges climbed 50.7 percent (70,700), growing at an average annual rate of 4.2 percent compared to a higher education annual growth rate of 4.5 percent. The proportion of females rose from 53.7 percent (74,884 of 139,444) to 54.6 percent (116,065 of 212,574) compared to a 0.9 percent decrease in the proportion of males. Graduate enrollment rose 231 percent, an increase of 11,145 students (Table 2), while undergraduate enrollment grew by 38 percent. Between 1970 and 1977, a 71.9 percent increase (14,778) was reported in the part-time enrollments of 100 black colleges; full-time enrollment grew by 22.1 percent (Williams 1980). New first-year students contributed to a mere 8.6 percent to the increase in students between 1966 and 1977.

Recent shifts in black college enrollment indicate the challenge these institutions will face in maintaining stable enrollments in the future. In fall 1978, the total enrollment of the black colleges (200,140) fell 5.8 percent (12,434) for the first time in a decade; first-year enrollment dropped 13.1 percent (6,460), while national black enrollment (14-to-34 age cohort) dropped 7.5 percent (U.S. Department of Labor, Bureau of Labor Statistics 1973 and unpublished 1980 data). In most instances, the across-the-board losses in black college enrollment were an extension of trends that had

been developing since 1976. In that year, four-year public enrollment declined for the third consecutive year (6.1 percent or 8,728);
four-year private enrollment fell for the first time since 1973. The
proportion of male students dropped precipitously in 1976, falling
below the 1966 level (45.3 versus 46.3 percent) and graduate enrollment declined by 25.1 percent. According to Mingle (1980), the
total number of black graduate students in higher education fell by
2.4 percent between 1976 and 1978.

TABLE 2

Percentage Change in Graduate Enrollments
at Black Colleges, 1967-77

Year	Number of Graduate Students	Percentage of Change
1967	8,488	—
1968	10,928	28.7
1969	12,003	9.8
1970	13,726	14.4
1971	15,505	13.0
1972	16,549	6.7
1973	19,919	20.4
1974	20,711	3.9
1975	22,233	7.4
1976	20,692	-6.9
1977	19,633	-5.1

Sources: E. Blake, Jr., L. K. Lambert, and J. L. Martin, Degrees granted and enrollment trends in historically black colleges:
An eight-year study (Washington, D.C.: The Institute for Services
to Education, 1974) and raw data derived from surveys of the Institute for Services to Education, 1974-78.

The continuing downturn of the economy with the accompanying
high inflation and high unemployment rates and the consequent retrenchment in federal support of higher education are primarily responsible for the recent crunch in black-college enrollment. It is
unlikely, therefore, that their enrollments will climb beyond 300,000
by the year 2000 without planned intervention.

Where Will the Students Come From ?

Although demography favors the black college-age cohort, the increasingly disproportionate ratio of black dropouts to graduates, declining college-going rates of black high-school graduates, and the growing competition for students in general will shrink the size of the traditional student markets of the black colleges throughout the remainder of this century.

During the first half of the 1970s, the total number of black high-school graduates increased by 22.2 percent (66,000) as opposed to a 16.7 percent (412,000) increase in white graduates (U.S. DOL, BLS 1973; 1978). The number of black high-school dropouts declined by 9.5 percent (16,000), the ratio of black high-school dropouts to graduates reached an all-time low of 42 percent, and the number of white dropouts increased by 6.2 percent. During the latter half of the 1970s, the enrollment patterns of both blacks and whites reflected the leveling off in the numbers of high-school graduates and the bulge in dropouts that had started in the late 1960s. In 1978, at the end of the nine-year period, the black dropout ratio had again climbed to 50 percent, as it was in 1972-73 and 1973-74.

Similarly, the college-going rates of black and white high school graduates were leveling off throughout much of the 1970s. This was particularly true for blacks in 1973, a depression year, when their college-going rate fell from 48 percent in the previous year to 35 percent. Nevertheless, the college-going rates of black and white secondary school graduates averaged 46 to 50 percent, respectively, throughout this period.

These comparisons illustrate the differential impact of the economy and other external forces on the progression of blacks through the educational system. During the 1969 and 1973 recessions, the high-school dropout and college-attendance rates of blacks fell precipitously compared to less dramatic changes in the rates of whites. During the latter recession, black participation in the military again began to increase, compared to that of whites. Further, the Bureau of Labor Statistics in 1974 reported that the majority of the 1973 black high-school graduates who did not go on to college were employed by October of that year, but at a significantly lower rate than that for whites (69 versus 82 percent) (U.S. Department of Labor 1974).

Reversing the Trend

Despite the dim outlook for an improved economy in the decades ahead, there are real possibilities for reversing this trend and broadening the clientele of the black colleges:

— Annually nearly a million black and low-income youths in
the 16-to-24 age cohort drop out of high school.
— The size of the black 18-24 age cohort of the civilian population has reached 3.6 million and will grow by 1.4 percent between now and 2000 (Carter-Williams 1978).
— Annually, more than a million recent graduates in the
16-to-24 age cohort do not enroll in college.
— Several states outside the South are expected to have large
increases in the black college-age population (18-to-24)
during the 1980s, including Arizona, California, Colorado,
Delaware, Indiana, Iowa, Massachusetts, Michigan, Minnesota, Nebraska, Nevada, New Jersey, New York, Oklahoma, Oregon, Rhode Island, Washington, and Wisconsin
(Henderson 1977).

Changing Attitudes

It is likely that growing changes in the attitudes of black students and parents toward the black colleges, especially of blacks in
predominantly white high schools, present opportunities for expanding the future student markets of the black colleges. A study
(Gaines 1979) by the Institute for Services to Education (ISE) found
that 33 percent of the students surveyed at three black institutions
preferred a black college. The majority reported that their choice
of institution was based also on the availability of strong academic
programs—a finding not only consistent with the college selection
criteria of entering students nationally, but also with those of both
black and white students attending predominantly white institutions.

The ISE study also noted the role of parental preference in
the college choices of these students. Twenty-seven percent of the
students sampled made their college choice based on their parents'
wishes. Yet, a recent sampling of 2,000 of the 5,000 participants
in a survey of the viewpoints of blacks on a wide range of social,
political, and economic issues demonstrates the ambivalent feelings
many black parents appear to have toward the black colleges (Black
Enterprise August 1980).

Although a large proportion of the participants (42 percent)
preferred that their child attend a predominantly black college,
more than half (54.9 percent) preferred other institutions. Simultaneously, more than 80 percent felt that these institutions serve
a purpose that cannot be addressed by other colleges. Ninety percent of them agreed that "there is a difference for the black student
who attends black colleges" (Black Enterprise August 1980, p. 82).
Unfortunately, the results of the study provided no clue to the
meaning of this finding.

Astin and Cross also noted the importance of relatives and significant others in influencing the college choices of blacks (Morris 1979). They found that, in addition to seeking good or special academic programs and low tuition costs, black male students depend heavily on the advice of relatives (15.8 percent), teachers (10.9 percent), former students (20.7 percent), guidance counselors (11.7 percent), and friends (12.6 percent). The advice of teachers, nonacceptance by any other institution, and low tuition appeared to be significantly less important to the institutional selections of black female students. These findings were less true for blacks in predominantly white institutions and least true for whites in similar institutions.

Racial Composition of High Schools

Although few studies address the importance of the racial composition of high schools in the college choices of black students, it appears that attendance at predominantly white high schools functions as a deterrent to the enrollment of black students into black colleges. For example, the Henning study of three generations of entering freshmen at historically black colleges found that nearly 50 percent of these students were from high schools which were "all black" or "two-thirds black" (Henning 1979). Only a little over one-fifth of them were from high schools that were two-thirds white (20.3 percent).

Two other studies tend to support these findings. In a demonstration study, Armor (1972) found that the black students who opt to attend predominantly white suburban high schools are more likely to choose to attend four-year colleges and more prestigious schools. When school district size and social class were held constant, Crain and Mahard (1978) found significant regional differences in the college attendance and survival rates of black graduates of predominantly white high schools. Northern black graduates were more likely than Southern blacks to pursue a college education and were almost twice as likely to have achieved junior status three years later. Of particular relevance to the issue of student choice was these authors' finding that the predominantly white high schools in the South send few black students to black colleges. They state:

> Black colleges have been the traditional form of
> higher education for black students in segregated
> schools. The remaining all-black high schools in
> the South still maintain a tradition of sending black
> students into these schools. The predominantly
> white schools generally do not. They send a some-
> what larger number of blacks to predominantly

white schools, but not enough to make up for the students who are not going to black colleges (Crain and
Mahard 1978, pp. 129-30).

Crain and Mahard go on to state that the racial composition of the
staff in desegregated schools is sometimes a more important factor
in the quality of the school's functioning than is the racial composition of the student body. They also indicate that when racial composition is controlled, there is a direct relationship between the
proportion of black teachers in the school and the grades and college attendance rates of black students in both the North and the
South. It appears likely, therefore, that the presence of black
faculty and counselors in predominantly white high schools has a
positive influence on the number of black graduates who matriculate
in black colleges.

Profile of Future Black-College Students

In the future, the profile of the "typical black-college student"
will change. Students attending these institutions will vary more
than ever before in age, race, academic achievement, and family
background characteristics. Less than 15 years ago, it was possible to say that the average student entering the historically black
colleges was female, black, 18 years of age, and from a family
with an income of $3,000 or less. Except for the continuing pre-
dominance of black-female students in these institutions, these are
no longer typical characteristics, and, as we move toward the end
of the twentieth century, they will become increasingly diverse.
In the Henning (1979) study of three generations of students
attending black colleges, he found that a significant change had
occurred in their demographic characteristics: fewer students
were matriculating immediately after graduating from high school.
Between 1969 and 1975, Henning's sample of 18-year-olds dropped
from 67 to 48 percent, while the cohort of students 20 years of age
and older grew larger. Although a significantly larger percentage
of these black students were from families with incomes of $10,000
and over, because of inflation, little change had occurred in the
income levels of their families over the six-year period. A 6 percent drop (from 68 to 62 percent) was noted in the percentage of
students who reported family income levels below $6,200 between
1969 and 1975.
The changing characteristics of students attending black colleges is most evident in those institutions that have become 30
percent or more white in recent years (Gaines 1979). Examples of

these schools are Bluefield State College (West Virginia), Bowie State College (Maryland), Kentucky State University, Delaware State University, and Lincoln University (Missouri). The white students attending such institutions are older (20 years and over), more independent, and career-oriented. The majority of them work full-time and are enrolled in graduate programs. They tend to commute, are married, have estimated family incomes of $15,000 and above, and do not rely on their parents for financial support. The black students, on the other hand, have the same demographic characteristics as those attending all historically black colleges.

Although a large proportion of the students attending black colleges will continue to perform poorly as measured by standardized tests, a growing number of them will represent the brightest and the best. This inference is based on several observations. The minimum competency testing movement, which has spread to approximately 33 states, may significantly reduce the illiteracy rates of individuals with low educational skills if the tests produce the expected results. This will happen if they are used for evaluation of students during their high school years and not as exit criteria. Moreover, the growing inclination of states to set standard admissions criteria for all public institutions will not only exert pressure on school systems to produce more young people proficient in the basic skills, but also on black colleges to include targeting high-ability students in their recruitment policies. Finally, declining national attention on equality of educational opportunity as evidenced by the decrease in federal support of higher education and plans to desegregate higher education may rekindle the commitment of the black middle class to the black colleges.

The future students of the historically black colleges will probably differ from their predecessors in two other important ways. Because of economic conditions and cutbacks in educational assistance, more students will drop out between their first and second years. This suggests that fewer black college students are likely to graduate over a five-year period. Additionally, more of them will have part-time status, not only because of a depressed economy but also because of age and family obligations.

The Effect of Public Policy on Future
Black-College Enrollments

Public policy will continue to pose one of the most serious threats to black-college enrollment. Desegregation policies (mergers, transfer of duplicate programs from predominantly black to predominantly white institutions, and vice versa), state-imposed

enrollment ceilings on out-of-state students in black public universities, admissions criteria, program cutbacks, and the decline of
federal support of higher education will sorely test the ability of
these institutions to attract and retain students. (See Chapters 10
and 11 for more extensive treatments of these issues.)

The potential danger of these trends is clear. In 1972, approximately one-half of the black students enrolled full-time in
public higher education in six of the Adams states (Arkansas, Florida, Georgia, North Carolina, Oklahoma, and Virginia) were enrolled in the black colleges, ranging from 26.0 percent in Oklahoma
to 62.5 percent in Virginia (Gaines 1979). Four years later, the
black colleges' share of full-time black students had declined by
14.4 percent. The number of black students in the black colleges
of Oklahoma and Virginia had dropped by 16.3 and 48.4 percent,
respectively. In fall 1978, similar declines in the enrollments of
black colleges in these states were noted (Gaines 1979).

Two related issues to the impending impact of desegregation
on future black-college enrollment are transfer of programs from
black to white institutions and vice versa, and enrollment ceilings
on out-of-state students. In Georgia the education program of
Savannah State, a predominantly black residential institution, was
exchanged for the business program of Armstrong State, a predominantly white urban institution. Haynes (1980) noted that this
action contributed to a significant decline in the fall 1979 enrollment
of Savannah State. At Florida A&M University (FAMU), a land-
grant institution, the agricultural and home economics programs
were transferred to predominantly white institutions. This action
by the Florida Regents "effectively circumscribed FAMU's ability
to develop into a comprehensive university" (Haynes 1980). And,
in Louisiana, 58 programs from ten public institutions in the state
were eliminated (Chronicle of Higher Education 1980). Grambling
State University lost ten of its master of science programs (mostly
in specialties in elementary education) and Southern in Baton Rouge
lost three of its education programs and master's programs in social sciences and administration and supervision. The elimination
of these programs will have a major impact on these two institutions' enrollments given the importance of teacher education to their
institutional missions.

Administrators at public black colleges also strongly believe
that ceilings placed on the number of potential out-of-state students
will prevent their institutions from selecting qualified applicants
from a national pool and prohibitively raise tuition fees for their
students (NAFEO 1977). Similarly, administrators surveyed by
NAFEO felt that states are not full partners in providing matching
funds required by the federal government for student financial aid.

Consequently, black colleges tend to use their operating funds to subsidize student financial aid, in addition to administration and management. As veterans' benefits and academic fellowships and internships have been reduced, and new criteria developed for the former Basic Educational Opportunity Grant program (now Pell Grants), black college enrollments have declined sharply. These reductions in government aid are true of most other federal student financial aid programs (supplemental educational opportunity grants, college work-study, national direct student loans, and guaranteed student loans); it will be difficult for students to support their education without other types of financial support.

Public policies regarding higher education will play a pivotal role in determining future black college enrollments. Although most of the issues that I have discussed have focused on students, equally important legislation has been enacted to aid the colleges. Title III of the Higher Education Act of 1965 has had a large impact on the enhancement of black colleges, academic programs, their marketability and, consequently, these colleges' ability to attract a larger and more diverse student body (see Chapter 10 for more on Title III).

RECOMMENDATIONS

Planned intervention will be key to sustaining and expanding gains in the enrollments of the historically black colleges. I recommend that:

• Comprehensive enrollment targets be set for the historically black colleges to ensure that their role in the future is better defined. Based on the near stabilization of the black colleges' share of black enrollment at approximately 20 percent during the past five years and a goal of 1.6 million black students in higher education by the end of the century, 330,000 students by the year 2000 is a reasonable goal for these institutions.

Specific targets must also be set for the makeup of the 330,000 students to offset the underrepresentation of males, middle-income students, bright students, and graduate students, and the overrepresentation of part-time students.

• The leadership roles of the black colleges be broadened to heighten their impact on the development of disadvantaged youths and communities.

There must be improved communication between these colleges and old and new feeder systems. These activities should include building productive partnerships with elementary schools and predominantly white high schools, assisting low-income junior high and high school students in identifying job opportunities, and identifying gifted and talented black students at an early age. The establishment of a stronger liaison with industry, churches, community-action agencies, and professional societies will be fundamental to expanding opportunities for articulation.

Systematic, well-planned recruitment programs (in-state and out-of-state) and retention programs are a necessity. In their recruitment activities, these schools must give equal attention to enrollment size and the characteristics of enrollees in order to counter, as suggested, the overrepresentation of women, low-income, and underprepared students. Schools with viable graduate programs must vigorously recruit graduate students.

• Given the fierce competition for students that will characterize future decades, improving black-college retention rates must be a priority. The incorporation of systematic evaluation components into these schools' already well-established developmental education and remedial programs will increase their ability to match student needs and learning systems as well as provide immediate feedback to their students. (See Chapters 9 and 13.) Retention studies must be a priority of the institutional research office to increase the availability of information needed by black-college administrators, faculty, and students to plan for improved retention.

• The black colleges must become experts in governmental policies pertaining to enrollment. The inclusion of a governmental affairs office in the administrative structure would provide the type of overall framework needed for them to enter the public-policy arena in a more significant way. This office would be primarily responsible for assisting college presidents to keep abreast of information and actions relating to enrollment, identifying emerging policy issues, and coordinating constituency- and coalition-building activities.

• The black colleges offering sound graduate programs must strengthen their academic research capability (see Part III in this volume). These schools sorely need research supports such as released time, research assistants and teaching fellows, clerical assistance, networking opportunities, data processing services, and library materials to enhance their credibility as producers of new knowledge pertinent to the national interest. Strong graduate programs in public affairs, public administration, governmental studies, industrial psychology, and operations research would be particularly useful in helping them address public policy issues affecting higher-education enrollments. The presence of policy institutes and centers on these campuses that include the study of enrollments and enrollment-related areas (e.g., employment, population, taxation) would also be useful.

• Networks of black colleges with expertise in academic areas (e.g., science and public policy) and nonacademic areas (e.g., recruitment, articulation, and grantsmanship) be established to assist these colleges in expanding their leadership roles. The centers should also be designed to offset costly duplication of efforts among the schools and to improve their efficiency.

A network of black colleges with demonstrated expertise in grantsmanship and fundraising should be among the first established. This network would concentrate on assisting to develop and implement strategies for generating the funding that is needed to expand enrollments. Such strategies would relate, for example, to support for student financial aid, program diversification, and recruitment and retention.

• The federal government reaffirm its commitment to black colleges and to equity in higher education in general. Title III and Title IV of the reauthorized Higher Education Act of 1965 must be carefully monitored by the government to ensure that recent changes in education policy, such as the introduction of the Middle Income Student Assistance Act, do not erode black-college enrollments. The "half-cost" provision of the Pell Grant Program should be withdrawn, veterans' benefits should be restored to pre-1976 levels, and the implementation of the Adams mandate (e.g., merger of predominantly black and white institutions, transfer and elimination of traditional programs) must not be carried out at the expense of black colleges. The 1890 land-grant institutions and Tuskegee Institute must have full access to the financial resources accorded them by the Second Morrill Act in order to become mainstream research universities. States must agree to comply with the enhancement clause of the Adams mandate as well as to eliminate restrictive enrollment ceilings and out-of-state recruitment policies. They must also be induced to provide their share of the cost of implementing state-imposed compensatory education programs and campus-based student-aid programs. It is extremely important that the federal government continue to promote existing special service programs such as TRIO programs and Job Corps and to introduce new funding programs designed to assist disadvantaged youths in catching up educationally, socially, and economically.

• Comprehensive research studies on the enrollment patterns of the historically black colleges should be done. Existing and potential student markets should be studied in order to learn more about the values, interests, and educational plans of potential enrollees.

• Approaches to the packaging of student financial aid in order
to facilitate the redistribution of educational opportunities in higher
education; the roles that alumni, professional societies, and industry can play in assisting the black colleges to build more competitive
student bodies; the interactive effects of diverse social policies
(education, science and technology, population control and health)
on the enrollments of the black colleges; forecasts of future black-
college enrollments and recommendations of alternative policies;
examining and forecasting the impacts of economic conditions (e.g.,
inflation, recessions, declining productivity) on enrollments; and
institutional practices (e.g., faculty attitudes, programming and
reward systems) and their impacts on student enrollment patterns
all demand increased research attention.

SUMMARY

The outlook for the future of black-college enrollment is
equivocal at best. Like national higher-education enrollments,
black-college enrollment is in transition due to the complex inter-
play of social, economic, and political factors, but the stakes are
higher for the black institutions. Hence, any predictions about the
future character of their enrollments must be made with caution.

The findings suggest a mixed picture. Total black-college
enrollment will probably remain below the 200,000 level throughout
this century due to the growing shortfall in student aid (including
veterans' benefits) and institutional assistance, as well as the
dwindling pool of high-school graduates and of those graduates who
go on to college. Debilitating desegregation policies, the declining
purchasing power of blacks resulting from high inflation and recessions, and the tendency of black graduates of predominantly white
high schools to attend predominantly white institutions will serve to
push black college enrollment down. It is more difficult to predict
whether the sporadic upsurges in the high-school completion and
college-going rates of blacks will be large enough to balance the
pull of low-cost two-year institutions and the intensive recruitment
efforts of predominantly white institutions. As black institutions
and black high-school counselors step up their recruitment efforts,
increasing numbers of white counselors may direct students to
black colleges.

The enrollment of graduate, full-time, and male students will
be hardest hit because of their vulnerability to major shifts in educational assistance. Larger proportions of the students attending
these institutions will likely be older, female, white, better prepared academically, and attend part-time. Because a dispropor-

tionate number of them will require student aid, withdrawal and dropout rates will reach unprecedented heights and the average number of years required for the typical student to graduate will exceed five.

Five sources of potential growth brighten the future outlook for these institutions: the enlarged pool of college-age blacks in and out of the South, high-school dropouts, black graduates who have not enrolled in college, the children of the black middle class, and students in predominantly white high schools. Two other sources of students which have not been addressed in this chapter are two-year institutions and the growing pool of foreign students.

This scenario clearly points to the pivotal role that public policy has historically played in shaping the destiny of black colleges. Unless these institutions become self-sufficient and active participants in formulating policies that affect them, the arbitrary choices of government in the areas of desegregation, student aid, institutional assistance, and testing and recruitment will determine whether they continue to exist or have to close their doors.

To a large extent, students function as the heartbeat of institutions of higher learning. As such, they alone determine new directions in college leadership, administration, programming, and outreach. The trends outlined in this chapter dictate dramatic changes in the future roles of black colleges. More subtly, they suggest that these schools must take on a new perspective—one that emphasizes the relationship of economic and political behavior to the larger social system and the inseparable character of equality of opportunity and equality of income. From this vantage point, black colleges will truly be in a position to control the status and makeup of their enrollments because of their orientation toward the integral relationship that exists between education and economic and political policy.

Hopefully, black-college enrollment trends do not signal the passing of the era of equality of opportunity in the United States or the denial of future roles that they might play in ushering blacks and other disadvantaged groups into the era of creative efficiency.

REFERENCES

Arce, Carlos Humberto. Historical institutional and contextual determinants of black enrollment in predominantly white colleges and universities, 1946 to 1974. PhD dissertation, the University of Michigan, 1976.

Armor, David J. "The evidence on busing." The Public Interest 28 (Summer 1972):90-126.

Astin, Alexander W. "The myth of equal access in public higher education." A paper presented at the conference on Equality of Access in Postsecondary Education, Atlanta, GA, 1975.

_____. Preventing students from dropping out. Washington, D.C.: Jossey-Bass Publishers, 1975.

Astin, Helen J., and Patricia H. Cross. "The impact of financial aid on persistence in college." Summary of preliminary findings prepared for the PAS/ACE Seminar, August 6, 1979.

Bayer, Alan E. The black college freshman: Characteristics and trends. American Council on Education Research Reports, Vol. 7, No. 3. Washington, D.C.: American Council on Education, 1972.

Belcher, Leon H. "Patterns of federal financial aid for students in predominantly black colleges." In Student Financial Aid—Two Analyses. Washington, D.C.: Institute for Services to Education, Summer 1975.

Black Enterprise. "Black Americans speak out on leadership, economics and race." Tenth Anniversary Issue. August 1980.

Blake, Elias, Jr., Linda Lambert, and Joseph Martin. Degrees granted and enrollment trends in historically black colleges: An eight-year study. Washington, D.C.: Institute for Services to Education, 1974.

Breneman, David W., Chester E. Finn, Jr., and Susan C. Nelson. Public policy and private higher education. Washington, D.C.: The Brookings Institution, 1978.

Brown, Diane, and Mary Carter-Williams. A case study of institutional change in two selected racially changing historically black colleges. An unpublished report of the Institute for Services to Education, 1979.

The Carnegie Commission on Higher Education. From isolation to mainstream. New York: McGraw Hill, February 1971.

Carnegie Council on Policy Studies in Higher Education. Next steps for the 1980's in student financial aid. San Francisco, CA: Jossey-Bass Publishers, 1979.

Carter-Williams, Mary. "Trends in the total enrollments of the black college, 1970 to 1977, with emphasis on male and graduate/ first professional enrollments." A paper prepared for the American Council on Education, Summer 1980.

_____. Profiles of enrollments in the historically black colleges, Fall 1977. Washington, D.C.: Institute for Services to Education, 1978.

Chronicle of Higher Education. Louisiana proposes compromise on higher education desegregation. June 23, 1980.

Crain, Robert L., and Rita E. Mahard. The influence of high school racial composition on black college attendance and test performance. Washington, D.C.: U.S. Department of Health, Education and Welfare, January 1978.

Folger, John K. The south's commitment to higher education: Progress and prospects. Atlanta, GA: Southern Regional Education Board, 1978.

Frances, Carol. The short run economic outlook for higher education, a chartbook. American Council on Higher Education, 1980.

Gaines, Lenita Y. Profile of enrollments in the historically black colleges fall 1978. An unpublished report of the Institute for Services to Education, 1979.

Haynes, Leonard L., III. "An update of desegregation planning and its effect upon historically black colleges and universities." A paper presented at the Annual Meeting of the American Association for Higher Education, March 7, 1980.

Henderson, Cathy. Changes in enrollment by 1985. Policy Analysis Service Reports, Vol. 3, No. 1. Washington, D.C.: American Council on Education, June 1977.

Henderson, Cathy, and Janet C. Plummer. Adapting to changes in the characteristics of college-age youth. Policy Analysis Service Reports, Vol. 4, No. 2. Washington, D.C.: American Council on Education, December 1978.

Henning, Herman. Profile of three generations of entering freshmen enrolled in the thirteen college curriculum program. Washington, D.C.: Institute for Services to Education, 1979.

Kumi, Linda, and Mary Carter-Williams. "Predicting the academic success of black students attending the historically black colleges." Unpublished report of the Institute for Services to Education, 1979.

Mingle, James. Black and Hispanic enrollment in higher education: Trends in the nation and in the South. Atlanta, GA: Southern Regional Education Board, 1980.

Morris, Lorenzo. Elusive equality: The status of black Americans in higher education. Washington, D.C.: Howard University Press, 1979.

NAFEO (National Association for Equal Opportunity in Higher Education). "State policy impediments to black colleges." A study project for the National Advisory Committee on Black Higher Education and Black Colleges and Universities, November 15, 1977.

U.S. Bureau of the Census. The social and economic status of the black population in the United States: A historical view, 1790-1978. Current Population Reports, Special Studies, Series P-23, No. 80.

_____. School enrollment—Social and economic characteristics of students: October 1979 (Academic Report). Population Characteristics. Series P-20, No. 355 Issues. August 1980.

U.S. Department of Labor, Bureau of Labor Statistics. "Employment of high school graduates and dropouts, October 1970." Monthly Labor Review. May 1971.

_____. "Employment of high school graduates and dropouts, October 1971." Monthly Labor Review. May 1972.

_____. "The high school class of 1971: More at work, fewer in college." Monthly Labor Review. June 1973.

_____. "Employment of high school graduates and dropouts, October 1973." Monthly Labor Review. September 1974.

_____. "Students, graduates and dropouts in the labor market, October 1974." Reprint from August 1975, Monthly Labor Review.

_____. "Students, graduates and dropouts in the labor market, October 1975." Reprint from June 1976, <u>Monthly Labor Review</u>.

_____. "Students, graduates and dropouts in the labor market, October 1976." Reprint from July 1977, <u>Monthly Labor Review</u>.

_____. "Students, graduates and dropouts in the labor market." Reprint from October 1979, <u>Monthly Labor Review</u>.

Van Alstyne, Carol. <u>Financing higher education: Basic facts underlying current issues</u>. American Council on Education, January 1977.

PART VI

TRANSFORMING BLACK COLLEGE MISSIONS INTO INSTITUTIONAL OBJECTIVES

The majority of the articles in this book focus on potential roles black colleges might play in U.S. higher education. Thus, the selections to this point have been largely speculative and the authors devote most of their attention to reasons why these institutions should take on the particular roles suggested. Henry E. Cobb's article is a mixture of prescriptions and hypothetical proposals for tying together an integrated structure of academic programs. The critical thrust of Sherman Jones' paper, which is largely historical, is that in order to achieve the missions of these and other postsecondary institutions it is imperative that there be strong leadership and effectual systems of governance and management.

Cobb sets the tone of his remarks at the outset by noting that the prosperous, and sometimes chaotic, years of higher education in the 1960s have passed and that higher education faces an uncertain future in the 1980s. For black colleges, he notes, the problems will be much more acute. Cobb believes strongly that an institution's prestigious reputation is inextricably linked to the quality of its academic programs. Using a hypothetical public black college, he develops a set of academic programs and identifies research issues that evolve from the process of establishing strong curricula.

The paper states that it is absolutely essential that certain aspects of the teaching and learning process, as well as the organizational structure of the university, be modified. Some of these possible changes include: reorganization of instructional units in order to bring supervision closer to classroom activities; establishment of new academic programs; the logical and educationally sound combination of disciplines; the initiation of a research structure that concentrates on all facets of the academic program; and the strengthening of academic support programs and networks for students.

Cobb offers goals and outcomes for the college, the student, the teacher, and the academic programs themselves. Of all of his recommendations, the one to which he seems to attach the greatest importance is the proposal for the initiation of a College of General Studies that would house a wide variety of developmental programs and serve not just freshmen but all undergraduate students. These developmental programs should be designed for academically talented students as well as those deficient in basic communication skills. Cobb also proposes a new divisional structure of learning units that will include a College of Arts and Humanities, a College of Education, and a College of Sciences. A rationale for each of these divisions is provided along with the departments that will comprise each unit. Toward the end of the paper he discusses the need for a Center for Black and Ethnic Studies and the importance of strong programs of academic support for students and more opportunities for faculty to retool their skills through development institutes. Finally, he recommends, for public black colleges particularly, a variety of new degree programs—bachelors, masters, and doctorates—and concludes by underscoring the need for revitalization strategies within the institution and the office of academic affairs, which would coordinate all academic services and maintain the accountability of the college's curricula.

Sherman Jones' article reviews the leadership, governance, and management patterns and styles of historically black colleges and compares them with those of U.S. colleges and universities in general. Jones asserts that, despite the stereotype that black colleges have been run dictatorially by presidents and boards of trustees, there is little difference between their governance patterns and those of predominantly white postsecondary institutions. He traces the growth of the administrative power of college presidents from the colonial period to the present day and discusses the degree of faculty involvement in the university's decision-making processes. In addition to the limited budgets within which the majority of the early presidents of colleges had to operate, Jones emphasizes that the early black college presidents also had to contend with a public that did not overwhelmingly support the higher education of blacks. Therefore, they expended much time and effort defending the existence of their schools and working diligently to make them survive with inadequate resources. Implicit in his paper is the fact that when funds are scarce, administrative power, not surprisingly, is centralized and vested mostly in the chief executive officer. Jones' own research of governance patterns at black and white institutions demonstrates that the most prevalent pattern today, and an effective one, at most colleges is the managerial model whereby the president and his senior administrative staff, rather than the faculty, manage their institutions.

At the end Jones makes some recommendations for college presidents in the 1980s, the most important being that they fully understand the academic enterprise and management, have expertise in financial matters, personnel administration, information systems, and institutional planning.

He discusses the source of the bulk of the funds of black colleges, the impact of federal and state government policies, and other factors such as desegregation and possible mergers in order to show that the leaders of these institutions must be able fund raisers, adept politicians, and, especially, outstanding educators. And finally, he offers a word of advice to boards of trustees who, he writes, should see that colleges are run well and also that faculty assume greater responsibility in decisions on academic and personnel matters. With this level of increasing involvement and effective presidential leadership, Jones believes viable institutions will emerge and survive during the difficult decade of the 1980s.

13

Developing Academic Programs in Public, Historically Black Colleges

Henry E. Cobb

Since 1965, changes in U.S. society and especially in higher education have shifted the focus of both immediate and long-range concerns of colleges and universities, especially with respect to academic programs. Gone from the scene are the bands of vocal youths demanding a share in governance. The sounds of the hammer, the saw, and heavy machinery preparing new dormitories for ever-increasing waves of young people who inundated campuses every fall are heard less and less. Administrators no longer worry about how to rid their campuses of recalcitrant students without violating due process, but about how to retain those who have elected to enroll in their institutions. Research professors no longer worry about which grant they will accept but rather about which grant they can get, to maintain a sufficient flow of grant funds to keep a few members of the small army of research assistants to whom they have become psychologically and intellectually accustomed.

The golden age of the 1960s has come to an end! The higher education industry has entered a "no-growth" phase. Educational planners and administrators who inherited generations of expansionist thought now have to deal with higher education in a contracting state. It is not surprising that they have not always handled their problems with the necessary speed and expertise.

As campus disruptions receded into the background, other problems surfaced to attract the attention of administrators and planners. The changing student clientele called for new or revised academic programs. The multiple effects of the economic crunch created tensions. As a result, teachers turned increasingly to unionization as they struggled to keep faculty salaries competitive with those outside higher education and to hold tenure rates at a level that would allow the infusion of new blood into faculty ranks. Because of these issues, plus legal and political problems, higher education currently faces an uncertain future.

CONSTRUCTING AN INTEGRATED STRUCTURE OF ACADEMIC PROGRAMS

All these problems affect higher education generally, but they have an even greater effect on black colleges that never experienced the "golden age" and that have traditionally been underfunded. Changes in the academic programs of black colleges must be made in light of these pressing realities. Their historical status as developing institutions and their future roles need to be appraised.

An institution's reputation for quality is inextricably related to the quality of its academic programs. Program quality, in turn, is almost always linked to the degree of excellence of the research component of the curricula. The 34 public black colleges have not developed reputations for excellence in academic programs and research. I believe that this circumstance is due, at least in part, to the failure of these institutions to organize their academic components in a manner which maximizes academic strengths, effects an easier synthesis of content for students, provides for optimal supervision, and stimulates research productivity.

This chapter presents a proposal to enhance the public black college, with special attention to the development of an integrated structure of academic and research programs. This program will substantially change the academic climate and other conditions under which teaching and learning take place in black public colleges. Among the priorities that must be established to effect these changes are:

— Reorganization of instructional units to bring supervision closer to classroom activities
— Combining disciplines for administrative purposes in a logical and educationally sound fashion
— Establishment of new program structures to achieve both mandated and perceived purposes
— Improvement of various institutional programs so that all graduates meet the academic and professional requirements of their fields
— Development of programs to meet the wide range and diverse options of students
— Providing students, especially in their first year, special experiences to broaden and improve their skills

— Establishment of, or improvement of, a research mechanism which is both empirical and action-oriented, focusing on all facets of the academic program
— Strengthening and synchronizing academic support systems for the implementation of new programs and servicing existing ones

This chapter reflects ideas from four major sources: theories of organizational development, studies of developing institutions, the social history of public black colleges, and the experiences and perceptions of the author who has had nearly 30 years of experience as a teacher, researcher, and administrator. Although the prescriptions in this chapter are designed specifically to enhance the academic program of a black public college, much of what is offered is equally relevant for the private historically black college and other postsecondary institutions with similar characteristics. Because of the need to generalize the prescriptions and at the same time avoid discussing any specific institution, I will refer to a hypothetical institution, "Public University No. 16" (PU-16). This university is typical of public black colleges (see Table 1).

BASIC CHARACTERISTICS OF PUBLIC UNIVERSITY NO. 16

Public University No. 16 was founded in 1880 during the Postreconstruction period, amid the reaction and racial unrest of those times. Like other institutions in its class, it owes its origin to the efforts of black politicians who wished to make a contribution to their people and leave a legacy of the power they once wielded. Over the last 100 years the institution evolved through the usual stages: first, basically a precollege institution; then, a normal school; then, a four-year college; finally, a university, with the addition of graduate and professional schools. During most of this period the institution had land-grant status.* It now holds a National Center for Higher

---

*The 1862 Act gave federal lands to the states for the establishment of colleges offering programs in agriculture, engineering, and home economics, as well as in the traditional academic subjects. Because of the act's emphasis on the practical arts, the land-grant system now includes practically all the nation's agricultural colleges and a large number of its engineering schools; in 1973 there were 70 land-grant colleges. Land-grant status is conferred upon institutions of higher learning by designation and by the mutual agreement of the state and federal governments. These institutions, including one in

TABLE 1

Enrollment Profile of Public Black Colleges for First Semester, Fall 1978

Name of Institution	Under-graduate	Graduate	Total Number of Students*
Alabama A & M University	3,286	1,002	4,425
Alabama State University	3,971	246	4,794
Albany State College	1,661	—	1,750
Alcorn State University	2,097	199	2,296
University of Arkansas at Pine Bluff	2,927	—	2,998
Bowie State College	1,519	685	2,722
Central State University	2,211	—	2,414
Cheyney State College	2,378	241	2,637
Coppin State College	2,266	170	2,874
Delaware State College	1,628	—	2,153
Elizabeth City State University	1,552	—	1,584
Fayetteville State University	2,012	—	2,125
Florida A & M University	4,873	658	5,882
Fort Valley State College	1,744	98	1,872
Grambling State University	3,327	197	3,623
Jackson State University	6,416	1,229	7,646
Kentucky State University	1,741	167	2,196
Langston University	940	—	942
Lincoln University (Missouri)	2,085	247	2,332
Lincoln University (Pennsylvania)	993	69	1,132
Mississippi Valley State University	2,821	78	2,899
Morgan State University	4,059	591	5,209
Norfolk State College	6,319	547	7,283
North Carolina A & T State University	4,577	695	5,385
North Carolina Central University	3,495	686	4,810
Prairie View A & M University	3,833	1,268	5,101
Savannah State College	2,066	163	2,229
South Carolina State College	2,898	359	3,437
Southern University System	10,353	718	11,463
Baton Rouge	6,956	718	8,061
New Orleans	2,710	—	2,710
Shreveport	692	—	692
Tennessee State University	4,071	860	5,537
Texas Southern University	7,469	1,001	8,802
Virginia State College	3,735	523	4,475
West Virginia State College	3,127	—	3,678
Winston-Salem State University	2,067	—	2,204

*The totals here may not equal the sums of the other two columns because the institutions also report students who are unclassified—neither undergraduate nor graduate.

Source: Derived from Andrew Pepin, The fall enrollment in higher education 1978, final report. Washington, D.C.: National Center for Educational Statistics, U.S. Department of Health, Education and Welfare, 1979.

Education Management Systems Classification III, which means that, although it has a comprehensive program, its only postbaccalaureate degrees are the master's and Juris Doctor. PU-16's other characteristics follow closely the Title III Eligibility Criteria for participating in the Developing Institutions Program.* These include certain qualitative criteria such as Full Time Equivalent (FTE) enrollment, enrollment trends, type of admissions policy, institutional personnel, and institutional vitality. The enrollment and the faculty come under the same quantitative requirements for participating in the Developing Institutions Program. For example, an institution is put into a certain category on the basis of its FTE enrollment; the faculty is categorized on the basis of the percentages with master's degrees and doctorates. Each institution is also judged on the basis of the number of volumes in the library, total educational and general expenditures, and percent of students from lower income families. Institutions are also classified on the basis of being public or private, two-year or four-year.

Goals for Public University No. 16's
Academic Program

The goals of an institution of higher education should be logical extensions of its mission to advance knowledge, humanize and liberalize students, and fulfill its social responsibility. They should address its major roles and provide the definitive and temporal framework in which the mission will be pursued. The goals of PU-16's academic program center around four major areas:

— To expand, enrich, and modernize the curriculum so that students will relate classroom work to life and have a large number of career options, especially in fields of high-employment opportunity.

Washington, D.C., must qualify under either the First Morrill Act of 1862 or the Second Morrill Act of 1890. Most black institutions that hold land-grant status qualified under the Second Morrill Act. See Mayberry 1966; Neyland and Riley 1963; Potts 1978; Trueheart 1979; Vincent and Woolfolk 1962.

*The basis of this classification is found in Federal Register, Vol. 40, No. 107, June 3, 1975, p. 23859. For a discussion of these criteria and their relevance for Title III Institutions in particular and higher education in general, see Cobb 1977.

— To broaden access to higher education for those who have been excluded because of low income and for other groups who, for various reasons, cannot take advantage of the regularly scheduled offerings.
— To initiate programs that will reduce the student attrition rate, and improve the skills of students with and without deficiencies at all levels of the academic program.
— To improve the quality of education at PU-16 by meeting appropriate accreditation standards and by introducing a campuswide program of research and creative activities.

The pursuit of this mission and the achievement of a reasonable portion of its goals should yield a number of desired outcomes. These will be useful not only in determining the efficiency of the academic structure, but also raise issues for possible research. Vigorous research efforts should study teaching excellence and other vital areas that will influence the character of intellectual inquiry throughout the institution. All programs of experiential education should demonstrate visible ties to the community and should include specific objectives that can be assessed both quantitatively and qualitatively in relation to curriculum, scheduling, locations, and populations served. The success of the academic structure will depend heavily on a College of General Studies that will function as a holding and retooling mechanism for those not enrolling in senior colleges immediately after their first year. When the academic structure is evaluated, the utility of this strategy should be fully tested so that a decision to retain, improve, or eliminate it may be made.

The Establishment of a College of General Studies

One vital clue to the effectiveness of academic programs is the manner in which they are integrated with each other. It is sometimes necessary to establish new structures to achieve this end, such as the College of General Studies at PU-16. Educators have long recognized the need for a structure to serve as the home base for an assortment of developmental programs and a general education core. There is a varied group of students who, for a number of reasons, are not moving immediately into a senior college. Such a structure would be especially useful to this group, including those students who have not decided on a major, who must build up their skills, or to transfer students who must earn additional credits before being accepted into their chosen disciplines. The existence of a College of General Studies allows the department in which the student intends to major to delay that student's entrance until he or she is qualified and ready. This policy should raise the performance level of the entire institution.

One of the most important features of the General College will be its administration of the Comprehensive Developmental Education Program discussed later in this chapter. The location of this program in the General College helps destroy the fiction that only first-year students need academic assistance since this retooling arsenal is open to the entire student body. At the same time, it reinforces the institution's commitment to positively changing the exit characteristics of its graduates.

Since the College of General Studies also houses and administers the general education prerequisites, there is no longer a need to crowd all nonspecialized learning into the first year. Further, it becomes easier and more in line with institutional goals to introduce special exit courses and activities that are geared toward improving skills.

The proposed College of General Studies is conceived as a complex organization that is not only the setting for programs for students' remediation, but also as the home of a number of programs and courses for the academically talented. Other courses and programs may have a special focus and operate on an experimental basis with different structures and with a varied system of academic credits. It will house other specialized, but nonmajor, courses designed to serve as electives or for both cultural and technical reinforcement. Like the basic course, they will be available to students on the recommendation of their departments or colleges.

The general education core should be shaped by the academic history of the students expected to enroll at PU-16 and the educational demands of the social role they hope to play. Most of the students who will enroll at PU-16 are black, about 90 percent are on financial aid, and more than one-half receive Pell Grants. Many students will enter PU-16 unprepared to carry a full load of college work. Substantial numbers will carry some of these deficiencies throughout their college career, deficiencies that show up notably in standardized tests. For years, we have known that major weaknesses exist at the college level in mathematics, science, social science, humanities, and communications. These deficiencies will be addressed through courses organized around particular themes in each of these subject areas. The courses will be competency-based and will be open to those who need them.

The general studies college is the appropriate location for university-wide quality control mechanisms, each of which should reflect the major goals and objectives of the institution. These evaluative processes include, for example, a continuing task force on teaching; they will probably function best through committees and will be useful in giving definition to specific aspects of the program and in preventing the occurrence of many instructional errors.

The Divisional Concept

A great deal of the literature on improvements in higher education discusses the necessity of upgrading teachers and instructional strategies. A major difficulty in dealing with that problem is that the deans in the larger black colleges are often removed from first-level supervision, yet too tightly bound by academic custom and tradition, administrative procedures, and human relations policies. Thus, they often do not know what is happening at departmental levels (Corson 1960). The department heads who furnish most of this information are frequently overburdened with other obligations. The remedy proposed here is that a divisional administrative unit be placed between the department and college structures, thus bringing another administrator, the division head, to the assistance of the department head and the dean. This type of organizational structure is especially appropriate for many black colleges where some departments are very small—only one to three faculty members. Since such a unit is too small to support a full-time qualified administrator, usually the ablest or the most senior professor is pressed into service as the head of the department. Professorial work, especially research, suffers; yet he or she cannot become a competent administrator either (Hungate 1964).

The case for the organization of learning units by divisions does not rest solely on the need for and ease of planning and supervision. There is mutual reinforcement when divisions are organized on the basis of closely related disciplines. In some instances, divisions are able to launch needed postbaccalaureate programs of high quality where one department or discipline might not have the requisite numbers of professors of sufficient distinction to launch such a venture. In this way, black colleges would be able to institute master's and doctoral degree programs. The divisional concept is proposed as one phase of the academic organizational scheme for PU-16. In this scheme the structure, course content, and methods of instruction are all geared to demonstrating the interrelatedness of knowledge. This brief exposition serves as the rationale for the proposal to restructure the colleges of Arts and Humanities, Education, and Sciences into a divisional organization (see Table 2).

TABLE 2

Proposed Divisional and Departmental Structures

College of Arts and Humanities	College of Education	College of Sciences	College of General Studies
Humanities English Language and Literature Mass Communications Philosophy and Humanities Foreign Languages	Elementary and Secondary Education Primary education and programs for exceptional students Early Childhood Education Elementary Education Reading Special Education	Psychological and Biomedical Sciences Biology Psychology Allied Health Studies	Developmental Educational Program Continuing and Experiential Education
Social and Behavioral Sciences Political Science Sociology History Geography	Curriculum and Instruction Mathematics Education Science Education Social Studies Education Music Education Art Education Library Science Foreign Languages	Exact and Natural Sciences Chemistry Mathematics Physics Computer Science	Honors Program Special Studies
Performing Arts Music Fine Arts Speech and Theatre	Vocational Education Vocational Agricultural Education Vocational Business and Office Administration Vocational Home Economics Education Vocational Trade and Industrial Education Industrial Arts Education		
	Foundations of Education Guidance and Counseling Educational Psychology Administration and Supervision Media		
	Physical Education and Athletic Administration		

The College of Arts and Humanities

The College of Arts and Humanities will be divided into three major divisions—humanities, social and behavioral sciences, and the performing arts—which, in turn, will be subdivided into departments. Each of the departments in the division utilizes similar analytical techniques of study to explore a common, broadly defined subject, namely, the human experience.

People need to learn to live as human beings. In the humanities, students will learn how different people in different times and places felt about important concepts such as equality, authority, and freedom, as well as the ethical and moral systems of various societies. The humanities can also reveal how different people solved or failed to solve problems growing out of these concepts.

The second division of the college is the social and behavioral sciences. This collection of disciplines is concerned with human beings as individuals and as groups, and how they interrelate.

The third division is the performing arts. The departments in this division have common ways of perceiving the physical and human environment. Including the performing arts in the College of Arts and Humanities is justified on the following grounds: They contribute to the esthetics of the educational environment, they serve as recreation for students and the community at large, and they contribute significantly to the creative experience.

The College of Education

Recent changes in society, declining enrollments, and new demands for educational accountability all point to the need for new management structures in colleges of education in black colleges. These structures must make sense educationally while at the same time respond creatively to the need to increase career options for education majors. The structure proposed for PU-16's College of Education includes the following divisions: Elementary and Secondary Education, Physical Education and Athletic Administration, Vocational Education, and Foundations of Education.

The reconstruction of colleges of education at black colleges is crucial to any redirection of teacher training. Changes in colleges of education will have wide-ranging ramifications for every level of the educational establishment because of the large number of students who elect to major in education.

The College of Sciences

The planned reorganization would include the departments of psychology, biological sciences, chemistry, computer science, mathematics, and physics in the College of Sciences. These five departments and allied health studies would be divided into two divisions: psychological and biomedical sciences and exact and natural sciences.

As a means of moving supervision and counseling closer to the teaching and learning process, the larger departments—biology, chemistry, and mathematics—should be divided into subdivisions. Coordinators of these subunits would be responsible for the supervision of certain faculty members, for specified activities within the subdivision, and would report directly to the department heads. The coordinators' activities and duties would be clearly defined. Under such an arrangement, department heads would share their responsibilities with the coordinators and would be expected to seek advice and information from them when making decisions about departmental programs, policies, and regulations.

A Center for Black and Ethnic Studies

Among the legitimate purposes of a public black college is the illumination of all dimensions of the black experience. This proposal calls for the establishment of a well-articulated Black Studies program within the framework of a center focusing on multiethnic concerns. Such a program would constitute a meaningful thread in the fabric of the social science and humanities disciplines, linking the teaching and research efforts already established in these departments. In addition, there would be a significant relationship between the program and the institution's need to meet its responsibility to find, codify, preserve, interpret, and make available for institutional and public use documents, artifacts, and other materials pertaining to the Afro-American heritage. From a scholarly point of view, the critical yield from such a program would be equally important. Ultimately the positive outcomes from such a thorough, relevant, high-quality program of black studies would include: an improved self-concept for black people, correction of the negative stereotypes that many people hold about blacks, and a move closer to the creation of a social order that freely recognizes differences in men and women, but strongly opposes inequality in their opportunities for development. It is especially important that the black colleges establish strong black studies programs since several of the better known programs are now found at predominantly white institutions.

This proposal directly relates to black studies, but it is also quite appropriate for a broader-based program of multiethnic studies. Research in the field clearly indicates that negative stereotypes have been developed for most ethnic minorities. Both literature and the arts have created a false image of superiority in the dominant group and are responsible for the creation of a negative self-concept among ethnic minorities.

I. A. Newby in his book Jim Crow's Defense (1965) provides a cogent analysis of anti-Negro thought, including negative stereotypes of blacks during the first 30 years of the twentieth century. Rayford W. Logan in The Betrayal of the Negro (1967) offers abundant corroboration of Newby's work. Both authors clearly demonstrate that negative images of blacks were found at all reading levels in popular magazines, serious literature, and scholarly works. The situation, though improving, still exists. The record must be corrected.

The Black Studies program proposed for PU-16 would be a part of a more comprehensive unit—an Ethnic Studies Center. This center would allow PU-16 to: (1) develop a curriculum to counter negative stereotypes; (2) provide students with a broader base of knowledge; (3) serve as a clearinghouse for material pertaining to ethnic groups in the United States; and (4) help to encourage in students and the larger community a positive image of all ethnic groups.

There would be a close operational interrelationship among the Black Heritage College and the PU-16 Library, the Center for Ethnic Studies, and the Graduate Studies Program. Because students who major in ethnic studies often take a graduate degree in social science with a concentration in history, political science, or sociology, they would be expected to use the documents located in the center in writing their theses. While the center would be available to the faculty and the general student body, it is expected that students in the social sciences, humanities, and education would spend more time working with the available materials. The type of center outlined here will fulfill the institution's mission in the community by serving citizens who may desire to use its resources.

PROGRAMS OF ACADEMIC SUPPORT

The clientele in higher education today is significantly different from that of the 1960s and even of the early 1970s. Today's average student is likely to be older, less well-off economically, and certainly less able academically when tested by standardized instruments. Thus, there is a need to provide academic supports in the form of developmental programs.

The Developmental Education Program (DEP)

At PU-16, the most significant academic support program is known as the Developmental Education Program. The rationale for the program is that many first-year students enter PU-16 lacking adequate educational preparation, specifically in communication and computational skills, and are unable to pursue college level courses successfully. It is clear that the existing developmental education courses and other enrichment programs cannot adequately eliminate the deficiencies of all students. Furthermore, these programs have not been sufficiently coordinated to achieve maximum effectiveness. Nevertheless, the planned reorganization and coordination of existing programs at PU-16 creates a need for a teacher-training program, a diagnostic-testing program, instructional modules, immediate and in-depth reinforcement of skills and materials presented in classroom settings, and personalized counseling and peer tutoring.

The student-centered aspects of the Developmental Education Program have as their major objective the development of competency levels in the following basic skills: the ability to speak, read, and write acceptable English; and the ability to solve problems requiring basic arithmetic skills.

The delivery system will include the careful delineation of a set of objectives and content to fit the contours of a competency-based model. The American College Test (ACT) will be used to provide a rough measurement of student ability, but the fine-tuning, for accurate prescriptions, should be arrived at by the use of other appropriate diagnostic tests. Teachers in each component, with the assistance of norms and advice from consultants, will determine the point at which a student is allowed to move from the DEP into a major course of study. A significant feature of the program is that its techniques may be applied at the upper levels for strengthening the skills bases of third- and fourth-year students.

The faculty-oriented aspects of the program involve the preparation and grading of materials and teaching. Each participating teacher is required to undergo intensive retraining in a Faculty Development Institute. The institute is a central aspect of the DEP and will provide for further development and retraining of teachers in pedagogical techniques. Faculty usually receive little or no formal training in the teaching of college students. The widespread need for special techniques to teach the educationally disadvantaged college student has come to national attention only in the past decade or so. There is a dearth of professional literature dealing with the comprehensive approach proposed here. While many experienced teachers at PU-16 will have developed special methods for teaching educationally disadvantaged college students, they have not had an opportunity to codify their techniques and to engage in the kind of experimental research that would validate their instructional strategies. Chapter 9 by John Monro deals perceptively and at some length with this problem.

Thus, an on-campus institute which would have as its central purpose the further development and retraining of teachers in pedagogical techniques is an efficient and economical way to provide these necessary skills to tenured teachers. The institute would bring campus specialists to PU-16, who would be able to assist teachers in developing the necessary competencies. In addition to the mathematics, reading, and English faculty identified initially, some senior members of the other departments would be expected to enroll to supplement the developmental staff while the latter is perfecting their pedagogical skills and learning the new tasks related to their new responsibilities.

The institute's program would link the professional development of teachers with the introduction to first-year students of both an innovative teaching methodology and an experimental curriculum. By teaching a selected group of first-year students who would be invited to the institution for the summer, the teacher-participants would have a laboratory for testing this methodology and curriculum. The institute should bear the cost of the summer program, insuring access to it by the students. The students selected to participate should have average academic profiles.

The proposed Experimental Summer Institute has several points of special significance.

- It will afford an opportunity to test a new approach to the teaching of linguistic and quantitative skills.
- The institute's extension over several summers, with periodic reinforcement during the regular school year, will build a reservoir of expertise on the PU-16 faculty for teaching students who come to college with less than minimum skills.
- The experimental format of the institute will permit careful evaluation, replication, and eventual codification of the success of these efforts. The result will be the development of an educational environment which will effectively interface with the emerging competency-based and test-taking orientation of the academic program at PU-16.
- The teachers undergoing this experience will be able to approach their work with the same kind of pride as those who have specialized in other fields.

Other advantages of the Experimental Summer Institute would be the establishment of a bridge for beginning students, a supportive atmosphere for experimentation, a noticeable rise in the achievement of upperclassmen after two years, and the development of a communication-oriented campus environment.

Language Skills Component

A spinoff of the DEP is the reinforcement of language skills at the upper level featured in the Language Skills Component. Assessments of reading and writing skills from all over the country reveal a continuing decline among U.S. students at all levels. Blacks and other disadvantaged students lead the list of those who exhibit major reading and writing problems. The evaluation of the reading and writing skills of PU-16 graduates clearly indicates the need for some modification of the Language Skills Program (see Chapter 9 for further discussion).

General institutional requirements should be expanded to include a continuing program of basic language courses consisting of grammar, composition, and reading at each college level. At present at PU-16, the reading and writing skills courses are given only in the first year; with the extended program, students would be required to take a basic English course of increasing complexity for each of their undergraduate years. The expectation is that this more comprehensive, annual reinforcement will result in measurable improvement in the students' language skills.

Testing

Educators recognize that there is a positive relationship between successful achievement on examinations, particularly on standardized exams, and "test sophistication" or a certain level of experience and skill in negotiation of various test instruments. Whatever problems students may have with substantive subject matter, many of them exhibit a relatively low level of proficiency in some of the key skills required to score high on standardized tests: understanding detailed instructions, budgeting response time, knowing when it is proper to guess, and handling test items that involve problems of association, logic, and application.

There should be concerted action throughout the institution to upgrade the test sophistication of all students. Specifically, teachers in each academic area should institute measures to expose their students to the test situations they are likely to face, with the long-range objective of overall improvement in the student's comprehension analysis and evaluation skills. However, each department must recognize that ineffective test performance is more a function of students lacking requisite knowledge and not merely the result of test-taking deficiencies. Thus, the first order of business in academic reform is to evaluate the effectiveness of existing programs.

Continuing Education

A viable Continuing Education Program seems imperative if an institution is to perform more efficiently its service role to the community. Colleges and universities are constantly asked to provide an increasing volume and variety of services and only recently have they found that prompt and effective response is possible. Further, the energy, educational insight, and commitment of the program personnel, and the schedule of projected activities indicate that continuing education will play a significant role in relating the institution to the community it serves. The weekend college, short courses, and special seminars for distinct populations on campus, combined with off-campus activities, will forge a bond between the community and the school.

Programs in Colleges with Special Missions

Improvements in the colleges of agriculture and home economics depend to some extent on the development of aggressive and effective recruitment practices. Both units will also profit from more effective public-service programs that would establish fruitful links with the community. Such contacts should positively impact curriculum development in these colleges and especially engineering, because of PU-16's land-grant status. As the largest of the 16 public black colleges and Tuskegee Institute in the land-grant group, PU-16 should exert a strong influence on black higher education, especially in the area of research. The college of agriculture is the center of this capability and much research can be conducted through the cooperative State Research Service administered by the Science Education Administration (see Chapter 3 for more on this program).

The colleges of engineering and business at PU-16 are growing units; their graduates are in great demand. These colleges are among the largest at PU-16 and face a common critical problem: staffing. They should give serious consideration to the vertical extension of selected programs so that they might produce high quality master's graduates. Such a move, which might well increase their drawing power, would allow senior professors to teach graduate classes and do research, and, in general, increase their contribution to the trickle of minority manpower available in these fields.

The college of education and the school of architecture, two professional units whose graduates have to be licensed to practice their art, have had difficulty producing graduates who can pass national examinations required for certification. This problem merits careful study and the determination of appropriate remedies.

New Degree Programs

The creation of new programs as well as the strengthening of existing ones is necessary to develop the kind of delivery system PU-16 needs. Several suggestions are mentioned below but all should be given serious consideration.

Associate Degree Programs

Eight programs are recommended to meet manpower demands and varied student interests and needs. The major fields are: teacher aide, computer scientist, agricultural mechanics technologist, clothing and textiles worker, business administrator, nutritionist, office administrator, and library technician.

Bachelor Degree Programs

Only two new programs, public health and bioengineering, are recommended, primarily to provide preparation for master's or doctoral programs.

Master's Degree Programs

These new master's degree programs are proposed: psychology, special education, criminal justice, community health, labor studies, industrial management, computer science, psychometrics, counseling, and agribusiness economics.

Doctoral Programs

Five new doctoral programs are recommended, including chemistry, language communications, biomedical sciences and allied health, social sciences, and education.

Professional Education

The majority of black colleges and universities do not have professional schools. Perhaps more than ever, black professionals play a significant role in community life. They are an important resource, which black colleges have traditionally trained. The professional schools have a mission to develop and improve their programs so that they will become leaders in their fields.

CONCLUSION

This proposal attempts to demonstrate an effective method of developing an integrated structure of academic programs for public black colleges. By implication, it also attempts to reveal fundamental questions to which the public black colleges must answer if they are to fulfill the roles assigned to them now and in the future. It delineates some of these roles and implies the need for research intervention to enhance them. Yet, the academic program which the proposal seeks to put in place must be sustained by constant revitalization and academic-support systems.

The proposal grows out of a firm conviction that improvement of the academic programs at PU-16 rests largely with the institution itself. Members of the institution may find it useful to employ research as an intervention strategy to enhance or sustain a high level of operation in the academic system. But if the faculty and other academic personnel predetermine the outcomes, they will be less likely to fall victim to the tyranny of research.

No academic enhancement plan will retain its vitality for long unless the faculty has significant opportunities for renewal. The best results are likely to come from a revitalization plan the faculty itself develops and manages. However, this type of plan is usually long-range and difficult to achieve. Alternative techniques such as short-term in-service faculty workshops or institutes are recommended. The general theme of teacher renewal should always be emphasized, but each workshop should have its own special focus. Those responsible for monitoring and revitalizing the program should be keenly aware of the need for special features and even remedies to the circumstance of the public black university—PU-16. Importing ideas and structures to fill the requirements of black colleges may be dangerous.

This chapter's principal objective is the identification and coordination of all academic-support systems in a single structural component under the supervision of an academician with direct responsibility to the chief academic officer. Such academic-support services would include the library, the computer center, student financial aid, recruitment and admissions, and the office of the registrar. Centralizing the services which are directly related to academic affairs would permit the maximization of the resources allocated for their performance. In addition, through the coordination made possible by this arrangement, there will be increased accountability for each component. Optimal use of academic-support services would positively contribute to the full development of the academic potential of each student.

REFERENCES

"American higher education: Toward an uncertain future." Daedalus
    I and II, 103 (1974).

Booth, David B. "Institutional disciplinary ideas for development." Educational Record 58 (Winter 1977).

Clark, Burton R. The distinctive college: Antioch, Reed and Swarthmore. Chicago: Aldine Publishing Co., 1970.

Cobb, Henry E. "Mission, status, problems and priorities of black graduate schools." In Minority group participation in graduate education. Washington, D.C.: National Board on Graduate Education, 1976.

_____. Report on an examination of the developing institutions program. Washington, D.C.: U.S. Department of Health, Education and Welfare, 1977.

Cohen, Michael D., and James G. March. Leadership and ambiguity: The American college president. New York: McGraw-Hill, 1974.

Commission on the Humanities. The humanities in American life. Berkeley, CA: University of California Press, 1980.

Corson, John. Governance of colleges and universities. New York: McGraw-Hill, 1960.

Dressel, Paul L. "A look at new curriculum models for undergraduate education." Journal of Higher Education 50 (July/August 1979): 389-97.

Dressel, Paul L., and Lewis B. Mayhew. General education explorations in evaluation. Washington, D.C.: American Council on Education, 1954.

Etzioni, Amitai. Modern organizations. Englewood Cliffs, NJ: Prentice-Hall, 1964.

_____. A comparative analysis of complex organizations. New York: The Free Press, 1961.

Fischer, Charles F., ed. Developing and evaluating administrative leadership. San Francisco, CA: Jossey-Bass, 1978.

Franklin, Vincent, and James D. Anderson, eds. New perspectives on black educational history. Boston: G. K. Hall, 1978.

Hodgkinson, Harold L., and Walter W. Schenkel. A study of Title III of the Higher Education Act: The developing institutions program. Berkeley, CA: Center for Research and Development in Higher Education (CRDHE), 1974.

Hungate, Thad L. Management in higher education. New York: Columbia University, Teachers College Press, 1964.

Jencks, Christopher, and David Riesman. "The American Negro college." Harvard Educational Review 37 (Winter 1967).

Keeton, Morris T., ed. Defining and assuring quality in experiental learning. San Francisco, CA: Jossey-Bass, 1980.

Lee, Eugene C., and Frank Bowen. Managing multicampus systems: Effective administration in an unsteady state. San Francisco, CA: Jossey-Bass, 1975.

LeMelle, Tilden J., and Wilbert T. LeMelle. The black college: A strategy for relevancy. New York: Praeger, 1969.

Logan, Rayford W. The betrayal of the Negro. New York: Collier Books, 1967.

Louisiana Board of Regents. The master plan for higher education in Louisiana. Louisiana Register (April 1978).

Maybery, B. D. Research at historically black land-grant institutions. Tuskegee, AL: Alabama Association of Research Coordinators, 1966.

Miller, James L., Jr., Gerald Gurin, and Mary Jo Clarke. Uses and effectiveness of Title III in selected developing institutions. Ann Arbor, MI: University of Michigan Press, 1970.

Mindel, Charles H., and Robert W. Habenstein, eds. Ethnic families in America: Patterns and variations. New York: Elsevier Science, 1977.

National Advisory Committee on Black Higher Education and Black Colleges and Universities (NACBHEBCU). Black colleges and universities: An essential component of a diverse system of higher education. Washington, D.C.: NACBHEBCU, 1979.

Newby, I. A. Jim Crow's defense: Anti-Negro thought in America, 1900-1930. Baton Rouge·, LA: Louisiana State University Press, 1965.

Neyland, L. W., and J. W. Riley. The history of Florida Agricultural and Mechanical University. Gainesville, FL: University of Florida Press, 1963.

O'Connell, William R., Jr., ed. On providing undergraduate education in the south. Atlanta, GA: Southern Regional Education Board, 1979.

Pepin, Andrew. The fall enrollment in higher education 1978, final report. Washington, D.C.: National Center for Educational Statistics, U.S. Department of Health, Education and Welfare, 1979.

Potts, John F. The history of South Carolina State College, 1869-1978. Columbia, SC: R. L. Bryan, 1978.

Rudolph, Frederick. Curriculum. San Francisco, CA: Jossey-Bass, 1977.

Simon, Myron. Ethnic writers in America. New York: Harcourt, Brace, Jovanovich, 1972.

Stent, Madelon D. "Education." In The state of black America, 1979. Washington, D.C.: National Urban League, 1980.

Stone, James C., and Donald P. DeNevi, eds. Teaching multicultural populations: Five heritages. New York: D. Van Nostrand, 1971.

Sucard, Alan R. "Educational development at a moderate-sized university." Institutional Renewal Through the Improvement of Teaching 24 (1978).

Trueheart, William E. "The consequences of federal and state resource allocation and development policies for traditional black land-grant institutions: 1862-1954." Unpublished doctoral dissertation, Graduate School of Education, Harvard University, 1979.

University of North Carolina Board of Governors. A comparative study of five historically constituent institutions of the University of North Carolina. Chapel Hill·, NC: University of North Carolina, 1976.

Vincent, Charles. A centennial history of Southern University A
and M College: 1880-1980. Baton Rouge, LA: Southern University, 1981.

Watson, Bernard. "Education." In The state of black America,
1978. Washington, D.C.: National Urban League, 1979.

_____. "Through the academic gateway." Change (October 1979).

Weathersby, George B., Gregory Jackson, Frederick Jacobs,
Edward St. John, and Tyler Tingley. The development of institutions of higher education: Theory and assessment of impact
of four possible areas of federal intervention, final report.
Cambridge.

Wharton, Clifton R., Jr. "Back to basic is not enough." Change
(November-December 1979).

Williams, C. A. "The potential of the historically black land-grant
universities of the United States in technological assistance to
less developed countries." Baton Rouge, LA: University of
Louisiana Press, 1979.

Williams, Thomas T., ed. Economic development experiences of
the Southern University System. Baton Rouge, LA: University of
Louisiana Press, 1979.

Willie, Charles V., and Ronald R. Edmonds, eds. Black colleges
in America: Challenge, development, survival. New York:
Columbia University, Teachers College Press, 1978.

Woolfolk, George R. Prairie View: A study in public conscience,
1874-1946. New York: Pageant Press, 1962.

Wright, Stephen J. The role of minority members of boards of
higher education. Washington, D.C.: Institute for Services to
Education, 1978.

14

Adapting Governance, Leadership Styles, and Management to a Changing Environment

Sherman Jones

This chapter reviews the governance, leadership styles, and management at historically black colleges. Whatever future tasks these institutions will be called upon to assume, effective management and leadership will be necessary to accomplish them.

There has long been a stereotype that the historically black colleges have been run dictatorially, with a strong and dominating president or board of trustees and a weak, incompetent faculty (Jones 1973). Like most stereotypes, this one, too, has a grain of truth to it, but it is essentially incorrect. But, if the stereotype were true it would not be enough merely to state it. It would be necessary to understand why so many of the early presidents at the historically black colleges were dictatorial and why others were not so. What was there about the environment in which these college presidents operated that influenced their management and leadership styles to give rise to this stereotype?

As one reviews the history of governance at black colleges and at the predominantly white colleges, it becomes quite clear that there has been very little difference in their structures. Indeed one finds that the evolution of governance and leadership at the historically black colleges parallels that among the historically white colleges. My thesis is essentially that, although black colleges may be distinctive in the educational role they play, they are subject to the same pressures facing all of higher education and accordingly have had to adjust their governance and management systems periodically to accommodate their environments.

HISTORICAL OVERVIEW OF CAMPUS GOVERNANCE

From the time the first U.S. university was established in 1636, the issue of how decisions were to be made became an issue of concern. Was it to be the state, the board of trustees, the institution's president, its faculty, or students who were to make the basic decisions affecting the life of the university? This debate over decision making in universities has continued to concern both participants and observers of higher education ever since.

The issue has assumed new importance in recent years as institutions of higher education have become more complex organizations with many more, often conflicting, demands being placed upon them by various elements of society. For example, colleges and universities now play a role in preparing young people for entering jobs in the professions, in promoting racial and sexual equality, in providing opportunities for those people who have been labeled disadvantaged or have low incomes, in solving social and economic problems, in performing a variety of service functions to government and industry, and in providing employment. Like other large organizations in today's society, institutions of higher education are compelled to comply with many federal and state regulations designed to promote and ensure social justice and the welfare of all citizens. Further, these same institutions are expected to pay decent wages, keep tuition low, provide a high quality of instruction, and provide cultural, athletic, and social services to their communities. Colleges and universities must necessarily be sensitive to their many constituencies—almost all of whom have some claim on the institution's resources yet also have competing interests. Our colleges and universities are quite different from the quiet educational communities of a few years ago, which had very focused interests and narrow constituencies. Accordingly, the methods of decision making have had to change in order to meet the challenges now faced by these institutions.

Faculties have sought a central role for themselves through much of the history of decision making. They have generally believed that they should make all major decisions about instruction, but their views have not always prevailed. Faculty's struggle for a central role invariably pitted them against other participants in higher education who sought an equally important role. Indeed, from the seventeenth century through the first half of the nineteenth century, colleges and universities were directed and administered by boards of trustees. Beginning in the latter part of the nineteenth century, control shifted to the hands of presidents and their adminis-

trative staffs. At most institutions, faculty have historically played
a limited but important role in institutional decision making.

In his landmark book, The Emergence of the American University (1965), Laurence Vesey states that the two most important
academic conflicts in the late nineteenth century centered on the
basic purposes of the new universities and the kind and degree of
control that would be exerted by the institution's leadership—the
state, the board of trustees, the president, and the faculty. The
issue of the goals of the university was dominant from the Civil War
until about 1890; after 1890, the emphasis shifted to a concern over
academic administration as factions arose in response to the growing administrative leadership exerted at many institutions. This
encompassed related issues of control of curricula, personnel policy, financing, and admissions.

Early in the twentieth century, the faculty began to exert itself
collectively, and finally in the 1960s students emerged as a new constituency who sought to be included in the decision-making process.
There have always been various bodies external to the university
with a continuing interest in the conduct of higher education: the
church, the state, alumni, and foundations, among others. Their
influence has varied, based on the degree of the colleges' dependence
on them for financial support. The governance problem for the 1980s
will be to reconcile the legitimate interests of each of these groups
in such a way that institutions are managed effectively.

The Colonial College

The boards of trustees of the early U.S. colleges did in fact
govern their institutions, often getting involved in their most minute
affairs. In many cases, these early colleges were under the control
of churches which were concerned not only with their students' academic development, but also with their moral development. Accordingly, boards of trustees of such institutions were intimately
involved in all of the institutions' affairs to ensure that the interests
of the church were not neglected (Rudolph 1962).

The board's close oversight was so easily accomplished, because in the seventeenth and eighteenth centuries colleges were not
complex institutions; they were usually small communities of scholars (teachers) and a few students. As Frederick Rudolph has written:

> In contrast with the modern university, the old college
> was a place where nothing happened and where the
> president by a kind of indifference or remoteness or

even superiority to mundane matters performed an ef-
fortless role in seeing to it that nothing did happen
(Rudolph 1962, p. 143).

The old-time college president was not an administrator, but was,
first and foremost, a teacher who lived at the college, traveled
little, and probably taught every member of the senior class.

The Emergence of Presidential Power

Boards of trustees maintained effective control over decision
making until the period just after the Civil War (Hofstadter and
Hardy 1952; Rudolph 1962; Vesey 1965). Events after the Civil War
resulted in the transfer of control to college presidents and their
emerging administrative staffs.

After the Civil War . . . the American college, with
more than two centuries of history already behind it,
now found itself in deepening difficulty because of declining enrollments, lack of financial support, and public indifference to the educational missions they had
defined for themselves. Ever since the Jacksonian
period, college enrollments had remained static amid
a growing population. In the years after 1865 these
discouraging figures drew more and more attention.
. . . During the 1870s, attendance at twenty of the
"oldest leading colleges" rose only 3.5 percent, while
the nation's populations soared 23 percent (Vesey 1965,
p. 14).

Sadly, the nation's colleges at that time were playing a minor role
in the life of the country.
    Fortunately for the future of higher education, a fresh group
of active, strong college presidents emerged in the latter part of
the nineteenth century who instilled new vitality into the old-time
colleges and the new universities and made these institutions responsive to the needs of the country. The stories of such men as
Charles Eliot at Harvard, Andrew White at Cornell, Woodrow Wilson
at Princeton, William Harper at Chicago, and Nicholas Murray
Butler at Columbia have been told by a number of historians. These
presidents endeavored to establish a collegiate structure that claimed
public respect and thereby obtained a new infusion of financial support. They did their job well; at the beginning of the twentieth century, enrollment at colleges and universities was 250,000—five times
more students than were enrolled in 1870.

Faculty played a relatively minor role in the transformation of the "college" into the "university":

> Below the president and his appointed deans stood the rank and file of the faculty. A formal subserviency was expected of them, as well as informal deference.
> The usual position of the American faculty was revealed by the fact that whenever an insurgent movement to "democraticize" the structure of an institution took place it was described as a "revolt." At the large universities faculty meetings were often tedious and relatively inconsequential affairs. . . . Faculty government, where it formally existed, served much the same function as student government. It was a useful device whereby administrative officers could sound out opinion, detect discontent so as better to cope with it, and further the posture of official solidarity by giving everyone parliamentary "rights" (Vesey 1965, pp. 304-5).

Unlike the old-time college leader, the president that emerged after the Civil War was an administrator, an executive expected, and indeed compelled, to exert institutional leadership. With this new concern also came increases in the size of administrative staffs— the additions of assistants to the president, registrars, deans, business-office personnel, and clerical support. In 1860, according to Rudolph, the median number of administrative officers in U.S. colleges was 4; by 1933, it was almost 31 (Rudolph 1962, p. 435). The size of administrative staffs has continued to grow ever since as institutions have developed into even more complex organizations.

Faculty Response to Administrative Power

This growth in the administrative power of the president did not go unchallenged by the faculty. Almost from the beginning, the concept of a controlling "administration" provoked intense resentment among faculty. In their eyes, then and now, the administration represented an alien and illegitimate force which "captured" the leadership of the university. As early as 1878, Alexander Winchell of Cornell had urged that professors, rather than presidents or trustees, ought to have "sole authority to expend the income of the university" (Vesey 1965, pp. 391-92).

The major drive for faculty control, however, did not come until the turn of the century, culminating in 1915 when the American

Association of University Professors (AAUP) was established. The organization's goals were to improve job security of college teachers, to enhance their professional status within society, and to secure a consensus on the legitimate role for faculty in the governance of their institutions.

The comprehensiveness of the faculty's demand for decisive participation in institutional governance at one campus is shown in the contents of a report of the Special Committee on Faculty Organization and Procedures at Cornell University (April 1957):

> This report on "The Functions of the University Faculty" claims responsibility for the faculty for initiating, considering, and making recommendations on questions of educational policy or problems arising therefrom whether concerning (i) current operations of the University or (ii) long-range policy (such as admissions policies, proposals for new degrees, establishment of new educational and research units, the size of the University, auxiliary cultural agencies, and questions concerning the status and privileges of the faculty). And the report interprets the term "questions of educational policy" broadly to include questions that involve (i) conditions facilitating instruction, study, research, publications and other scholarly activities of faculty members and students or (ii) the general welfare of the academic community (Corson 1960, pp. 98-99).

The faculty's right to be consulted and to make decisions on educational questions is universally acknowledged. Faculty influence in matters of governance was repeatedly challenged, however, as institutions grew larger and more complex and administrative demands created central staffs around the president and the deans, tending to increase their decision-making authority. The faculty's influence has been further reduced by the apparent lack of concern and unwillingness of many faculty members to devote time to consideration of governance questions. It is inherently difficult for a number of persons, whether faculty or any other group, to arrive at decisions in a timely fashion; but institutions often need such prompt decisions.

The establishment of the AAUP represented a response on the national level to faculty desires to participate in the governance of institutions of higher education. Over the years, the AAUP has developed a number of procedures to aid it in this task. Late in the 1950s, the AAUP established a Committee on College and University Governance which submitted a report in 1960, setting forth a statement of principles for faculty participation in university governance. This statement declared that the basic functions of a college/university were performed by a community of scholars who must be free to exercise their independent judgment in planning and executing their educational assignment. It recognized three groups as having important roles to play in the governance of institutions: the faculty, the administration, and the board of trustees. The statement called for a careful delineation of the role of each group in university governance, declaring that no one group had exclusive claim to power. In fact, the report went on to propose what was called the "joint authority" of faculties, administrators, and governing boards in all areas of university governance.

A short time later, the AAUP invited the American Council on Education and the Association of Governing Boards of Universities and Colleges to join it in preparing a joint position on college and university government. This statement was published by the AAUP in 1966 and, like the earlier one, emphasized that governance was a joint endeavor, stressing the faculty's primary responsibility in matters of faculty welfare/status and the educational program. Unlike the 1960 report, this statement recognized a limited role for students in matters of governance in areas that involved their particular interests.

One outcome of these activities was the emergence on many campuses during the 1960s of groups variously called "academic senates" or "university councils" which sought to put into effect the concept of joint or shared decision making. In his 1975 study of campus senates, Hodgkinson found that 85 percent had been in existence for less than eight years. Usually these groups were quite large and were comprised of representatives of faculty, administrators, and students, with the faculty in the majority. At many institutions they were viewed as forums where decisions were to be made, not as advisory groups.

As institutions have become more complex and have taken on a variety of roles, it has become more difficult to reconcile the theory—the normative model—of faculty participation in governance with the actual practice of such participation. As professional workers in white-collar professions, faculty members feel that they should play a major role in the affairs of their institutions; they view themselves as more than merely employees of these organizations, but rather as the embodiment of the organizations. Thus, there is the desire to control the affairs of the institution in a more authoritative way than in the past. One response of some faculty to this dilemma has been to turn to collective bargaining, but in my view, collective bargaining is not now a significant force in higher education governance.

Recent Patterns of Governance at the
Historically Black Colleges

The history of governance and management at historically
black colleges has not differed greatly from that at white institutions. The emergence of black colleges, like white ones, depended
upon the leadership of strong executives such as Samuel Chapman
Armstrong, Booker T. Washington, John W. Davis, John Hope,
Mordecai Johnson, Charles Wesley, and Thomas Elsa Jones, two
of whom were white. Unlike their white college counterparts, these
presidents had to exert their leadership within the framework of a
racially segregated society. Indeed it was within such a segregated
and racist framework that the image of the dictatorial presidents of
black colleges developed. In an environment in which the existence
of higher education for blacks was not widely accepted, presidents
of black colleges were called upon to defend the existence of their
institutions and, more importantly, to ensure peace on their campuses.

Dr. Bledsoe of Ralph Ellison's Invisible Man might well serve
as the archetype of the president of a black college in the early years
of these institutions. In Bledsoe's words:

> Negroes don't control this school or much of anything
> else—haven't you learned even that? No, sir, they
> don't control this school, nor white folk either. True,
> they support it, but I control it. I's big and black and
> I say "Yes, suh" as loudly as any burrhead when it's
> convenient, but I'm still the king down here. I don't
> care how much it appears otherwise. The only ones
> I even pretend to please are big white folk, even those
> I control more than they control me. And I'll tell you
> something your sociology teachers are afraid to tell
> you. If there weren't men like me running schools
> like this, there'd be no South, nor North either. No,
> and there'd be no country—not as it is today (Ellison
> 1947, p. 140).

Samuel Chapman Armstrong, founding white president of
Hampton Institute in 1869, or Booker T. Washington, president of
Tuskegee Institute, established in 1881, were real-life prototypes
of the early presidents of black colleges. But one should be re-
minded that the presidential styles of Bledsoe, Armstrong, or Washington were not peculiar to black colleges. Indeed the pattern of
leadership in all of higher education in this period was for presidents to assume strong leadership roles.

Quite often, the president was the only person of any education and social standing on the campus in these early years of the development of the U.S. college and university (Rudolph 1962). It was not unusual for the faculty of an institution to consist of a president who had higher-education training and a number of tutors with little academic training. Accordingly, it was not unusual for college presidents to dominate the campus; they had neither equals nor near-equals among their colleagues. In many church-related institutions, presidents of the colleges were also ministers—demanding respect by their position in the church.

It should not be considered peculiar then that black colleges, especially during their emerging years, had strong executive leadership. But writers on the management of black colleges have not often taken this view. An example is Ambrose Caliver writing about the management of the historically black college in 1942 in the Third National Survey of Higher Education of the Negro:

> It is a generally recognized principle of college organization that within a democratic frame of reference the faculty is the legislative authority for matters concerning the general academic affairs of the institution. In practice, the faculty organization in the institutions studied does not conform to this principle; rather the organization is authoritarian, and important decisions relative to academic matters are made by administrative officers (Caliver 1942, p. 27).

Earl McGrath expressed this same view in his 1965 book, The Predominately Negro College in Transition: "Heavily dependent on the goodwill of influential private benefactors or local political powers, they have tended to remain 'presidential' institutions."

Writers such as these would lead readers to conclude that strong executive leadership was a phenomenon peculiarly associated with black institutions. The Carnegie Commission on Higher Education in its 1973 book, The Governance of Higher Education, concluded, however, that the "internal practices of governance vary by type of institution. For example, faculty authority tends to be comparatively great at the leading research institutions and at the academically most prestigious liberal arts colleges." What the commission leaves unstated is that faculty authority is often subordinate to administrative authority at almost all other institutions of higher education. No historian of U.S. colleges would label Cornell, Harvard, Columbia, Wisconsin, or even Johns Hopkins faculty-dominated institutions during their emergence as universities in the late nineteenth century. They became faculty dominated after they had emerged as strong, well-financed institutions.

For example, after a detailed study of governance of both black and white institutions, this author concluded that the basic model of governance and decision making is not the so-called "collegial model" with the faculty dominating campus decision making (Jones 1978). Rather, the most common governance system on college campuses is one which can be called a "managerial model," in which the president and his senior administrative staff do in fact manage their institutions.

It may well be as true today as it was when Earl McGrath wrote in 1965 that:

> . . . [if the historically black colleges] expect to compete for faculty members of superior qualifications, most of whom have become accustomed to the freedom and self-determination in the great centers of learning, they will have to provide similar conditions of academic life on their own campuses. Both those faculty members who go away for advanced training and return, and those who come in as exchange professors will find authoritarian leadership uncongenial (McGrath 1965, p. 124).

McGrath, like others, associates strong executive leadership with authoritarian leadership, but the two are not necessarily interrelated. A strong executive can be effective without being a dictator, a point which he fails to acknowledge.

As individual black colleges have increased their academic strength, financial viability, and moved closer to the main currents of American higher education, they have experimented—like their white counterparts—with various governance and decision-making models. For example, Fisk University in the early 1970s experimented with a university assembly composed of faculty, administrators, students, and board members whose purpose was to make basic decisions for the university. By 1977, the university had returned to a more conventional management organization which recognized the president as its chief executive officer, while allowing for broad participation of faculty, students, and administrators in governance and management. Among the 100-plus historically black colleges, the amount of faculty influence in decision making is as diverse as among all institutions of higher education. The exceptions are the most prestigious liberal-arts colleges and the leading research universities. Many of the same influences affecting campus governance patterns at historically white colleges will affect such patterns at historically black colleges.

FACTORS AFFECTING MANAGEMENT PATTERNS

Given the crucial influence that external forces have had on campus governance and management at the historically black college in the past, one must expect that such forces will continue to have a significant influence on the colleges throughout the 1980s. Three forces that have already had a strong influence are recent patterns of financing, the impact of the federal government and state systems of higher education, and desegregation of higher education.

Recent Trends in Financing

The financing patterns of the black colleges from the 1920s until after World War II were fairly well set by well-established conditions and trends. After World War II, the federal government began to play a larger and, more recently, an essential role in the financing of all of higher education. Recent statistics show that in 1975 the federal government provided 38 percent of the total income of independent black colleges and universities and over 21 percent of the total income of state-assisted colleges and universities. This includes both direct institutional support and student-aid monies obtained indirectly through the federal student financial-aid programs. Stated another way, the federal government accounted for 46 percent of the educational and general income of independent black colleges and 28 percent of such income at the state-assisted institutions. Indeed, for the periods shown by Tables 1 and 2, the federal share of the mean income at these colleges actually increased. As of fiscal year 1980, the federal government probably accounts for over 60 percent of the income at a number of the private black institutions and over 40 percent at the public black institutions.

Contrary to popular belief, black colleges receive relatively little of their income from direct institutional grants or from research programs. The primary reason for the growth in federal funds at the historically black colleges has been the growth in the federal student financial-aid programs and the large proportion of students at black colleges who are eligible for such funding. This heavy reliance on one primary source of income for the historically black colleges poses a number of problems. First, the colleges are caught up in the sometimes whimsical preferences of bureaucrats and politicians; second, federal government regulations call for financial and management audits that require more sophisticated accounting than most colleges can provide, given their limited resources; third, audits of students eligible for federal financial aid can delay funds going to students to pay their bills and indeed might

TABLE 1

Mean Income by Source in 1970 and 1975 for
Public Black Colleges and Universities

Source	1970		1975	
	Amount	Percent	Amount	Percent
Federal government		18.5		21.5
Aid to students	$ 562,805		$ 991,647	
Aid to institutions	369,195		939,931	
Sponsored research	0		240,185	
State government		53.1		44.7
Aid to students	38,520		66,110	
Aid to institutions	2,637,986		4,456,105	
Tuition and fees paid by students	150,081	3.0	264,439	2.6
Endowment	1,658		2,048	
Gifts, grants	28,114	0.6	100,641	0.1
All other income for educational and general expenses	0	0	765,428	7.6
Auxiliary enterprises	1,023,289	20.3	1,501,753	14.8
Student aid	228,674	4.5	591,655	5.8
All other income	0	0	189,211	1.9
Total	$5,039,322	100.0	$10,109,153	99.0

Source: Reprinted by permission of the publisher from Sherman J. Jones and George B. Weathersby, "Financing the Black College," in Black Colleges in America, edited by Charles V. Willie and Ronald R. Edmonds (New York: Teachers College Press, copyright 1978 by Teachers College, Columbia University), pp. 118, 119.

TABLE 2

Mean Income by Source in 1970 and 1975 at
Independent Black Colleges

Source	1970 Amount	1970 Percent	1975 Amount	1975 Percent
Federal government		33.8		38.0
Aid to students (75% of tuition and fee income)	$ 649,831		$ 950,515	
Aid to institutions	207,951		664,025	
Sponsored research	0		120,248	
State government		2.7		3.9
Aid to students (5% of tuition and fee income)	43,322		63,368	
Aid to institutions	25,290		116,437	
Tuition and fees paid by students	173,288	6.8	253,471	5.5
Endowment	112,247	4.4	130,786	2.9
Gifts, grants	448,827	17.7	737,150	16.1
All other income for educational and general expenses	0	0	163,695	3.6
Auxiliary enterprises	589,966	23.2	816,403	17.9
Student aid	289,292	11.4	526,086	11.5
All other income	0			
Total	$2,540,014	100.0	$4,564,615	99.4

Source: Reprinted by permission of the publisher from Sherman J. Jones and George B. Weathersby, "Financing the Black College," in Black Colleges in America, edited by Charles V. Willie and Ronald R. Edmonds (New York: Teachers College Press, copyright 1978 by Teachers College, Columbia University), pp. 118, 119.

even deny funds to some students who were allowed to register because they seemed to meet the requirements. Now that student aid
and all federal funds have been cut back, the outlook is bleaker.

Bishop College almost closed its doors between 1978 and 1980
after an alarming decrease in its enrollment. Federal financial-
aid funds were cut off because of allegations of malfeasance and mis-
handling of these funds by university officials. This experience represents one of the worst dangers of the increasing reliance of the
historically black colleges on the federal government as a source of
income. This reliance on the federal financial-aid programs places
a premium on annual enrollment increases to ensure growth in annual income available to the colleges. This is especially evident at
those institutions where almost all of the student body has substantial financial aid underwritten by the federal government; that is,
the amount of tuition and fees that the colleges can charge is limited
by what their students can pay. By definition, students receiving
almost total financial aid cannot pay any more than the amount of
their financial aid and this amount cannot be increased until the federal government increases the limits on its own programs.

The Impact of the Federal Government

Besides the role that the federal government has recently assumed in financing historically black colleges, it has had an important influence on the development of the colleges in other ways. The
black land-grant institutions were established as a result of the initiative of the federal government; the surveys of the education of
blacks in the nineteenth and early twentieth centuries were instrumental in the development of black schools and colleges and bringing
greater financial support to these colleges in the 1930s, 1940s, and
1950s. One of the primary goals of the Title III program established
in the 1960s was to bring black colleges "into the mainstream of
American higher education." Since its establishment, the Title III
program has assisted the nation's black colleges to clarify their
missions and to strengthen their management and academic programs. More recently, a stated objective of the executive branch
of the government has been to increase the participation of the historically black colleges in the programs of the federal government.

Thus, there is the potential for an even closer relationship
between the nation's black colleges and the federal government.
The programs a college offers are typically those which provide
education, public service, and research. At the present time, the
federal government gives its principal support to black colleges for
their educational programs; it provides very little support for their

research and public service programs. This situation will change
only when the colleges become actively involved in the political
process to ensure that their vital interests are being considered.

State Systems and Desegregation of
Higher Education

Over the past ten years, a number of states have moved to
unitary systems of public higher education. Such systems normally
rely on a state board to coordinate and make final decisions on the
direction and nature of higher education in the state. A major consequence of this new organizational pattern is that, to varying degrees, individual state institutions have lost a part of their authority to determine their futures. Further, the effective management
of a state system of higher education demands common management
information systems, policies, and practices governing all of the
institutions in a system. The result is that a state system requires
better administration of the colleges.

Many of the public black colleges and universities are now a
part of state systems. One of the dilemmas facing the presidents
of these institutions is, on the one hand, to maintain some sense of
their historical clientele and missions and, on the other, to resist
becoming just another one of the public higher-education institutions
in the state.

At the same time that a number of the public black colleges
have become part of unitary systems of higher education, they have
confronted the consequences of the legal requirement to dismantle
segregated systems of higher education in those states where such
systems exist.

PRESIDENTIAL LEADERSHIP AND
GOVERNANCE IN THE 1980S

Given the array of obstacles to be confronted in the 1980s,
what kinds of presidents will be needed if the black colleges and universities are to become stronger, more viable institutions? The
Carnegie Commission on Higher Education has come out very strongly in support of active presidents for colleges and universities:

> We believe that the present periods call for substan-
> tial changes on campus and in the relationships of the
> campus to society. This, in turn, will require greater
> presidential influence to initiate and to guide the changes.

It is also a period of more than usual conflict on campus
that requires understanding and action. Additionally,
fiscal stringency requires more administrative authority. We believe, consequently, that boards should seek
to appoint active rather than passive presidents, presidents who will lead rather than just survive. They
should also give presidents adequate authority and staff,
and their own support in the difficult task of encouraging constructive change—realizing that periods of
change are also periods of unusual tension—and of effectively resolving conflict (Carnegie Commission 1973,
p. 37).

Five years later John Millett supported this position in his
book on campus governance and concluded:

The structures of campuswide governance developed in
the 1960s were conspicuous in their studious avoidance
of instruments or agents of leadership. In this sense
the status and authority of presidents were secure.
The reformers of the 1960s had no alternative to propose to presidential leadership; they seemed to want
no leadership at all. As a consequence, campuswide
governance arrangements ended up for the most part
confirming presidential leadership but seeking to attach certain limitations to its exercise. By the late
1970s the indispensability of presidential leadership
was again rather generally acknowledged, if not always appreciated (Millett 1978, p. 268).

A number of former and current black college presidents,
members of boards of trustees, and other leaders of historically
black colleges concur with these conclusions. They acknowledge
that the president of any college in the 1980s has to be a person
with an understanding of the academic enterprise and management—
knowledge of financial affairs, personnel administration, information systems, planning, and controlling. In addition, a president of
an independent college, far more so than the president of a state-
assisted college, will have to be an effective fund-raiser, possessing all those intangible skills that increase the flow of private gifts
and grants to a university. The college president of the 1980s,
especially at a state-assisted institution, will also need to be effective in federal and/or state government circles to ensure that the
political and bureaucratic decisions made are beneficial, or at least
not detrimental, to institutions of higher education. Finally, while

college presidents are playing the roles of managers of a purposeful organization, fund-raisers, and politicians, they must not for-
get that they are, above all, educators. They must be able to communicate effectively with faculty, students, their administrative
staff, support personnel, community groups, alumni, friends of the
institution, and with anyone else interested in the college.

The old-time college president could attend to the most minute
details of the college. Even in the 1960s there were still many old-
time college presidents leading institutions. But few of them remain.
We all know that no one person can do all the above tasks well. Accordingly, during the 1980s, I would expect that more and more colleges will adopt modern management concepts for directing their institutions. These would include developing clear policies and procedures to guide their organizations, decentralizing responsibility and
authority, establishing a top management team, and improving financial management and control. At some institutions, the president's
emergence as a kind of "Mr. Outside" has led these institutions to
create a new administrative position, a vice-president or executive
vice-president, who functions as a "Mr. Inside." Such an organizational arrangement permits the president to function primarily in an
external role emphasizing the public functions—fundraising, making
friends for the college, speaking to various groups that may have an
interest in the college—and policy-making functions of the president's office. Meanwhile, the vice president attends to the daily
administration of the institution.

Boards of trustees must devote more attention to providing
for effective governance of the institutions than, as they once did,
in attempting to govern themselves. The Carnegie Commission
(1973) suggests that they should not run colleges, but rather should
assure that colleges are run well.

Up to the present, faculty collective bargaining has been an
issue at only a few of the historically black colleges. I would expect that this will continue to be the case. Further, it would seem
that, as historically black colleges adopt modern management models
and structures, their faculties will assume greater responsibility for
governance and decision making, particularly in academic affairs
and faculty personnel matters. Some tension is bound to arise between the forces desiring faculty power and those supporting presidential leadership. Yet, only those institutions with strong, effective
presidential leadership will survive as viable institutions.

The implications for the management of black colleges of the
increasing reliance on federal monies, particularly financial aid, are:

— A need for efficient and effective management of federal
  financial-aid programs

— A need for accounting and financial systems that can with-
stand the scrutiny of government guidelines
— A need to maintain enrollment levels
— A need for compliance with the appropriate federal regulations

In the past, such needs for increased administrative detail have led
to the growth in staffs to perform the new tasks. I expect this growth
to occur at the historically black colleges just as it has occurred at
the white colleges.

REFERENCES

Caliver, Ambrose. National survey of the higher education of
Negroes. Washington, D.C.: U.S. Government Printing Office,
1942.

Carnegie Commission on Higher Education. Governance of higher
education. New York: McGraw-Hill, 1973.

Corson, John. Governance of colleges and universities. New York:
McGraw-Hill, 1960.

Ellison, Ralph. Invisible man. New York: Vintage Books, 1947.

Hodgkinson, Harold L. Institutions in transition: A profile of
change in higher education. New York: McGraw-Hill, 1971.

Hofstadter, R., and C. D. Hardy. The development and scope of
higher education in the United States. New York: Columbia
University Press, 1952.

Jones, Ann. Uncle Tom's campus. New York: Praeger, 1973.

Jones, Sherman. "Faculty involvement in college and university
decision-making." PhD dissertation, Harvard University,
1978.

McGrath, Earl. The predominately Negro college in transition.
New York: Columbia University, Teacher's College Press, 1965.

Millett, John. New structures of campus power. San Francisco,
CA: Jossey-Bass, 1978.

Rudolph, Frederick. The American college and university. New York: Vintage Books, 1962.

Vesey, Lawrence. The emergence of the American university. Chicago, IL: University of Chicago Press, 1965.

Willie, Charles V., and Ronald Edmonds, eds. Black colleges in America. New York: Columbia University, Teachers College Press, 1978.

PART VII

SUMMARY

15

A Creative Minority
in the World
of Higher Education

Jane Browning

As in many other academic inquiries, this book focuses on the support and strengthening of a basic tenet held by its authors: historically black colleges and universities are viable institutions of higher learning and therefore should be maintained. This issue was discussed at great length by all the participants at the two working meetings and the final seminar where the highlights of each of the commissioned chapters were discussed.

Participants examined perspectives on current and potential roles for black colleges previously identified by the editor through meetings and conversations with black-college faculty and administrators and other higher-education researchers. They discussed issues related to these roles in order to develop research recommendations. The authors addressed the historical significance of black colleges and developed theories for determining and initiating research strategies for survival in order to maintain the founding mission of these institutions.

RESEARCH STRATEGIES FOR SURVIVAL

Why was research strategies for survival chosen as a crucial seminar question? Research is the cornerstone for quality academic instruction and has been shown, in large research institutions, to guarantee the presence of well-prepared and dedicated faculty. This, in turn, attracts bright students who perform well while in college. Moreover, ongoing research, that contributes to the improvement of the human race, produces financial rewards that allow an institution to function as a community and educational resource. The

authors developed research strategies which not only would identify
the characteristics that distinguish black colleges from other postsecondary institutions but also those which would strengthen these
colleges. The purpose of this summary is to analyze the major re-
curring themes and to review several of the suggested research
recommendations. The themes were derived from the authors'
selection of relevant issues. They are:

— American higher education is in a period of transition.
— Black colleges are mainstream colleges.
— The traditional missions of black colleges should be maintained.
— Research efforts designed to strengthen black colleges provide the most effective means of ensuring their survival
  during the transition period.
— Research centers and institutes are viable structures for
  initiating sustained quality research in black colleges.
— The federal government has an important role in assisting
  large-scale quality research in black colleges and universities.

AMERICAN HIGHER EDUCATION IN TRANSITION

Colleges and universities throughout the United States are in
a period of transition which reflects the changes taking place in U.S.
society. During the 1970s there was a redefinition of priorities and
goals for higher education, a redefinition which is continuing in the
1980s. The overuse of energy resources in the middle of the century, for example, has created problems that directly affect and determine the future lifestyle of the general population, with minority
populations acutely affected. The future directions of higher education curricula and research emphases are interwoven with the shifting nature and needs of U.S. culture. And black colleges, more
than white colleges, should address the difficulties of changing
priorities.

Mainstream Institutions

Black colleges are mainstream institutions subject to the same
academic and administrative pressures faced by the majority of postsecondary schools. In the 1980s and 1990s, colleges and universities
will confront issues that will affect approaches to administration,
curricula, enrollments, and alumni affairs. The problems of higher

education are chiefly those of society at large and include urbaniza-
tion, rural development, health care, career development, economic
and political development, the roles of men and women in society,
and many other issues relating to quality of life. In response, black
colleges, like all colleges, are concerned with defining and achieving institutional goals and objectives appropriate for today's world.

Maintaining Traditional Missions

Maintaining the traditional missions of black colleges is a re-
current theme throughout the book. These missions are best summarized as providing a quality undergraduate experience for the
poorly qualified, preparing leaders for society (particularly for the
black community), delivering services to the community, and providing graduate and professional education for blacks who otherwise
would not have such opportunities.

During the seminars, the participants agreed that the black
colleges' missions do not need to be altered over the next 10 to 20
years. For one thing, the majority of the student population of these
institutions remains black, with students coming from predominantly
black public schools. The current and potential roles of black colleges remain appropriate for this slowly changing population.
Charles Smith warns us, however, that the transition period requires new strategies for developing stronger institutions in a competitive environment of academic instruction, community service,
and research.

Research to Strengthen Black Colleges

The most effective means of coping during the transition
period is through research designed to obtain information which will
influence the quality of education provided at black colleges. Increased quality research will strengthen scholarship, promote movement into the mainstream, guarantee competition, and maintain well-
trained faculty. The presence of research is an essential key to the
survival of black colleges, since research does not only play a
major role in determining the future of these schools, but also as-
sists in the formulation of policy affecting blacks in the U.S. and the
nation at large. The barrier to promoting research on black college campuses is that grants go primarily to teachers who have a
track record in research. To correct the present situation, Branson suggests that black colleges not be isolated from sources of research funds or other research institutions. This would allow their

faculties to grow intellectually, pursuing federal and other fiscal support consonant with their skills and interests. Specifically, he would promote the single researcher and small research teams, working in basic areas such as molecular biology and energy as they relate to physical and social problems.

Daniel Thompson states that only 2 to 3 percent of teachers in black colleges are involved in serious research. He provides a summary of the reasons why it is difficult to obtain a balance between teaching and research: black college faculty are engaged in endless tasks related to the survival of the colleges themselves; they devote their time to community and race-related problems; they are concerned with a lack of sufficient funds for administering the institutions; and they have heavy teaching loads. The irony, Thompson writes, is that the absence of research in black colleges causes the institutions to be viewed by outsiders as subordinate to all other colleges and universities. Thus, there is an immediate challenge to find means and resources for black college faculty to do research and change this negative and false image.

Research Centers to Initiate Research

Another theme repeatedly discussed throughout the chapters and in the seminars was the need for research centers, forums, and institutes to house and support major research efforts at black colleges. These centers would operate independently or in cooperation with research projects at white colleges to produce significant findings that might be of use to the public and private sectors. The centers would be the principal voice from the black-college community contributing to the formulation of policy related to national and international affairs. The centers would also foster student participation in research on both the undergraduate and graduate levels and assist in improving communication between the campus and the surrounding community.

The Federal Government

For some black institutions, the role of the federal government in funding research is equal in importance to their other concerns. The authors stress that federal funds remain the major source of financing research efforts in the United States. The federal government, therefore, will have to encourage research in these colleges through financial and technical assistance. Only in this way will the colleges be able to encourage faculty-research projects and develop centers that will address some of the complex social, scientific, economic, and international problems this nation faces.

DIRECTIONS FOR RESEARCH AND PUBLIC
POLICY ON BLACK COLLEGES

The authors present convincing arguments for possible research on the future and potential roles of black colleges. This research should be designed to gather data pertinent to the future of these institutions and to their communities. A few research recommendations drawn from the preceding chapters merit additional comments. These recommendations are: (1) the need for strategies to develop quality research capabilities at black colleges; (2) the need to establish centers for housing and monitoring research efforts at black colleges; (3) the need for improved scientific instruction at black colleges; and (4) a review and reassessment of the function of public-policy analysis in determining public opinion and government responses to black colleges.

Strategies to develop quality research capabilities at black colleges are essential to initiating studies and, in some instances, restructuring the large volume of serious research already in existence. At the seminar the authors discussed the constantly changing nature of socioeconomic and political issues, both internal and external to the institutions, and emphasized the need for a governance structure that will be flexible enough to respond to these changes. Presidents and other administrators can benefit most from research that is responsive to the daily needs of their institutions. In addition to issues of governance, more attention must be given to academic instruction, a changing student population, and fiscal and community affairs. The research, therefore, has to be designed to correlate overlapping areas of concern for black-college development. For example, how can the curriculum meet the instructional needs of a changing student population? What will happen to the student population as a result of dwindling financial assistance? And, how might research at the colleges benefit internal development and assist in the solution of community problems that are an integral part of the college's mission, for example, leadership development? Research at and about black colleges must, therefore, be constructed to yield answers to the essential questions in a way that will benefit administrative planning and the academic program for students.

Research Centers

Centers, forums, and institutes are mechanisms through which a college or university can establish research priorities, negotiate and determine policies, and affect decision making relevant to an institution's survival and maintenance. Maintaining the historical missions of black colleges in a desegregating society is another topic referred to often in the book and one that needs to be examined in detail. Thus, the black colleges will continue to pursue the dual goal of addressing academic topics such as international affairs, especially as concerns the Third World, while simultaneously dealing with issues that bear directly on the lives and conditions of black U.S. citizens.

One such immediate topic is the energy crisis. Poor and disadvantaged people bear the brunt of costly gas and electrical consumption. Two authors suggest that addressing these energy concerns would be a natural research interest for institutes at black colleges. The research center, as a strategy, thus becomes the vehicle for providing research opportunities for faculty and students, for collecting and analyzing data on blacks and other populations, and for developing communication between the campus and the public, all with the intent of determining public policy.

Research centers and institutes also have the potential for strengthening academic instruction in the natural sciences at black colleges. More graduates of black colleges will have the opportunity to participate in the science-related professions. In order for black-college graduates to qualify for management or policy positions in industry today, they must receive special instruction to counter historical deficiencies in the learning process, especially in the hard sciences and mathematics. Research on teaching the educationally disadvantaged student is an important topic for these centers to address, either as a major effort or by means of small research teams. In the research centers, students will be able to apply principles learned in the classroom to test concepts and design and complete, with adequate supervision, independent research projects. The outcome will hopefully be graduates better prepared for jobs requiring a strong scientific background and research assistants, particularly at the graduate level, for the often overworked faculty at black colleges.

The Impact of Public Policy

Finally, public opinion and policy have created the environment in which black colleges currently exist. Public policy, as adapted by federal and state governments, has been designed to in-

fluence and, in most cases, determine the academic and fiscal decisions of black-college administrations over the past two decades.
But the question remains whether academic priorities and internal
administrative policies at black colleges truly reflect what those institutions want to do or should be doing, as opposed to what they
consider necessary to avoid losing federal funding. One can question if the right policy questions have even been asked.

Of even more importance is the need to address the division
in public opinion over whether predominantly black colleges should
exist in a desegregating society. Public opinion influences the support of black colleges by legislatures and private funding sources;
furthermore, public opinion helps shape the decisions of students
to attend and of faculty to work at these institutions. The historic
and future effects of public policy and opinion filter through the
black-college environment and have a direct impact on curricula,
fiscal policies, student enrollment, and college involvement in state
activities.

Black colleges and universities have been creative in their
response to public policy. They have been able to maintain quality
education while preserving the founding mission of teaching the educationally disadvantaged, of developing leadership, and of promoting
community involvement by supporting instruction and cooperative
ventures designed to enhance the Afro-American experience.
Throughout the last three decades, meeting national requirements
has been the exhaustive and exhausting task of these institutions.
This task will become even more demanding since the occupational,
educational, and social communities are desegregating at a more
rapid pace than the historically black colleges and these institutions
are being pressured to justify their existence in the face of spiral-
ing tuition costs and budget cuts.

Confirming the need for the continuation and strengthening of
the historically black colleges should begin with research designed
to provide policymakers with information on their validity. This is
the message of the seminars and this book. The seminar participants, particularly Stephen Wright and Kenneth Tollett, emphasized
the necessity for the colleges to be creative in administrative affairs.
For instance, they note that middle management must be trained and
allowed to take full responsibility to implement policies set by the
boards and senior administrators, so that senior officers can spend
adequate time with the external affairs of the institution.

Black colleges and universities face a new challenge to become
once again unique examples of creativity in providing proven administrative strategies for survival in a rapidly changing postsecondary
environment. This challenge is invigorating because it allows black
colleges, as examples to all of higher education, to find the answers
to quality academic performance despite scarce resources.

Index

About the Editor
and Contributors

SIDNEY J. BARTHELEMY is an assistant professor of sociology and director of the Urbinvolve Program at Xavier University, as well as Councilman-at-large in New Orleans, Louisiana. Barthelemy is a former Louisiana State Senator and was director of the New Orleans Department of Welfare from 1972 to 1974.

HERMAN BRANSON is president of Lincoln University in Pennsylvania. Prior to his appointment at Lincoln in 1970, he served as president of Central State University in Ohio and taught physics and mathematics at Howard University from 1941 to 1968 and briefly at Dillard University. Branson is a member of numerous professional associations and has published more than 90 articles on a variety of topics in biophysics, physics, and science education.

JANE SMITH BROWNING is director of Inroads/Atlanta, Incorporated. After receiving her EdD from Harvard, she served as director of freshman studies, assistant professor of sociology, and later assistant to the president at Spelman College. She has also served as assistant vice-president for research and development at Atlanta University.

HENRY E. COBB is a professor of history at Southern University in Baton Rouge, Louisiana, where he previously served as vice-chancellor for academic affairs and dean of the graduate school. He also taught history at Tuskegee Institute and was professor of history at Florida A&M University from 1952 to 1957. Cobb has an extensive background as a researcher and director of curriculum projects and has published books and articles on Afro-American history, black colleges, and the Far East.

JOHN W. DAVIS, who died in 1980 at the age of 92, was president emeritus of West Virginia State College. After his retirement from West Virginia State, he served as special director, Teacher Information and Security Programs, of the NAACP Legal Defense and Educational Fund and director of research for Prince Hall Masonry. He was a member of Phi Beta Kappa and Sigma Pi Phi honor societies.

G. FRANKLIN EDWARDS has been a faculty member in the Department of Sociology and Anthropology at Howard University since 1941. He participated in the work of the Negro Land-Grant Cooperative Research Project (1944-46) and was a member of the Research Advisory Committee for the Cooperative Research Project of the U.S. Office of Education (1962-65). Edwards is the author of numerous articles, The Negro Professional Class, and editor of E. Franklin Frazier on Race Relations.

ANTOINE GARIBALDI is chairman and associate professor of education at Xavier University in New Orleans, Louisiana. Prior to his current position, he was a research associate for five years at the National Institute of Education on the Postsecondary Organization and Management Studies Team, director of the St. Paul (Minnesota) Urban League Street Academy, a school psychologist, a teaching and research assistant at the University of Minnesota, an elementary school teacher, and a lecturer of educational psychology at Howard University. He is the author of chapters and articles on discipline, cooperation and competition, science education, desegregation, and alternatives to suspension, as well as an instructor's manual for an educational psychology text (Prentice-Hall, 1979) and editor of In-School Alternatives to Suspension (Government Printing Office, 1979). He has also been a consulting and associate editor for the American Educational Research Journal.

MELDON S. HOLLIS is Special Assistant to the President at Harvard University. During the 1981-82 academic year, he was vice president for development at Texas Southern University and prior to that was special assistant to the Assistant Secretary for Education and director of the White House Initiative on Black Colleges and Universities during the Carter Administration. Hollis is a graduate of Harvard Law School, attended the U.S. Military Academy at West Point, and holds BA and MA degrees in government and politics from the University of Maryland.

FREDERICK S. HUMPHRIES is president of Tennessee State University in Nashville, a position he has held since 1974. After receiving his PhD in physical chemistry from the University of Pittsburgh, he served as a professor of chemistry at Florida A&M University and as an assistant professor at the University of Minnesota. He is a former vice president of the Institute for Services to Education and the author of numerous scientific and educational articles.

WILLIAM M. JACKSON is professor of chemistry at Howard University. Prior to his present position he was affiliated with the Goddard Space Center (NASA) as a staff (1964-69) and senior chemist (1970-74) and was a visiting associate professor in the Department of Physics at the University of Pittsburgh (1969-70). A member of many scientific and honor societies, he is the author of more than 50 articles, many in the field of photochemistry.

SHERMAN JONES is executive vice-president at Tuskegee Institute. Prior to his present position, he was vice-president for administration and served as acting dean of academic affairs at Fisk University and was affiliated with the Academy for Educational Development and Cresap, McCormick and Paget, management consulting firms. He received his BA from Williams College, and MBA and EdD from Harvard University and has written articles on various aspects of higher education.

JOHN MATLOCK is chief administrative assistant to Congressman Harold Ford of Tennessee. He is a former director of institutional research and planning at Tennessee State University and served as manager of research and planning at the Tennessee Valley Center in Memphis. While completing his PhD at the University of Michigan, he taught journals courses and graduate courses in organizational research and planning.

JOHN U. MONRO is professor of writing at Tougaloo College in Mississippi. He was director of freshman studies at Miles College in 1967 and professor of English in 1977. A graduate of Harvard College, Monro served in various capacities at his alma mater from 1947 to 1967, including counselor for veterans, assistant to the provost, director of financial aid, and dean of Harvard College from 1957 to 1967.

JEWEL L. PRESTAGE is professor and chair of the department of political science at Southern University in Baton Rouge, Louisiana. She has also served as an associate professor of political science at Prairie View A&M in Texas, and has held numerous offices in professional political science organizations including the presidency of the Southwestern Social Science Association, the Southern Political Science Association, and the National Conference of Black Political Scientists. A former vice president of the American Political Science Association, she has published extensively and is coauthor, with Marianne Githens, of A Portrait of Marginality: The Political Behavior of the American Woman.

CHARLES U. SMITH is dean of graduate studies, research and continuing education, and professor of sociology at Florida A&M University. He is also an adjunct professor of sociology and a research associate at Florida State University. He is past president of the Southern Sociological Society and of the Association of Social and Behavioral Scientists, and president-elect of the Conference of Deans of Black Graduate Schools. Smith has authored more than 50 research articles in education and sociology and coauthored six books, including New Careers and Curriculum Change and Black Sociologists: Historical and Contemporary Perspectives.

MADELON DELANY STENT is a professor at the City College of the City University of New York. Stent also served as acting vice-president of academic affairs at the University of the District of Columbia in 1977-78. A recipient of degrees from Sarah Lawrence College, Wellesley, and Columbia University, she is the coauthor of Minorities in U.S. Institutions of Higher Education and Cultural Pluralism in Education: A Mandate for Change.

DANIEL C. THOMPSON is professor emeritus of sociology and former vice-president for academic affairs at Dillard University. Dr. Thompson has served as an instructor at Clark College (Georgia), a researcher at the Tulane University Urban Life Research Institute, and has also taught at Howard and Loyola universities. He has written widely on such topics as leadership, race relations, and poverty and is the author of the following books: The Eighth Generation, The Case for Integration, The Negro Leadership Class, Private Black Colleges at the Crossroads, and Sociology of the Black Experience.

KENNETH S. TOLLETT is distinguished professor of higher education and director of the Institute for the Study of Educational Policy at Howard University. Before his present position, he was dean and professor at the Texas Southern University School of Law, visiting fellow at the Center for the Study of Democratic Institutions, and a member of the Carnegie Commission on the Future of Higher Education. Most of his publications have been in the areas of equal educational opportunity and affirmative action.

MARY CARTER-WILLIAMS is a senior fellow at the Institute for the Study of Educational Policy at Howard University. Her professional experiences include: director of policy analysis and research at the Institute for Services to Education; educational and management consultant at the Sterling Institute and Gill Associates;

and elementary teacher in New York City and Washington, D.C. Her books and articles are on minority education, desegregation, and the use of computer-based information systems for improved instructional decision making.

JOHN B. WILLIAMS is a lecturer and research associate at the Harvard Graduate School of Education. Prior to his appointment there, he was an assistant professor at Vanderbilt University and research associate at the Vanderbilt Institute for Public Policy Studies. He has also taught at Fairleigh Dickinson University and Boston State College and held positions in state government in New Jersey and at the National Institute of Education in Washington. Williams recently completed a study of court-ordered desegregation in six higher education systems and assisted with a national study of the impact of recent reductions in federal student financial aid.

STEPHEN J. WRIGHT has recently been senior advisor to the president of the College Entrance Examination Board, an organization he has been affiliated with for ten years. Prior to that, he was president of the United Negro College Fund (1966-69), president of Fisk University (1957-66), and president of Bluefield State College (1953-57). Wright has written extensively on education and completed his undergraduate and graduate work at Hampton Institute, Howard University, and New York University.